The Present and the Past

Modern China
A History

Edwin E. Moise

Longman
London and New York

Longman Group Limited
Longman House, Burnt Mill, Harlow
Essex CM20 2JE, England
Associated companies throughout the world

Published in the United States of America by Longman Inc., New York

First published 1986

British Library Cataloguing in Publication Data
Moise, Edwin M. *1946–*
　Modern China: a history. – (The Present and the
　past)
　1. China – History
　I. Title
　951　　　DS735
　ISBN 0 582 49076 6
　ISBN 0 582 49077 4

Library of Congress Cataloging in Publication Data
Moise, Edwin E., 1946–
　Modern China, a history.　ESSEX COUNTY LIBRARY
　(The Present and the past)
　Bibliography: p.
　Includes index.
　1. China – History – 20th century.　I. Title.
II. Series.
DS774.M58　1986　　　951.05　　　84–27857
ISBN 0–582–49076–6
ISBN 0–582–49077–4 (pbk.)

Set in 10/12pt Palatino Roman
Produced by Longman Singapore Publishers (Pte) Ltd.
Printed in Singapore.

Contents

List of Maps

List of Figures

Acknowledgements

We are grateful to Alfred A. Knopf Inc for permission to reproduce extracts from pp 132 & 134/5 *Son Of The Revolution* by Liang Heng & Judith Shapiro. Copyright © 1983 by Liang Heng & Judith Shapiro. We are also grateful to the following for permission to reproduce plates: the Anglo-Chinese Educational Institute (8.1); Associated Press (5.1, 5.2, 5.3, 6.2, 8.2, 8.3, 8.5, 9.1, 9.3(a), 9.3(b), 9.4, 9.6, 9.7); the British Museum (1.5); the BBC Hulton Picture Library (1.4, 1.6, 1.7, 2.2, 2.4, 3.1, 4.1, 6.3); Courtesy of the Freer Gallery of Art, Smithsonian Institution, Washington, DC (2.1); John Hillelson Agency/Magnum Photos (6.1, 7.1); Hsinhua News Agency (2.3, 4.3, 5.5, 8.4, 9.5); The Institute of History and Philology, Academia Sinica, Taipei (1.1); Novosti Press Agency (3.2); and The Photo Source (1.2, 1.3, 3.3, 4.2, 5.4, 9.2).

Introductory note: Chinese names and Chinese geography

Writing Chinese names

This study will emphasize general policies more than the individuals who made those policies. This will be helpful to readers not already familiar with China, since variations in the way Chinese names are spelled in English, and cases in which none of the spellings seem to the English speaker to match the way the name is actually pronounced, can cause considerable confusion. A few years ago the English-speaking world used what was called the 'Wade–Giles' system to write most Chinese names. In the Wade–Giles system the pronunciation of consonants often shifted drastically depending on the presence or absence of an apostrophe. Thus the word pronounced like 'bye' was written *pai*, while the word pronounced like 'pie' was written *p'ai*. The names of provinces and major cities, however, were written in a different system. Sometimes the same sound was written in two different ways depending on whether it appeared in the name of a person or a place, and neither spelling corresponded to the way it was actually pronounced.

Recently we have shifted to a new system called *pinyin*, for the names of both people and places. The *pinyin* system is a bit more rational, but there are still some cases in which the sound indicated by the letters is not what the average English speaker would guess. The table below shows the relation between the new spelling, the old spelling, and the actual pronunciation for the letters most likely to cause confusion. The *pinyin* spellings will be used in this book, but the first time a particular name appears the former spelling will usually be added in parentheses. Names will also appear in the index under both spellings.

Pinyin spelling	Wade–Giles spelling	Pronunciation
a	a	a as in p*a*pa
b	p	b as in *b*oy
c	ts', tz'	ts as in sho*ts*
d	t	d as in *d*og
g	k	g as in *g*ood
i	i, ih, u	ee as in f*ee*t after b, d, j, l, m, n, p, q, t, and x
		i as in sh*i*rt after c, ch, r, s, sh, z, zh
ia	ie	ye as in *ye*s
iu	iu	yo as in *yo*ke
j	ch	j as in *j*eep
p	p'	p
q	ch'	ch as in *ch*eap
r	j	approximately, though not exactly, like the English letter r
t	t'	t
x	hs	sh as in *sh*e
ya	ye	ye as in *ye*s
z	ts, tz	ds as in od*ds*
zh	ch	j as in *j*oke

The names that will appear most often in this book in *pinyin* are:

- Beijing, pronounced 'bay-jeeng', the capital of China. In Wade–Giles it would have been Pei-ching, but it was traditionally written Peking.
- Deng Xiaoping, pronounced 'Dung Shyao-peeng'. A leading member of the 'moderate' wing of the Chinese Communist Party (CCP), he was twice purged by the radicals, but returned to become the most powerful figure in the Party after Mao Zedong died in 1976. Formerly written Teng Hsiao-p'ing.
- Guangdong, pronounced 'Guahng-dong', the south-coast province that was headquarters for the Guomindang and the CCP in the mid 1920s. Formerly spelled Kwangtung.
- Guangzhou, pronounced 'Guahng-joe', an important seaport, capital of the south-coast province of Guangdong. It is often called Canton.
- Guomindang, pronounced 'Guo-meen-dahng', the name of the Nationalist Party which ruled China from 1927 to 1949. Formerly written Kuomintang.

- Jiangxi, pronounced 'Jyahng-shee', a province in South-central China where the Communist Party established a base area in the early 1930s. Formerly written Kiangsi.
- Mao Zedong, pronounced 'Mao (a single short syllable) Dzuh-dong', head of the CCP from 1935 to 1976. Formerly written Mao Tse-tung.
- Qing, pronounced 'Cheeng', the Manchu Dynasty which ruled the Chinese Empire from 1644 to 1911. Formerly written Ch'ing.
- Shanghai, pronounced 'Shahng-hai', the largest city in China, on the coast near the mouth of the Yangzi River. Former spelling the same.
- Yanan, a city in Shaanxi province (Northwest China) that served as headquarters for the CCP from 1937 to 1947. Formerly written Yenan, which matches the actual pronunciation.
- Yangzi, pronounced 'Yahng-dzih', the great river that flows from west to east through the middle of China. Formerly written Yangtse.
- Zhao Ziyang, pronounced 'Jao Dzih-yang', became Premier of the People's Republic of China in 1980. Formerly written Chao Tzu-yang.
- Zhou Enlai, pronounced 'Joe En-lie', Chinese Premier until his death in 1976. A moderate leader who managed to stay on good terms with Mao Zedong all through the Cultural Revolution. Formerly written Chou En-lai.
- Zhu De, pronounced 'Jew Duh', Commander-in-Chief of the Chinese Red Army (later renamed the People's Liberation Army). Formerly written Chu Teh.

There are a few people and places that have long been known in the West not simply by a different spelling, but by a significantly different name from that given them in modern standard Chinese. To avoid excessive confusion, this book will use the familiar English names for Hong Kong, Tibet, and Manchuria, for the Guomindang Party leaders Sun Yat-sen and Chiang Kai-shek, and for the philosophers Confucius and Mencius, rather than giving the names currently used in China (Xianggang, Xizang, Dongbei, Sun Zhongshan, Jiang Jieshi, Kongzi, and Mengzi).

Chinese names almost always consist of a one-syllable surname, which comes first, and is followed by a two-syllable personal name. Thus Mao Anying was the son of Mao Zedong, and both of them would be found, in an alphabetical index, listed under 'Mao'.

Map 1.   China: regional geography and population density.

Areas disputed with India

Population density
Per Sq. km   Per Sq. mile
0–10   0–25
10–98   25–250
over 98   over 250

kilometres
0   600   1200
0   400   800
miles

Manchuria

Inner Mongolia

Outer Mongolia

Xinjiang

Tibet

Beijing

Yellow R.

Nanjing

Wuhan

Yangzi R.

Chongqing

Shanghai

Guangzhou

Hainan

Taiwan

50°   120°   100°   80°   50°
30°   30°

Regional geography

China proper, the area that has for centuries had a dense population of ethnic Chinese, can be divided into three major regions:

1. North China. The most conspicuous feature of this region is the Yellow River. It follows a wide, looping path through the arid hills of the northwest, and finally crosses the North China Plain (largely created by the silt it has laid down) to reach the sea. It is not navigable, and it is very difficult to control; it lays down so much silt that the bed of the river tends to rise with the passage of time, and the water must be kept in its course by high dikes on either side. Eventually, the bed of the river may rise until it is considerably higher than the surrounding countryside. When the dikes break and the river flows down onto the lands around it, the task of putting it back in its elevated channel is difficult, sometimes impossible. Thousands die in the resulting floods. Three times in the past 150 years the river has changed its course very drastically, with the point at which it flows into the sea being altered by hundreds of miles.

    The area along the Yellow River is the original home of Chinese civilization. The soil is relatively rich, but harsh winters and sparse rainfall limit agricultural production.
2. Central China. The dominant feature is the Yangzi River, which is navigable far into the interior. The provinces along the Yangzi and its tributaries form the most populous region of China.
3. South China has no single unifying feature; it is cut up by a number of small mountain ranges. However, despite the uneven terrain, its generous rainfall and mild climate have made possible a productive agriculture that supports a large population.

In addition, there are peripheral areas which have not been inhabited by many ethnic Chinese for most of history, but which have been controlled by the Chinese government when that government was strong. The main ones are:

4. Manchuria. This was a fringe area for the Chinese Empire for most of its history, but a flood of Chinese settlers during the past 100 years has made it essentially Chinese today. The principal unifying feature in modern times has been not natural but manmade: the South Manchurian Railway, running north from the port of Dalian (Dairen) through the major cities of

Manchuria. This region has been one of the main centres of Chinese industry.

5. Mongolia has always been too arid to support a dense population. It was under the control of the Chinese government for a considerable time, but early in the twentieth century Outer Mongolia became a separate country, the Mongolian People's Republic, under strong Russian influence. Inner Mongolia has remained part of China.

6. Xinjiang (Sinkiang) is mostly mountain or desert, with a few areas of fertile oases. The indigenous population, quite sparse, is largely Muslim.

7. Tibet is mountainous and inaccessible; the population is very sparse. Of all the regions listed, this is the one where Chinese influence has traditionally been the weakest.

_1

The Chinese past

Most of the world has changed very drastically in the past 100 years, but few areas have been altered more than China. First the imperial government was brought down by internal decay and foreign pressure, and replaced by a republic. Then central authority collapsed completely, and the country was divided among provincial warlords. Incapable of organized defence, China became the prey of foreign powers whose 'spheres of influence' sometimes approached the status of outright colonies. Corrupt officials, marauding armies, and natural disasters periodically ravaged the peasantry.

China's recovery began under the Guomindang, or Nationalist Party, which ruled from 1927 to 1949. It eliminated most of the foreign spheres of influence and unified significant portions of the country. The Communist Revolution of 1949 carried on with these tasks, creating the first really effective central government since the middle of the eighteenth century, and pushing economic development far enough to eliminate mass starvation if not poverty. The Communists, however, then began struggling savagely among themselves.

A very large proportion of this book will be devoted to events after 1966, simply because so much happened in China after that year. China probably underwent greater changes between the 1960s and the 1980s than Britain or the United States have since the 1920s.

At first glance, everything in today's China seems new. If we can accept some oversimplification and look at the post-1966 political struggles in terms of two major tendencies, we will find that both of the trends involved were twentieth-century in their essence. One regarded modernizing China – creating a strong, wealthy, technologically sophisticated nation-state – as its main goal. We can find roots for such an attitude reaching back to about 1860, but its main development came after 1900. The other trend was preoccupied with Marxian class struggle; such attitudes had only been a factor in Chinese politics after about 1920.

Much of this book will be devoted to the interaction between these two trends, with the advocates of Marxian class struggle found within the Chinese Communist Party (CCP), while the advocates of modernization and nationalism have been found both inside and outside the Party. For a while, in the 1940s and 1950s, the CCP seemed to have learned to reconcile the two approaches to revolution, and apply both of them simultaneously. However, in the 1960s a savage conflict broke out between advocates of the two approaches, which finally ended in a victory of the group called pragmatists, moderates, or rightists – the people who thought of Communism essentially as a technique for making China a richer and stronger nation.

Given that China has changed so much in recent decades – far more than Britain, France, or the United States – one could almost consider writing a history of modern China without reference to the past. Everyone writing a history book must decide how far back in time he or she will go in searching for the causes of later events. Some date must be the earliest date mentioned. Why not write a history of modern China in which the earliest date mentioned is 1900, or even 1921 (the year in which the CCP was founded)?

The simplest and most obvious reason why we should not do this is that not even the most drastic upheaval changes everything. Continuities with the past do exist, especially in thought and attitudes. They will be discussed at various points in this book.

An equally important reason for remembering the past history of China is that the Chinese themselves remember it, and react to it. They are a historically minded people. If we wish to know why Chairman Mao and his radical followers attacked the intellectuals so savagely between 1966 and 1976, it is not enough to understand what the role and status of the intellectuals had been in 1966, or even in 1936. We must also know the role of the intellectuals in the imperial governments of past centuries, because Mao himself knew, and this knowledge helped to shape his actions.

It is sometimes said that the Chinese 'abolished history' during the years of the Cultural Revolution, from 1966 to 1976. This is true in the sense that there was not much historical writing done in this period, and that what little was published was mostly propagandistic hackwork. However, this did not mean that the Communist Party leaders no longer cared about the past. On the contrary, they were sure that events of the distant past could have a direct and immediate relevance to the present; the reason they clamped down on historical research was that they feared *the wrong things* might be said about the past.

One fairly important official of the CCP was disgraced and imprisoned partly for having written a play about a Ming Dynasty official who had died in 1587. His enemies charged that it was in fact an allegory about a 1959 power struggle in the CCP.

In 1974, the CCP declared that contemporary political issues had roots going back to ancient times. The political struggles surrounding the collapse of the Qin Dynasty, in the third century BC, were solemnly rehashed in the press. When the workers in a railway station in the city of Tianjin (Tientsin) formed a historical study group, the *People's Daily* declared:

> The struggle between the Confucian and Legalist schools over the past 2,000 years or so still has its influence at present and has continued to this day . . . The workers, peasants and soldiers can use Marxism to study and learn history. Liberate history from the confines of the historians' lecture rooms and textbooks, and turn it into a sharp weapon in the hands of the masses.

A Chinese-American woman who visited China during this period told me that her hosts, trying to decide whether she was still basically a Chinese, or had been so westernized as to be just an American with the ancestry and physical appearance of a Chinese, used knowledge of Chinese history as their touchstone. When the train on which she was riding passed a location where something important had happened more than 1,000 years before, would she know what had happened there and be excited about actually seeing the place? If so, they would consider her to be a real Chinese. This is not the behaviour of people who have abolished history, or would even consider abolishing it.

If we wish to understand modern China, therefore, we should start by learning at least a little about the origins and development of this very ancient culture.

The birth of China

The civilization we know as China originated in the area of the Yellow River, in the northern part of the country. Traditional texts list rulers going back to almost 2700 BC, but the earliest kings whose

1.1   Shang Dynasty 'Oracle Bone'. When the Shang kings wanted knowledge about the future, they had a question inscribed on the flat-bottomed shell of a tortoise or on the shoulder bone of a cow. Heat was then applied until the shell or the bone cracked; the shape of the cracks was supposed to indicate the answer to the question. The inscription on this tortoise shell asked whether it would rain soon; the cracks indicated that it would.

existence has actually been verified by archaeology lived probably between 1300 and 1200 BC. Their dynasty, the Shang, ruled a substantial portion of northern China. The people of the Shang used a writing system recognizably related to the characters of twentieth-century Chinese, but in other respects (such as frequent human sacrifices) they were strikingly different from later Chinese cultures.

The Shang rulers were overthrown by a group called the Zhou (Chou), who had lived on the western fringe of the Shang domain and had a similar culture. This probably occurred around 1040 BC, though estimates of the date range from 1122 BC to 1018 BC. The Zhou kings maintained fairly effective control of the area around the Yellow River for a few generations, but then gradually lost their grip. After 770 BC real power was divided among a number of states. The typical state was a city, with some greater or lesser amount of the surrounding territory under its control. The rulers of these various states paid nominal allegiance to the Zhou kings, but the kings retained only a small territory under their actual control. The culture of Zhou China, however, was spreading even while its political structure was disintegrating. As time went on, areas along the coast and the Yangzi River, which had not been part of the Shang or the early Zhou, began adopting some cultural traits of the Yellow River states and joining their political struggles.

The period from the sixth to the third centuries BC, although characterized by interstate warfare that had many Chinese in despair, was intellectually one of the most productive eras in Chinese history. A tremendous variety of philosophers and thinkers propounded various ideas. Chinese tradition refers to 'the Hundred Schools', but three major groups eventually emerged, which remained central to Chinese thought down to the twentieth century: Confucians, Daoists (Taoists), and Legalists.

Confucianism

Confucius was an itinerant teacher of the fifth century BC. He travelled from one state to another, talking with his disciples and with any rulers who might be willing to listen.

Our knowledge of Confucius' actual teachings is somewhat vague. Like Socrates, he taught face to face rather than writing books, so we are dependent on accounts by his students. Even for these we cannot be sure we have reliable texts. A considerable portion of the book known as the *Analects* really does come from accounts of his teachings written by his students, but other sections were inserted into the work long afterwards. While scholars today can sort much of the *Analects* into genuine and spurious sections, there are some passages about which doubt still exists.

Confucius was sure that his teachings provided the key to good and effective government, but no ruler was sufficiently convinced to give him a position of real power and let him show what he could do.

Confucian doctrine evolved gradually as later writers, of whom the most important was Mencius, extended and modified the original teachings. The general thrust of Confucianism was the importance of proper human relationships. Subordinates should be reverent and obedient towards their superiors, while superiors should be benevolent and just. In one sense, it was an optimistic doctrine – it claimed that human beings have a natural sense of what is good. However, Confucianism did not support the idea of progress; it suggested that people wanting to improve society should look to the past for their models, rather than trying to devise something new. Confucius advocated adherence to old customs and old rituals. Among the Confucian ideas that have particular importance for the later history of China are:

1. Confucianism treated the family as the key unit in human society, and filial piety – loyalty and reverence towards one's parents – as the most important part of family relationships. A man's loyalty to his parents was supposed to take precedence over everything else, including loyalty to his children, his wife, or his ruler.
2. Confucianism took a basically hierarchical view of society. One should note that of the five key human relationships in Confucian doctrine, four are relationships linking a superior to a subordinate: father to son, ruler to subject, husband to wife, and elder brother to younger brother. Only the relationship of friend to friend is between equals.
3. Confucianism argued not only that a ruler has an obligation to behave in a good and humane fashion, and provide decent living conditions for his subjects, but also that this is profitable for the ruler; the subjects will respond with loyalty and obedience. It is imperative that a ruler keep the confidence of his people. If they are poor and miserable the ruler will lose the mandate of heaven; he deserves to be overthrown, and he probably will be.
4. Power should be exercised by people who have been educated

in the proper way of exercising it. Confucius himself never attained the position of power for which he yearned, but he felt that he was training his students to be officials, and eventually (many centuries later) a Confucian education became, in fact, the main pathway to power in the Chinese government.

Few rulers actually behaved in the high moral fashion that Confucian doctrine prescribed. Many Confucians, therefore, developed a low opinion of the governments with which they had to deal, although the Confucian prescription of loyalty to rulers usually kept them from engaging in active opposition.

There is an anecdote about Confucius, which though it probably is not true, illustrates this strain in Confucianism. According to the story, the sage was once passing through a mountainous area with some of his disciples. They came upon a woman mourning by the grave of her son, who had been killed by a tiger. She told them that her husband and her husband's father had previously suffered the same fate. When asked why she lived in a place that had so many tigers, she explained that in this place there was no oppressive government. The moral Confucius is supposed to have drawn for his disciples is that oppressive government was worse than a tiger. The unspoken implication was that governments were so universally oppressive that the only way this woman's family had been able to escape oppression was to live in the wilderness where there was no effective government at all.

Legalism

Another school preached not moral obligations but naked self-interest. The legalists argued that human beings are fundamentally amoral, that they cannot be moved by moral example. The only way to make them behave correctly is by a strong legal system, which enforces correct behaviour through rewards and punishments. If even minor infractions are ruthlessly punished, then nobody will dare to commit serious crimes. The philosopher Han Fei Zi (Han Fei Tzu) argued that while there might occasionally be an individual who was naturally good, and did not need to be coerced into good behaviour, 'the intelligent ruler will not prize him. The reason is that the law of the state must not be sidetracked and government is not for one man.' The ruler must apply coercive laws to everyone; what difference does it make that this one individual would have behaved properly without being forced to do so?

Map 2.   The early expansion of the Chinese state.

....   Zhou Dynasty, 11th century BC.

—×—×—   Zhou Dynasty, C. 800 B.C.

—··—··—   Empire of Shi Huangdi, 211 B.C.

————   Portion of border defended by the Great Wall

kilometres
0   600   1200

miles
0   400   800

Han Fei Zi was contemptuous of the idea that the ruler should consider the opinions of his subjects. He claimed that legalist government would benefit the people, but he was sure that the people were too stupid to recognize good government even when living under it. His contemporary Li Si (Li Ssu) went further, and argued that the ruler could ignore not only the opinions but also the welfare of his subjects. The purpose of government was to serve the interests of the ruler, not the common people. 'If a ruler will not . . . utilize the empire for his own pleasure, but on the contrary purposelessly tortures his body and wastes his mind in devotion to the people – then he becomes the slave of the common people instead of the domesticator of the empire. And what honour is there in that?'

The legalists were future-oriented; they had no respect for tradition, and felt they could devise techniques of government superior to anything that had been known in the past.

Daoism

The Daoists preached harmony with the forces of nature. They doubted the value either of will-power or of too much thinking; life is to be enjoyed, and should be kept as simple as possible. They agreed with Confucius about the deplorable quality of existing governments, but where Confucius had been eager to achieve high office so he could carry out reforms, the Daoists rejected position and power. They argued that the wise man minds his own business, ignores the government, and hopes that it will ignore him. There is a story that the King of Chu, a very powerful state on the Yangzi River, once sent two officials to offer a senior position in his government to the sage Zhuangzi (Chuang Tzu). He was sitting by a river, fishing, when they found him and made their offer.

> Zhuangzi held on to the fishing pole and, without turning his head, said, 'I have heard that there is a sacred tortoise in Chu that has been dead for three thousand years. The king keeps it wrapped in cloth and boxed, and stores it in the ancestral temple. Now would this tortoise rather be dead and have its bones left behind and honoured? Or would it rather be alive and dragging its tail in the mud?'
>
> 'It would rather be alive and dragging its tail in the mud,' said the two officials.
>
> Zhuangzi said, 'Go away! I'll drag my tail in the mud!'

On another occasion, offended by a rumour that he was scheming to attain the position of Prime Minister in the state of Liang, he wondered why a person of taste and discernment should be suspected of lusting after a piece of carrion.

Daoist philosophy later mingled with medical knowledge, popular religious beliefs, and other elements of folk culture. The products of such mingling included a Daoist religion, with organized worship of numerous deities, and also the martial arts discipline known in the West as Kung Fu.

The unification of China

The wars between the various states grew increasingly violent. Finally, the state of Qin (Ch'in) conquered the others and its ruler became Qin Shi Huangdi (First Emperor of the Qin Dynasty). He controlled not only the original home of Chinese culture – the area around the Yellow River – but also the Yangzi Valley and even a portion of the south coast, reaching down to the borders of Vietnam. This new empire benefited from improved communications, standardized coinage, a standardized writing system, and so forth, but it was soon groaning under a legalist regime of unparalleled severity. Li Si (quoted above on the foolishness of trying to serve the interests of the common people) was the First Emperor's Prime Minister. The government's demands on the people were massive, and any failure to meet them brought severe punishment. Earlier rulers of several states had built walls to guard their northern borders against attack. Shi Huangdi organized incredible numbers of labourers to strengthen these walls, and link them together, to form what we know as the Great Wall of China. Many of those conscripted for this work failed to survive; their sufferings became part of Chinese legend.

The First Emperor launched a ruthless persecution of Confucianism. He was probably motivated partly by worries over the political threat posed by any comparison between his own savagery and the Confucian doctrine that a tyrant would lose legitimacy in the eyes of heaven, and partly by the intolerance of an arrogant man for any ideas different from his own. He may also have been egged on by legalist bureaucrats who resented the

1.2   When Shi Huangdi died, an army of at least 6,000 life-size pottery figures was buried with him. The figures are not identical; each has its own individual face. The first was unearthed in 1974.

1.3   One of the individual life-size pottery figures from the tomb of Shi Huangdi.

Confucians as would-be competitors for office. Confucian books were burned, and Confucian scholars were executed.

The Qin Dynasty lasted less than twenty years. Its fall was caused partly by power struggles between top officials after the death of Shi Huangdi in 210 BC, and partly by revolts of subjects who found the savagery of legalist government unendurable. According to tradition, the first major uprising was begun by some men who had been ordered to report for duty at a military post on a certain date. When floods rendered the roads impassable, they realized that they would not arrive in time. In accord with the legalist principle of ruthless punishment for even minor infractions, the penalty for tardiness was death, and no excuses were accepted. The men decided to rebel, despite the likelihood that they would fail and be killed, because they had nothing to lose.

The fall of the Qin Dynasty did not destroy the idea of a unified China under a single emperor. A new dynasty succeeded the old one, and despite occasional periods of division, unified imperial government existed for most of the next 2,000 years.

Major dynasties showed a fairly regular life-cycle. Every dynasty started out with competent and vigorous leadership; without such strengths a dynasty could not obtain control of China. However, the vigour of imperial leadership generally declined sooner or later, and the bureaucracy decayed. Great landowners were increasingly able to evade taxation, and such taxes as were collected tended to remain in the hands of corrupt officials instead of being passed on to the Emperor.

The wealth of the great landholders usually increased during the course of the dynastic cycle. In the beginning, if many such landholders of the preceding dynasty had lost their wealth during the collapse of the preceding dynasty, most of the land might be in the hands of small farmers. This eased the problem of tax collection; the land had to support only the government and the farmers themselves. Small farmers generally lacked the power and influence to evade taxation effectively. As time went on, however, families influential in the new dynasty accumulated land, and the surplus produced by the peasants who worked that land had to support them as well as the government. The richer these families became, the better they were able to bribe or otherwise influence tax-collectors, and shift their tax burden on to people having less influence than themselves. Government revenues therefore declined, even as the burden placed on the remaining peasant smallholders grew heavier. Some peasants were driven into banditry, which a decaying government with declining revenues could not easily suppress.

The pattern of decline might be reversed only briefly by strong leadership in the capital. Hunger and anarchy would soon be spreading again, and the dynasty would lose the 'Mandate of Heaven'. After its fall the country would go through a period of conflict, seldom very long, at the end of which a new dynasty would arise. The fact that the overall history of any particular dynasty was a history of decline encouraged the tendency of the Confucian scholars to praise the past rather than thinking in terms of progress.

One should not be misled by the recurring patterns of the dynastic cycle; China was not fundamentally an unchanging society. Every major dynasty came eventually to suffer from most of the same weaknesses, but in other ways they were very different from one another. The structure of government, the economy, and the relationship of government to society underwent substantial long-term changes.

The first major dynasty to go through the dynastic cycle was the Han. A man named Liu Bang (Liu Pang), one of the rebels who overthrew the Qin, founded the Han Dynasty in 206 BC. Shi Huangdi's ban on heterodox philosophical writings was lifted, and various scholars either removed old texts from places of concealment, or tried to write them out from memory. Confucian ideas eventually became quite influential at the Han court, even though much of the Han government structure was legalist.

The Han Dynasty lost power for a few years in the first century AD, but was soon restored under the same name, and did not finally disappear until AD 220. Central government collapsed with the Han, and was not restored for almost 400 years. However, the Chinese Empire, unlike the Roman, did not fall back into barbarism when it lost its political cohesion. When the brief Sui Dynasty (581–618) restored central authority, it controlled a civilization on roughly the level of the Han. The Tang Dynasty (618–907) carried Chinese culture to the highest peak it had yet attained in art and poetry as well as in wealth.

The coming of Buddhism

In the late years of the Han, and during the period of division that followed, the Buddhist religion was filtering into China from India. This was the only occasion before the modern era that Chinese culture was heavily influenced by the culture of a foreign country.

Buddhism had originally been essentially a set of prescriptions about how humans should approach the world. Buddhism taught that life in this world is essentially miserable, and that there is nothing that can be done to make it other than miserable. Nothing endures; everything changes, decays, and is eventually destroyed. People are born, grow old, sicken, die, and are born again in other bodies in an endless cycle of misery. The goal of all sensible people should be to break the cycle of reincarnation, to free themselves from the ties that bind them to the world. Upon attaining true enlightenment, a person will lose all desire for the things of this world. The lack of such desires means that after death, such a person will not be pulled back into this world to be born in another body for another life of misery. Instead, he or she will remain forever in the state of bliss known as nirvana. The man known historically as 'the Buddha', who is believed to have lived in northern India around 500 BC, was supposed to have been such a one.

This original doctrine, known as Theravada or Hinayana, was individualistic; it showed how each person could save himself or herself from the misery of earthly existence.

The schools of Buddhism that spread most widely in China and Japan, known as Mahayana, gave more emphasis to the ways human beings could obtain help from outside themselves. Mahayana thinkers criticized Theravada doctrine for its selfishness. Surely a person who had attained enlightenment would not simply escape from the world to enjoy the peace of nirvana as an individual, but would remain active in the world to help those less fortunate. He or she would become a Bodhisattva. Most Mahayana sects worshipped Bodhisattvas as if they were gods, and ascribed to them the sort of supernatural powers that other religions ascribe to gods. Ordinary humans could pray to them for assistance in matters both earthly and spiritual.

The Bodhisattva Amituofo (A-mi-t'o-fo, Amitabha, Amida) presided over what was in effect a heaven – a 'Pure Land' into which people could be reborn after death, in which they could be permanently safe from the suffering of earthly life. To be reborn in the Pure Land, by aid of the Bodhisattva, seemed a far more attainable goal than to achieve enlightenment by one's own efforts and thus avoid any rebirth. Chinese Buddhism eventually became more preoccupied with praying for the aid of Bodhisattvas than with efforts to achieve nirvana.

The doctrine attained its greatest strength during the Tang

1.4   A life-size sculpture in stone of the Buddha (technically Bodhisattva) Amitrofo, from the Chinese art of the Tang Dynasty.

Dynasty. It declined thereafter, but it did not disappear; instead it was absorbed into the mixture of traditions that came to characterize China.

Some Chinese were exclusively Buddhist or exclusively Confucian, but most saw no reason to choose a single set of beliefs. The Chinese worshipped a tremendous variety of gods. Many were

Bodhisattvas. Some were Daoist in origin. Some represented a combination of Daoist and Buddhist ideas. Each city had its own city god. The 'God of War' Guan Di, to whom prayers were directed not only by soldiers but also by ordinary people with problems such as illness, was an actual general of the late Han Dynasty, deified long after his death. Few people felt compelled to restrict themselves to a single deity, and there was seldom friction between worshippers of different gods.

The Confucian scholar could work all day as an official in a government that was essentially legalist in structure, then go home, have some wine, and write poetry that was Daoist or Buddhist in inspiration. The various schools learned to get along so well, in fact, that people sometimes forgot that there ever had been serious conflict. The legalist attack on Confucianism under Shi Huangdi was too dramatic to be forgotten, but men accustomed to the idea that the Confucian bureaucrat became a Daoist when the working day was over have sometimes had difficulty understanding certain old documents containing Confucian criticisms of Daoist ideas.

Popular religion remained strong, if not well organized, down to the twentieth century. Élite culture and élite philosophy became essentially secular, however, as they had been in the Zhou period. Confucius, when asked about the gods, had simply refused to answer. By about AD 1000, the strength of Buddhism had faded enough so that serious philosophy was coming once more to be concerned primarily with things of this world.

The later dynasties

Chinese urban culture reached a peak in the late Tang and then in the Song (Sung) Dynasty, AD 960–1279. A wealthy and vigorous merchant class developed commerce both within China and with Southeast Asia. The apparatus of government came for the first time really to be dominated by educated Civil Servants, men who had passed state examinations based on the Confucian classics. However, while civil culture throve, China's military strength declined. During the late Song period the nomads to the north began moving south into China. Finally, in 1279, the Mongols under Kublai Khan conquered all of China. Under the Mongol rulers (referred to in Chinese as the Yuan Dynasty), China was incorporated into a Mongol Empire which for a while covered most of Asia.

1.5　Song (Sung) Dynasty landscape painting.

1.6   Kublai Khan, Emperor of China. Chinese traditional painting.

Mongol rule lasted less than a century. In 1368, Chinese rebels were able to expel the Mongols and establish the Ming Dynasty.

Chinese society was dominated by Confucian scholars under the Ming Dynasty even more than it had been under the Song. Almost all positions in government were filled by men who had passed written examinations, administered by the government, which tested literary ability and knowledge of the classics. The scholar-bureaucrats who had passed such examinations formed the main ruling class of China from the early Ming up to the nineteenth century. However, the structure of government retained a strong legalist element. The Ming emperors, who used Confucian scholars in government more than most previous dynasties, were at the same time more brutally and arbitrarily despotic in their own behaviour than the rulers of the Han, Tang, or Song.

Confucian doctrine stressed harmony, loyalty, and trust. Actual government practice under the Ming involved elaborate techniques of 'divide and rule' by which despotic emperors broke up all concentrations of power and maintained their own control over their subordinates. The emperors worried that if bureaucrats were appointed to important positions in their home provinces, or if they served in any one place for too long, they might use the networks of contacts and friendships they built up to serve their own interests rather than the interests of the throne.

Rulers had learned the tremendous value of Confucian officials as tools of government, but a man true to Confucian ideals of moral government could find himself facing the same dilemma that had frustrated Confucius – immoral rulers may not be enthusiastic about officials who want to practise moral government. One famous clash occurred in 1565, when an official of legendary rectitude, named Hai Rui (Hai Jui), submitted a written protest to the Emperor about his disgraceful behaviour. Realizing what kind of reaction he could expect, Hai Rui had first purchased a coffin for himself and made arrangements for his funeral. He was indeed arrested and tortured; his life was saved only by the timely death of the Emperor he had offended. Most officials, however, were more flexible.

In the view of the scholars, society was made up of four major classes. In the order of their worth, these were: (1) The scholars themselves, who by virtue of their education and culture were fit to rule over the others. (2) The peasants, who grew the food without which nobody could survive. (3) The artisans, who made things somewhat less vital than food but still of considerable value. (4) The merchants, who made nothing, and lived simply by shuffling goods around from one place to another.

The real status of the merchants was higher than this theoretical scale would suggest; their wealth guaranteed them a certain amount of respect. However, the merchant class never regained the position it had held in Chinese society under the Song. Many successful merchants, instead of wanting their sons to follow in their footsteps, had them educated as scholars in the hope that they could join the bureaucracy, the real ruling class of China.

The Chinese reaction against Mongol rule gave Chinese culture an isolationist bent. The Ming rulers were less friendly towards foreigners than the Song rulers had been. Furthermore, the high proportion of foreigners among the merchant community at the time when China was under Mongol rule may have contributed to a decline in the prestige of the merchants.

Under the Song, Chinese diplomats had been quite active in Southeast Asia, promoting Chinese commerce in the area. The Ming Dynasty was not interested in encouraging such commerce. Early Ming emperors built a large navy, and sent fleets through Southeast Asia and on across the Indian Ocean as far as Ceylon and East Africa. However, they quickly lost interest in such projects. In the end they not only stopped maintaining a powerful navy, but also forbade Chinese merchants to build large ocean-going vessels.

China's relations with lands overseas were conducted through the tribute system. Other countries were expected to acknowledge the superiority of Chinese civilization and the Chinese Emperor, and present tribute. A good deal of commerce continued to take place, some of it conducted by foreign missions whose official excuse for coming to China was the presentation of tribute. However, the Chinese government did not place a high enough value on commerce to treat it as a purpose of the tribute system.

It was unfortunate that European ships began to arrive at this particular time, when Chinese attitudes towards both foreigners and commerce had become so negative. The first Portuguese sailors reached the south coast of China in 1514, and soon they were trading on a regular basis. The Chinese regarded them as barbarians; they looked odd, had a strange language and customs, and showed little respect for Chinese law. They also smelled disgusting, since sanitary conditions aboard most Portuguese ships were terrible. They were eventually allowed to establish a trading base at Macao, a peninsula on the south coast near the city of Guangzhou. The peninsula was walled off from the mainland of China.

Contact was restricted essentially to commerce until the 1580s, when a Jesuit missionary named Matteo Ricci began a determined effort to penetrate China. He studied the Chinese language, adopted the clothing and to some extent the customs of the Chinese upper class, and carefully dissociated himself from the disreputable Portuguese merchants at Macao. By 1598 he won permission to visit the capital at Beijing for a short period, and he lived in Beijing from 1601 to 1610. He made a number of converts to catholicism at the imperial court. Jesuit priests became a fixture at the court from

Ricci's time onward, though they had little impact on Chinese culture.

The overall rate of advance of Chinese civilization slowed dangerously during the Ming Dynasty. Under the Song, China had been among the leading cultures of the world, far superior to Western Europe in wealth, technology, and science. By the Ming period, stagnation was setting in. The causes are numerous and some are still subject to dispute. The decline in the position of the merchant class and the reduction in foreign contacts were probably important factors. The scholars' concentration on study of the classics diverted their interest away from science and technology. Changes in the structure of the Chinese economy have also been blamed. But whatever the causes, Chinese technology and science lost their previous dynamism.

The Ming Dynasty, like previous ones, eventually fell into decline. The Manchus, a semi-civilized and quite un-Chinese group living to the northeast, took advantage of this situation. Raiding parties were getting past the Great Wall into China proper by 1629. Manchu leaders progressively strengthened their political and administrative system, and in 1636 they began calling themselves the Qing Dynasty. In 1644, taking advantage of the collapse of the Ming (Chinese rebels had actually seized Beijing), they launched a massive invasion of China. Their control was fully consolidated by 1681.

Government and society under the Qing

The Manchus got along with their Chinese subjects far better than the Mongols had. They adopted many Chinese cultural patterns and were to a considerable extent assimilated by the people they had conquered, so by the year 1800 the empire was run in much the same way that indigenous dynasties had run it in the past. The Qing Dynasty emperors were Manchu, but Chinese was the language of administration, and many of the officials, even in very high positions, were Chinese.

Chinese emperors had traditionally worried about the danger

1.7   The Great Wall. The Ming Dynasty rebuilt and strengthened the Great Wall for defence against the Manchu nomads to the north. However, the Wall could block invaders only if it were effectively manned. In 1644, with the Ming Dynasty collapsing, the Chinese general assigned to defend a crucial section of the Wall decided to let the Manchus in, and to join their conquest of China instead of fighting to keep them out.

that officials who became too strong might someday turn against the throne. This problem was especially serious when the Chinese officials in question were serving an alien Manchu emperor. When the Manchus first established their control in China they allowed some of the Chinese who had collaborated with them in the conquest to exercise great powers. Three of these men rebelled in 1673, and eight years of warfare were required to put down the rebellion. From this point onward, the Qing rulers were more careful to keep their officials from becoming too strong. The form of government organization was determined as much by the need to prevent certain things from happening as by the need to make sure that the things that were supposed to happen did happen.

The empire spread far into central Asia; it was larger than it ever had been under an emperor who was actually Chinese. Aside from the areas where the Chinese people themselves had traditionally lived, it included Manchuria (the home of the Manchus) in the northeast, Mongolia in the north, Xinjiang (Sinkiang) in the northwest, and to some extent even Tibet in the southwest. The great majority of the empire's population was Chinese, but the sparsely populated non-Chinese border areas made up more than half of its land area.

Governmental power was as centralized as the emperors could make it. Provincial officials were not local leaders; they were men who had passed the Civil Service examinations based on the Confucian classics, and had then been appointed to office by the central government, usually in some location far from their original homes. However, this bureaucratic system did not stretch down below the county level. The county magistrate appointed by the Emperor had to work through local people in actually running the villages. The most important of these were the 'gentry', the people who had enough education to have passed at least the lower stages of the Civil Service examinations. (Note that the Chinese 'gentry' did not bear much resemblance to the gentry of traditional England.) At any given time the number of people who had passed the lower examinations and thus acquired gentry status was much larger than the number actually holding bureaucratic appointments; the ones not in office formed the leadership of local society.

The emperors tried to emphasize impersonal norms, but purely personal relationships played a tremendous role. The Chinese élite was bound together by a web of personal relationships (*guanxi*) based on kinship, shared educational background, and past favours given and received. Doing favours for one's friends often took precedence over adherence to imperial policy. The emperors made a point of not appointing Civil Servants to positions in their home provinces, because this was where they had the most and the closest personal relationships.

By the nineteenth century, as the Qing Dynasty weakened and its officials grew lax or corrupt, the gentry became a little more independent of the central government, but they still, to a considerable extent, formed a national rather than a local élite. A member of the gentry had far more in common with people of his own class in other provinces than with peasants who lived in his immediate neighbourhood. The main factor setting the gentry off from the masses was knowledge of classical Chinese,[1] the language of literature and scholarship. There were many dialects, sufficiently different really to constitute separate languages, spoken in different areas of the country. Scholars communicated in an ancient tongue, no longer spoken by the common people anywhere, but known to educated men everywhere. All respectable literature, and writing on politics, philosophy, and other important subjects, was in classical Chinese. It was used much the way Latin was in medieval Europe, but classical Chinese was a more difficult language than Latin.

The way the élite used a quite different language from the common people, which could be acquired only through long and usually expensive study, was symbolic of the great social inequalities that existed throughout Chinese society. Class structure was not frozen by heredity. If the son of a poor peasant were sufficiently intelligent, and somehow managed to get a good education, he could be accepted as a full member of the ruling class. Many children of the gentry, conversely, sank down among the commoners. However, the fact that individuals could cross the gap between élite and masses should not lead us to suppose that the gap was small. People who laboured with their minds felt they were born to dominate those who laboured with their hands. In most human relationships it was clearly understood that one person had a higher rank than the other, and the differences in rank were very important.

Simple inequalities in wealth were substantial (though not nearly as great as in some other societies of the same period, notably Russia). The landlords and officials could live in luxury while many of the peasants were on the edge of starvation. Living standards for the common people were not very good even in the eighteenth century, the high point of the Qing Dynasty. In later years, as overpopulation and a low level of technology were exacerbated by corruption and decay, things became very unpleasant indeed for them.

Psychological inequalities – differences in status – were even more extreme. One hears a lot about 'face' in Chinese society. The Chinese were very sensitive about their personal dignity, and would go to great lengths to avoid situations in which they were likely to 'lose face'. In most contexts, people were careful not to arouse enmities by causing others to lose face. However, the other side of the coin was that people with a high rank were sometimes quite ruthless in feeding their own pride by humiliating their inferiors. It is no accident that China, a place where people were extraordinarily concerned about their personal dignity, was also the place where top government officials were expected not merely to bow but to prostrate themselves on the floor when presenting themselves before the Emperor.

The central institution of Chinese society, the primary locus of loyalties, was the patrilineal family. For a man not to have a son was a disaster; there would be nobody to carry on his family line, nobody to care for him in old age, nobody to perform the ancestral ceremonies for him after his death. In order to have a son a man needed a wife. While some Chinese men were simply unable to marry, hardly any remained single by choice. However, marriage did not mean that bride and groom were creating a new family; it meant that the bride was becoming a member (not necessarily even an important member) of the family into which her husband had been born. Family structure was supposed to be based not on the bond between husband and wife, but on the line of descent from father to sons. If possible, husband and wife were supposed to live with the parents of the husband, or with his brothers if his parents were dead. In such an extended family, a young married man's primary loyalty was supposed to be to his parents and brothers rather than to his wife. In practice, however, the extended family was found mostly among the well-to-do; young men of limited wealth were often forced by circumstance to set up households separate from those of their parents.

Most marriages were arranged by the parents of the people involved. It was considered perfectly normal for the bride and groom to be strangers, and to meet one another for the first time during the marriage ceremony.

The status differentiation in Chinese society extended to family relationships, where old people ranked higher than young ones and men higher than women. The worst treatment was reserved for young females. As infants they were sometimes killed, or just allowed to die of neglect, if the family did not feel it could afford to feed the extra mouth. As children, most of them had to bind their feet – to wear tight wrappings which prevented the feet from growing to normal size, and distorted the skeletal structure. The result was 'lily feet', which made them sexually more attractive to their future husbands, but made walking difficult. As young wives they could be abused unmercifully, especially by their mothers-in-law. They were sometimes regarded less as members of the family into which they had married than as property owned by that family. A family containing a young man in need of a wife might buy one for him, and if things went wrong she might even find her husband, or her husband's family, selling her again to some other family.

The only way a woman could attain a position of power and security was through a relationship with a male. Sometimes she could attain a sufficiently good relationship with her husband, but the system of arranged marriages and the subservience most husbands showed towards their parents, especially their mothers, kept this from being the norm. The typical woman had to endure years of abuse by her mother-in-law, and achieved a strong position only when her son became important enough in the family to give her some leverage. When her son became the nominal head of the family she might in fact rule it through her control over him; she could then shower on younger women, if she chose, the sort of abuse she had once endured.

By the nineteenth century, the Qing Dynasty was beginning to decay as others had before it; Chinese who knew their own country's history could recognize the signs. However, Chinese society and culture seemed very stable. Hardly anyone in China suspected that the fall of the dynasty, when it came, would be accompanied by massive alterations in the whole structure of their civilization.

Notes

1. Classical Chinese is also called classical Mandarin, literary Chinese, and *wenyan*. Do not confuse it with modern Mandarin, which is the everyday language of most of northern China, and is the main language of education and government in China today.

2

The collapse of the old order

By the middle of the nineteenth century, the Manchu government of China was under severe pressures both internal and external. Its longstanding policy of isolationism was beginning to break down in the face of European military superiority; the Opium War of 1839–42 was only the first of a series of Chinese military defeats. In the 1850s and 1860s, the Taiping Rebellion almost destroyed the dynasty from within.

The Manchus were very reluctant to carry out any extensive reforms in the face of these threats. They had barely begun to attempt serious modernization when they were overthrown by the Revolution of 1911. The revolution aroused high hopes, but within about five years central government collapsed completely, and China was divided among various warlords. The challenge of establishing an effective government, capable of restoring order and defending the country against foreign encroachment, remained unmet.

The first Western impact

The general attitude of both Manchus and Chinese was that China had the highest, and in a sense the only, true civilization. They were willing to have contact with foreign cultures only on the assumption that the foreigners were barbarians who acknowledged the superiority of Chinese culture and the Emperor of China, and presented tribute to the Emperor as a sign of submission. China's immediate neighbours, such as the Vietnamese, Burmese, and Koreans, had generally been willing to give at least lip-service to this doctrine. The Jesuits won acceptance partly through their scientific knowledge, especially in astronomy, but the main key to their success was that they complied with Chinese expectations by adopting many aspects of Chinese culture. Eventually, in fact, the Pope became disturbed by the question of who was converting whom. In the early eighteenth century, when the Pope began ordering the Jesuits to behave more like Christian missionaries and less like Confucian scholars, their influence at the imperial court declined.

However, in the early nineteenth century the Europeans, and in particular the British, became unwilling to accept the system and the rather insulting restrictions that went with it. Western trade was permitted only at the south-coast port of Guangzhou, and the European merchants were not permitted year-round residence even there. Western diplomats had contact only with provincial officials in Guangzhou, not with the central government in Beijing. Christian missionary activity was forbidden. Britain, the greatest trading power in the world, wanted the right to trade more freely, to maintain an ambassador in Beijing, and to send missionaries into China.

Friction over these issues was exacerbated by the problem of opium. For many years European merchants seeking tea, silk, porcelain, and other luxuries had bought more from China than they sold, and paid for the difference in gold and silver. This was where much of the wealth that the Spanish had taken from Latin America had eventually gone. But early in the nineteenth century the British had begun selling tremendous quantities of opium, acquired from their new possessions in India, to China. Soon the balance of payments had shifted, and gold and silver were flowing out of China. This caused an economic crisis as well as a tremendous drug-abuse problem.

In the late 1830s the Chinese government made a serious effort to eradicate the opium traffic. An energetic and competent administrator named Lin Zexu (Lin Tse-hsu) was sent to Guangzhou to manage the campaign. Officials there had already launched an effective drive against the Chinese smugglers who had been distributing opium within China; Lin decided also to go after the foreign merchants (most of them British, but some from the United States and other nations) who had been supplying the Chinese smugglers. In March 1839, Lin placed about 350 foreign merchants under a polite sort of siege in their compound in Guangzhou. They were not physically harmed, or cut off from food supplies, but their Chinese servants all had to leave the compound, and the hostage merchants were not allowed either to trade or to leave until the merchant community had handed over its opium stocks to be destroyed. The British government's representative on the scene, Captain Charles Elliot, collected more than 1,000 tons of opium from the merchants and handed it over to Lin.

Lin had a more sophisticated understanding of the foreigners than most Chinese officials, but he had no conception of how important the opium trade was to the economy of the British Empire, or of how powerfully the British could and would react to any threat against their merchants. He had started what became known as the Opium War. For China it was a disaster from beginning to end. The British Navy roamed the coasts at will. Even on land the Chinese Army was inferior in weapons, training, and discipline, besides being riddled with opium addiction. Most of the officers were hopelessly incompetent, as one might expect in a society where it was said that one does not waste good iron by making it into nails, or good men by making them into soldiers. By 1842 China was forced to submit. Britain acquired the island of Hong Kong and an indemnity. Missionaries and merchants were henceforth allowed to live, trade, and preach in five 'treaty ports' along the coast.

Later negotiations with other Western powers, plus wars in which China was defeated by Britain and France (1856–60), France (1883–85), Japan (1894–95), and Britain, France, Japan, Russia, and the United States all together (1900), led to further privileges for the foreigners, under what became known as the Treaty System. The list of treaty ports expanded steadily; by 1917 there were ninety-two of them. (Most of these 'ports' were in fact ports, either along the coast or on the Yangzi River, but some were landlocked cities.) Foreign influence was substantial in all treaty ports; portions of Shanghai and fifteen other treaty ports were placed under outright foreign administration, mainly British.

Christian missionaries could move freely throughout China, and merchants could circulate to a considerable extent. The 'most favoured nation' principle ensured that any privilege given to one European power also went automatically to the others. Under the principle of extraterritoriality, no Westerner accused of a crime in China could be tried under Chinese law; Western courts were established in the treaty ports to try such cases. The tariff that China could collect on its imports was limited by treaty to 5 per cent, and in practice it often was below even this limit. The Maritime Customs Service, which collected the small permitted tariff, was run by foreigners (mainly British). Eventually, significant numbers of Western troops began to be stationed in China as protection for

Western residents and as guards on foreign-owned railroads. Foreign warships operated not only off China's coast, but even on her inland waterways.

Internal problems

The dynastic weakness that made China vulnerable to these foreign incursions also increased her susceptibility to internal rebellion. The population had increased dramatically under the Qing; it probably reached 400 million some time between 1800 and 1850. Traditional forms of technology were not capable of providing a decent living for so many people. At the same time the government was growing lax. Local officials, who had collected taxes primarily as agents of the central government early in the dynasty, were now keeping most of what they got and passing on only a fraction of their take to the Emperor. Wealthy individuals acquired greater influence over local administrators and thus became increasingly able to evade taxation, throwing the burden onto the poor. The peasants, short of land, paid increasingly heavy taxes while the amount of revenue actually reaching the Emperor declined. Poverty drove thousands to banditry. The Manchu army, its original spirit sapped by generations of garrison duty within China, had deteriorated badly; many units were almost useless. As the government's ability to maintain order declined, local leaders began raising their own militias to protect their villages.

Dynastic decay had gone far enough to permit a serious rebellion by the 'White Lotus' Buddhist sect in Central China at the end of the eighteenth century. The outbreak of the Taiping Rebellion in the mid nineteenth century led to an even greater crisis. It began in the hills of South China, where a religious visionary claiming to be the younger brother of Jesus Christ founded a sect incorporating elements of Christianity. His movement spread, came into conflict with the government, and developed its own army. Soon it was calling itself the Taiping Tianguo, or 'Heavenly Kingdom of Great Peace'. Sweeping north and east into the basin of the Yangzi River, the richest and most populous region of China, the 'Heavenly King' established his capital at Nanjing (Nanking) in 1853. He could not take the Manchu capital at Beijing, but the government armies proved equally incapable of destroying the rebels.

The Manchus then turned to regional militias formed by the local gentry, and allowed some of these militias to develop into real armies. This was a step they were very reluctant to take; they had not forgotten the lesson they had learned in the rebellion of 1673. However assimilated they might be to Chinese culture, the Manchus knew that they were in fact a small number of aliens dominating a large number of Chinese, and that if armed forces grew up under purely Chinese leadership, outside the established structure of Manchu power, those forces might sooner or later turn against the dynasty. One of the basic principles of the Chinese government, for many centuries, had been to break up all concentrations of power that might threaten the Emperor's control. However, the Qing Court preferred to place a dangerous amount of power in the hands of Chinese who at least seemed loyal, rather than wait passively to be destroyed by the Taipings. In the end the gamble paid off; the regional armies that grew up outside the regular chain of command put down the Taiping Rebellion, and other smaller rebellions in other regions of China, and remained loyal. The Westerners also provided the Qing government with some useful support against the Taipings, feeling that it was worth working with the existing government despite the fact that they did not really like it. One should particularly note the 'Ever-victorious Army', a small Chinese force commanded originally by an American named Frederick Ward, and later by a British officer, Major Charles Gordon. It was very successful in fighting against the Taipings near the mouth of the Yangzi River. Such Western intervention, however, was much less important than the support provided for the Qing by the regional armies.

The leaders of these regional armies acquired tremendous power. The greatest of them, Li Hongzhang (Li Hung-chang), in the late nineteenth century, took a large part of the responsibility for conducting China's foreign relations. He had his own army, under officers he had chosen and promoted, equipped to a considerable extent from his own arsenals. He also controlled much of China's naval forces. He was governor-general of a province, and had privileged access to tax revenues from other provinces to pay for his military forces. He sponsored several efforts to introduce modern technology into China. He would have been in an excellent position to lead a rebellion against the Manchus, but instead he and others like him formed the main bulwarks of the Qing Dynasty in the late nineteenth century.

Some Chinese were beginning to feel that they needed to learn from the foreigners, but this awareness developed very slowly. The idea of learning from foreigners seemed very abnormal in the light of Chinese tradition. In the English-speaking world today, most children grow up knowing that they use an alphabet developed in Italy, a political system whose origins go back to Greece, and a religion that comes from the Middle East. Their very ancestry can be traced more often than not to immigrant stock – Angles, Saxons, Danes, Normans, and so forth – who invaded Britain after the fall of the Roman Empire, and various groups that have migrated to the United States, Canada, and other English-speaking countries within the past 400 years. The ancestors of the modern Chinese, by contrast, had lived in China for all of recorded history. They had only once in their history engaged in large-scale borrowing from abroad, when they had adopted Buddhism. As far as most Chinese knew, the biggest foreign-inspired modification that had occurred in their culture in the past thousand years had been the imposition by the Manchus of a new hair style on their subjects (the Chinese were required, under the Manchus, to wear their hair in a single braid, called a queue, hanging down the back). Most Chinese still believed that it was the foreigners who needed to copy the superior civilization of China.

The Chinese had been shocked by the defeats they had suffered at the hands of the West, but they did not respect the military profession enough to feel that someone who was militarily strong was necessarily worthy of respect or imitation. What they most valued was the literary and philosophical knowledge, especially of the Confucian classics, that both defined the gentleman and formed the qualifications for high office in the government. When the Manchu warriors had conquered China, it had been they who had imitated and been absorbed by the Chinese, rather than the other way round.

Initially some men, especially leaders of the regional armies, tried to introduce particular Western devices without imitating the West in any more basic way. Rifles and Western-style cannon came first; steamships, railroads, and telegraph lines followed. The policy was to use Western techniques as tools while retaining Chinese culture as the fundamental basis for all activity. This policy showed a distressing lack of success. For one thing, the foreigners had to be handled and dealt with, and this required far more than knowledge of a few techniques. Chinese officials had to know Western languages, commercial practices, behaviour patterns, and concepts of international law before they would be able to understand what the foreigners wanted, and how it could be either granted or refused with minimal cost to China. Moreover, even simple matters of technology did not work very well when taken out of their cultural context. The Chinese could manufacture artillery to Western designs, but it was not actually much use in battle as long as it remained, to the troops, an essentially alien device. The same applied in other areas. Superficial adoption of a few Western techniques could not even begin to save the country from the degree of peril facing it.

By the end of the century a few influential people were beginning to realize that China would have to copy the West in fundamental matters, but they did not find their position popular; most Chinese who had an opinion of the foreigners detested them. This was partly a response to genuine injuries and slights suffered at the hand of the West, ranging from the Opium War down to incidents of petty racism. The Europeans showed a conspicuous lack of respect for Chinese law and the Chinese people. In Shanghai, the richest city in China, there was a public park for the exclusive use of Europeans. (There is dispute among historians as to whether there was actually a sign at the entrance stating that 'No Dogs or Chinese' were permitted in the park.) But beyond such issues, which created much well-founded Chinese resentment, there were rumours attributing quite imaginary crimes to the foreigners. Many Chinese were convinced the Christian religion was based on black magic, and that Western missionaries were using Chinese children as victims in rituals involving human sacrifice. The notion that the Chinese should become students of Western culture seemed odd even to many of the more sophisticated Chinese; to those who believed the wilder of the anti-foreign rumours, it appeared positively obscene.

The Empress Dowager Cixi (Tz'u-hsi) dominated the imperial court. She had not been particularly powerful as the wife of an emperor, but when her husband died in 1861 and her five-year-old son inherited the throne, she was able to seize effective control of the government. When her son died some years later she arranged, in violation of the normal rules of succession, that the throne should go to a three-year-old boy who was her nephew, and she continued to rule in this young Emperor's name. Certainly she was intelligent and strong-willed. Otherwise she could hardly have dominated a society as male-centred as China for forty-seven years. However, she was also short-sighted, self-centred, and thoroughly ignorant of the Western world which posed such a threat to the country she ruled. She would not willingly support any drastic programme of reform or modernization.

Islands of modernization began to appear in some places, under the aegis of various Chinese officials. Regional leaders like Li Hongzhang not only tried to modernize the armed forces under their control, but sometimes went beyond to sponsor commercial enterprises – shipping lines, factories, and so on. However, the

2.1 The Empress Dowager Cixi.

merchants who managed such enterprises were subjected to much interference from their political masters, and many of the enterprises suffered from corruption and nepotism.

A more vigorous and far-reaching form of westernization occurred in the treaty ports and in Hong Kong, where Western influence was strongest. Christian missionaries set up schools and colleges. Chinese businessmen not only learned foreign business techniques and technology, they were able to apply their knowledge in an environment far more friendly to commercial enterprise than that found in the bulk of China. The competition of Western business firms with superior financial resources was sometimes a problem, but on the other hand many Chinese businessmen were able to

2.2   Public execution during the Boxer Rising. A Boxer beheaded in front of European troops.

borrow operating capital, through intermediaries, from Western banks. In any case, foreign competition posed fewer problems than the extortionate bureaucrats of cities not under foreign control. Later nationalist scholars have looked down on the 'compradors', Chinese businessmen who acted as agents or partners of foreign merchants, but these people played an important role in introducing Western knowledge to their country.

In 1898 a scholar named Kang Youwei (K'ang Yu-wei), who had rather startlingly reinterpreted the Confucian classics, making Confucius an advocate of reform and change rather than a preserver of tradition, won the ear of the young Emperor. Kang and the Emperor launched a remarkably broad campaign of reform and modernization. However, within a few weeks conservative elements at the court, led by the Empress Dowager, had regained control. The brief period of Kang's ascendancy was later known as the 'Hundred Days'. Kang fled abroad; other leading reformers were executed, and the Emperor spent the rest of his days as a prisoner of his aunt the Empress Dowager.

Western pressure increases

The final outburst of traditional Chinese xenophobia came in 1899. A group generally called the Boxers, basically a secret society, began attacking missionaries and foreigners in general. They claimed that the mysterious powers of Chinese martial arts could defeat the firearms of the foreigners and drive them out. The Boxers originally had anti-Manchu tendencies, but the Empress Dowager and the court, hating the foreigners and in any case fearing to antagonize the Boxers, decided to co-opt them and gave them a certain degree of support. The Boxers killed missionaries and Chinese Christians, and besieged the foreign legations in the capital of Beijing. The result was what might have been expected, given China's repeated defeats earlier in the nineteenth century. A joint force of the major Western powers plus Japan marched in, defeated the Boxers and the government army that had been half-heartedly supporting the Boxers in their attack on the foreign legations, captured Beijing with much destruction and looting, and extracted a massive indemnity from the government.

Fortunately, the fighting was limited to the northern part of the country. Key provincial governors in central and southern China understood the power of the Europeans far better than did the Empress Dowager; they ignored her decision to support the Boxers, and maintained the fiction that the Boxers were rebels against the Qing Dynasty. They were thus able to avoid becoming embroiled in the hostilities. Eventually the victorious Westerners also decided to accept this fiction, which is why books published in the West often refer to the whole affair as the 'Boxer Rebellion'. The Westerners did not want to destroy the dynasty, but simply to manipulate and exploit it, so they allowed it to save face by disavowing its erstwhile Boxer allies.

The competition among the imperialist powers for 'spheres of influence' in China had become acute in the late 1890s. It seemed for a while that China might be reduced to colonial status. Within their spheres, the various powers' investments and commercial activities were usually backed up by control of communications, especially railroads, and by the presence of armed forces. China's helplessness was revealed during the Russo-Japanese War of 1904–5. Much of the fighting between Russia and Japan occurred within the borders of the Chinese Empire, in southern Manchuria, but the Chinese government remained an essentially passive spectator.

In the end China was not carved up; the spheres of influence did not become foreign colonies. Partly this was because China was too large for any one power to take, and for a foreign power to convert influence into full *de facto* rule was difficult, in any particular area, as long as there existed a Chinese national government lying outside the foreign power's sphere of influence. Partly it was because the various powers interfered with one another's ambitions. Complete control of an area by any of them would have implied locking out the others. The 'Open Door Policy', announced by the United States in 1899 and 1900, was the most formal statement of this principle. This policy ordained that the control exercised by foreign powers over their spheres of influence should not be carried to such a point that the commerce of other nations was excluded, or that the sphere of influence ceased to be a part of China. One should not overestimate the impact of this American policy. The USA was not prepared to enforce it, but only to declare a wish that other nations should obey its principles. Furthermore, even had it been enforced, it would not by any means have constituted a guarantee of Chinese independence. Chinese enthusiasm for the Open Door was limited; most Chinese, given a choice, would have preferred a closed door with the foreigners on the outside.

In the first years of the twentieth century, shaken by the disaster of the Boxer incident and by the scramble of the imperialist powers for concessions in China, the Qing Court finally took drastic steps to preserve China's independence. The court tried not only to negotiate an increase in tariff levels, but also to regain control of the Maritime Customs Service that collected those tariffs. It tried very hard to negotiate an end to foreign importation of opium into China. It began modifying the principle of extraterritoriality, under which Westerners in China were immune to Chinese law. It pushed effective administration into remote border areas to which it had previously never paid much attention, to make sure that they would not be nibbled away by the foreigners.

Even more important, the Qing Court embarked on a drastic programme of modernization and westernization within China. The traditional system of Civil Service examinations was abolished, and the education system was modified to take in Western knowledge. Provincial governments were ordered to select promising students for study abroad. Efforts were made to modernize many military units. These 'New Armies' differed from the traditional units not only in their training and equipment, but also in that their soldiers were better educated, and came in many cases from fairly respectable backgrounds. Administrative structures were reorganized on Western lines, and the court even announced a plan to introduce constitutional government. Provincial assemblies were elected in 1909; the following year a National Assembly was convened, with half the members selected by the provincial assemblies and the other half chosen by the court.

These steps towards modernization, however, weakened the dynasty's political position rather than strengthened it. The Manchu ruling class had neither real enthusiasm for the changes that had been forced on it, nor great skill at carrying them out. It was not capable of carrying the westernization programme through to rapid and massive success; it is hard to see how any national leadership could have done so. The government's initial steps towards modernization drastically increased the number of people who expected rapid progress, and many of them turned against the dynasty when their expectations could not be met. Soldiers of the New Armies, because of their higher educational level, were much more receptive to revolutionary propaganda than the soldiers of traditional units had been.

Talk of constitutionalism inspired the provincial gentry to hope for a considerable expansion in their political power. Voting for the provincial assemblies had been limited to people of considerable wealth or education, and not surprisingly the gentry had emerged with control of these assemblies. Representatives of the gentry were then able to take control of the National Assembly also, despite the fact that half its members had been appointed by the Court. However, the provincial assemblies had been given only limited powers, and the National Assembly had not yet been given any real power. Members of the assemblies, and their supporters among the gentry, petitioned for the National Assembly to be converted into a genuine parliament, and were deeply offended when the court not only rejected the petitions but forbade further petitioning. Promises of constitutional government lost much of their credibility as conservative Manchu leaders at the court restricted the newly elected assemblies mainly to advisory functions. Indeed these leaders, increasingly worried about threats to their control of China, seemed to be tightening their grip on the government rather than loosening it.

Forty years earlier, during the suppression of the Taiping Rebellion, the court had allowed the rise of regional leaders like Li Hongzhang. These men, usually holding the title of provincial governor or governor-general, had their own armed forces backed up by substantial economic resources. They were entitled to most of the credit for whatever dynamism, and whatever capacity to learn from the West, the Qing government had possessed in the late nineteenth century. In the first years of the twentieth century there were two such great regional leaders. Zhang Zhidong (Chang Chih-tung), in Wuhan, controlled a vital territory in the heart of the Yangzi Valley. A younger man, Yuan Shikai (Yuan Shih-k'ai), held what had formerly been Li Hongzhang's power base in the north. Yuan had built, and was steadily expanding, the most powerful of the New Armies.

Both Zhang and Yuan were removed from office in 1907. The court was trying to strengthen its position; it no longer wished to allow any regional official to be so powerful. However, the actual effect of this move was to weaken the government. Such great regional lords had been bulwarks of the dynasty for the past forty years. Zhang and Yuan had both played key roles in saving the Manchus from the consequences of their decision to support the Boxers against the Europeans a few years before. They possessed the greatest concentrations of power outside Beijing, and the court, following the long-standing Chinese tradition that the way to attain safety in politics is to break up potentially hostile concentrations of power, wished to be rid of them. However, if they had been allowed to remain they might have been very useful to the court in its efforts to control the other elements of the Chinese élite – lower ranking government officials, merchants, gentry, modern-style intellectuals, and officers of the New Armies. Most of these people had fewer ties to the national government, and far less sympathy for the problems it faced, than Zhang and Yuan. They had been growing stronger for decades; the creation of elected assemblies was about to give them a public forum, and help both to unify and to legitimize them.

The Revolution of 1911

The final collapse of the Qing Dynasty was to a considerable extent inspired by a revolutionary from southern China named Sun Yat-sen. He was a Methodist Christian who had travelled widely outside of China, had received much of his education in Hawaii and Hong Kong, and had been almost totally converted to Western ideas. He wanted to make China a republic on the European model. His belief in the easy conversion of one civilization to the practices of another was rather naïve, but he was able to build up a secret society called the Tongmenghui (T'ung Meng Hui, in English usually called the Revolutionary Alliance). Its optimistically vague programme called for overthrow of the Manchus, restoration of Chinese independence, establishment of a republican form of government, and development of a modern economy. Its membership remained small, and it was riven by factionalism. Much of Sun's financial support came from the Chinese communities in various foreign countries; dislike of the Manchus was a long-standing tradition in these communities. Between 1906 and 1911, his followers failed in numerous armed uprisings against the Qing. None of these efforts drew in many participants, but the revolutionaries kept trying.

The final crisis began with a dispute over the control of China's railways. Many Chinese regarded foreign control of the railway network as one of the major threats to Chinese independence, and they had succeeded in having the right to build some key lines returned to Chinese ownership. These lines were intended to link the city of Wuhan, on the Yangzi River in central China, with Guangzhou in the south and Sichuan province in the west. Members of the local gentry had then put up substantial amounts of capital for railroad construction. However, the amount raised would not have been adequate even if properly managed, and much of it was dissipated through inefficiency and corruption. In 1911 the central government, which could see that financing and management organized on a provincial basis were not getting the lines built, and which did not care to see such vital facilities under provincial control in any case, obtained a foreign loan to pay for nationalization of the lines.

There was immediate rage in the provinces affected, both because the foreigners whose money was now paying for the railways seemed likely to emerge with ultimate control, and because those among the gentry who had already put in capital to begin construction were not being given what they regarded as fair compensation. In Sichuan province particularly, disorders and riots had escalated to outright rebellion by the autumn of 1911. The government moved in troops from neighbouring Hubei province, and rebellion then broke out there also.

Units of the New Armies in Wuhan (actually a collective name for three adjoining cities, one of which is the capital of Hubei province), had been heavily infiltrated by revolutionary organizations. The revolutionaries there called themselves a branch of the Tongmenghui, but they had in fact no contact with Sun Yat-sen and only a loose sort of liaison with some other Tongmenghui leaders. They had originally planned to spend a long time preparing for an uprising, but the crisis in Sichuan forced them to speed their schedule. Then the police arrested several of the ringleaders and captured a list of those involved in the plot. The remaining conspirators decided to move immediately, in however disorganized a fashion, rather than wait to be arrested in their turn.

No top leader of the revolutionary movement was in Wuhan, and many of the second-level leaders were in jail, so the rebels went to the highest ranking army officer they could catch, a colonel named Li Yuanhong (Li Yuan-hung), and forced him to accept the role of leader in the uprising. He had no previous record of sympathy for the revolutionary cause, and had to be threatened with execution before he agreed to take command of the movement, but he became more enthusiastic as it gained strength. (From this unlikely beginning, he rose over the next five years to become the nominal president of the Republic of China.) China was ripe for even such a weak and disorganized revolutionary movement as this. There was no effectively organized opposition in Wuhan, because both the commander of the armed forces of the province and the head of the civil administration had fled in panic when the rebellion began. The successful uprising in Hubei quickly inspired imitation; and within a few weeks, revolutionaries of various sorts had taken much of central and southern China. A revolutionary government, established in the city of Nanjing in central China, elected Sun Yat-sen as its President.

The imperial court, in desperation, turned to Yuan Shikai. He had built the strongest army China then possessed, and he was now the best man the Manchus could think of to command this army,

2.3   Dr Sun Yat-sen. On 29 December 1911, those provinces which had declared independence from the Qing Dynasty met in Nanjing to prepare the establishment of central government. At the same meeting Dr Sun Yat-sen was elected Provisional President.

despite the way they had removed him from command four years before. Yuan extracted very broad powers from the court before accepting command. He then made a deal with the revolutionaries, under which he supported the conversion of China into a republic in return for being made its first President. The true weakness of the revolutionaries now revealed itself. The Manchus had fallen because they were weak, not because Sun Yat-sen or any other revolutionary leader was strong. The armies of the Qing Dynasty, now commanded by Yuan Shikai, controlled much of northern China. In many areas where the Qing had been overthrown, revolutionary regimes were led by members of the gentry, or army officers, who were not affiliated with the Tongmenghui and did not take Sun Yat-sen's orders. In Wuhan itself the Tongmenghui had little influence over the revolutionary government, and the main power struggle was that between the forces of Li Yuanhong and Yuan Shikai. Sun did not control China and saw no way he might obtain control; the best course available to him was to make a deal with General Yuan.

Yuan Shikai and the warlord era

The Republic of China operated on an *ad hoc* basis for about a year; an elected Parliament finally convened in February 1913. The most powerful party in it was the Guomindang or Nationalist Party, which was in large part derived from Sun's old Tongmenghui, reoriented and drastically expanded. Sun himself was no longer the central figure; he did not have the skills of a party politician, nor any great desire to acquire them. Sun took a nominal post in the Guomindang but devoted most of his attention to planning the development of China's railway network, while a man named Song Jiaoren (Sung Chiao-jen) became the effective head of the new party.

Unfortunately for the Guomindang, having control of Parliament did not confer control of China. The holders of real power, notably the military commanders, had little desire to submit to any elected body, and support for Parliament within Chinese society was not sufficiently massive to force the military to recognize its authority. The electorate had been much more broadly based than in the elections of 1909, but it had still been limited to a minority of the population. Most Chinese had not been asked to vote for Parliament, and many were not even really aware of its existence.

2.4   General Yuan Shikai, who became President of the Republic of China in 1912.

Yuan Shikai took advantage of divisions in the Guomindang, and quickly established full control over the central government. In March 1913 Song Jiaoren was assassinated, probably at Yuan's instigation. Guomindang sympathizers in several central and southern provinces rebelled against Yuan in July, but were easily suppressed. At the end of the year Yuan outlawed the

Guomindang, and in January of 1914 he dissolved Parliament. The political machine Sun Yat-sen and Song Jiaoren had built was capable of winning elections, but it was not capable of forcing a man like Yuan Shikai to hold elections if he did not wish to. Even when Yuan overreached himself by assuming the title of Emperor, and then died in 1916, Sun Yat-sen could do little to influence events.

Yuan had never really been dictator of China; his control over most provincial governments had been too weak. When he died, central authority in China collapsed completely, and the country was divided up among various generals. China entered a decade of warlord rule. There continued to exist in theory a Republic of China, with a President and a Prime Minister in Beijing. It had one duty of real importance – handling China's relations with the foreigners. This gave it access to the customs receipts from the foreign-operated Maritime Customs Service, or at least to foreign loans for which the receipts were pledged as security. (In some years the customs receipts went entirely for debt payments.) It contained a certain number of capable officials who genuinely wanted to use their positions to promote the national welfare. However, over most of China it had no genuine control whatever. On the contrary, it often seemed little more than a pawn of whatever warlord or coalition of warlords controlled the city of Beijing.

For China as a culture the warlord era was one of great progress. Businessmen were taking over foreign production techniques, especially in the treaty ports where foreign influence was strongest. The First World War temporarily distracted the Europeans and allowed Chinese capitalists to make considerable strides, with much less competition from foreign imports. The new knowledge imported from the West was being assimilated, and significant numbers of Chinese were acquiring a steadily deeper understanding of it. Beijing and Shanghai were especially important as centres for the new learning. This trend was not an unmixed blessing – by the late 1920s and early 1930s, the colleges of China were turning out many graduates whose education had been so totally Western that they had little knowledge of or interest in the problems of their own society – but a substantial degree of modernization and westernization were necessary for China's survival.

For China as a nation the warlord period was a time of disaster. The upper classes, in general, lost much of their legitimacy. In the old order the core of the élite had been made up of educated men, who had acquired official status by a long and difficult course of study in history, philosophy, and classical literature. Their indoctrination had included many injunctions to care for the welfare of the common people. They had not always behaved in accord with the ideals in the works they had studied, but at least they had known that the Emperor would be annoyed with them if they abused the peasants so badly as to cause a revolt. In the warlord era almost all power was derived simply from the possession of money or military force.

A man could start out as a bandit, expand his force until he had effective control of a small area, and regularize the procedure by which he extracted wealth from the population until he could call it taxation instead of looting. He would then start to negotiate deals and alliances with the military forces in neighbouring areas. He could, in short, convert himself from a bandit to a minor warlord, and if he were sufficiently competent and lucky he might someday rule a province.

The central government no longer had either the will or the ability to protect the people against the rapaciousness of provincial élites. The poor suffered terribly, whether they were workers in the growing textile mills of Shanghai, or tenant farmers beset by landlords, tax-collectors, soldiers, and bandits.

Peace and order had been breaking down in the Chinese countryside for a long time; the Revolution of 1911 released a flood of violence. The struggles that began in 1911, most of which involved armies that were far from first-rate by world standards of the time, and in which bribery and intrigue often played a more important role than actual combat, can be described in comic-opera terms. There were extremely humorous incidents, including the cases of bandits who rose to warlord status, and Li Yuanhong being forced against his will to lead the rebellion of 1911 in Wuhan. There was nothing even faintly comic about the killing, however. People died by the hundreds of thousands, perhaps by the millions. Chinese rebels slaughtered Manchus. Soldiers of the Qing Dynasty, and later of the Republic of China and the various warlords, slaughtered rebels and people suspected of being rebels. Soldiers killed bandits or suspected bandits; the bandits killed those who got in their way. Warlord armies fought one another, seldom competently, but still with a substantial level of bloodshed, which increased over time as the armies expanded and their weaponry improved.

What little progress China had made in combating foreign encroachment, in the last days of the Qing Dynasty, was reversed. Much of the country fell within the sphere of influence of one foreign power or another, and Western military forces were stationed rather widely within China to defend foreign interests. The Japanese were particularly aggressive. They declared war on Germany soon after the First World War began, moved into the German sphere of influence in Shandong province, and then demanded a substantial degree of control over China as a whole while the Europeans were distracted and unable to interfere. The 'Twenty-one Demands' which Japan presented to Yuan Shikai in January 1915 called not only for Japanese influence over very broad areas of China, but also for the presence of Japanese advisers in several crucial branches of the Chinese government including the police. The Japanese cannot have seen much that was extraordinary in their demands; this was the way the Great Powers had been treating less developed countries for many years. However, Japan's policy was understandably offensive to Chinese public opinion. Yuan Shikai, despite a tremendous public outcry, did not have the power to resist very effectively. He rejected the demand for Japanese advisers to the Chinese police, but gave in on most other issues. The last straw for China came at the peace conference after the war. The Chinese, who had declared war on Germany and had made some minor contributions to the war effort, had expected that in accord with Wilson's Fourteen Points they would obtain more independence and respect after the war, or at least that the German sphere of influence in Shandong would be returned to Chinese control. But the Versailles Treaty left the question of Shandong unsettled (in other words left the Japanese in control), and many of the other Chinese requests never even got on to the agenda of the conference.

The May Fourth Movement

In the nineteenth century, resistance against foreign incursions had usually taken the form of simple xenophobia; the Chinese had expressed a general distaste for things European and had wanted the foreigners to go away. By the end of the First World War a more modern style of nationalism was spreading, phrased in Western terms and concentrated among the most westernized elements of the population. When protests broke out in May 1919 against the lack of consideration for Chinese interests in the Versailles Treaty, and especially against Chinese officials who accepted foreign encroachment on China, the students and faculty at Beijing University played a major role. The period of ferment known as the

May Fourth Movement, which took its name from these demonstrations, included not only political protest but also literary and scientific developments involving considerable importation of Western ideas.

The concept of democracy gained in popularity among the intellectuals, both because of its inherent attractiveness and because they were aware that the most successful Western powers had been moving towards elected government during recent decades. In some aspects of life Western notions of equality went beyond the stage of being mere ideas for discussion, and began actually to be put into practice. The status of women rose; a small but increasing proportion of them obtained formal education, and the custom of foot-binding began to decline. Major intellectual figures began writing in a language much closer to that spoken by the common people, thus bringing closer the day when their writings could be read by a mass audience. Within a few years modern Mandarin, a North Chinese dialect spoken as a mother tongue by a large portion of the Chinese population, and not too difficult for speakers of other dialects to learn, replaced the fantastically difficult classical language as the medium of communication for educated people. This shift in language made mass education far easier than it could have been before, thus reducing the difficulty both of modern economic development and of creating a more equal society. Less than fifteen years before, the imperial government (thinking in terms of education in classical Chinese) had regarded raising the national literacy rate to 5 per cent as a goal that would take several years to accomplish.

The movement towards greater equality was more important than many of the intellectuals may have realized. The Chinese élite through all its history had been a thin stratum, arrogantly convinced of its own superiority, ruling over a great mass of relatively uneducated peasants. The bulk of the population, even in 1919, had hardly been touched by the currents of modernization, and endured a level of poverty which the citizens of modern industrial societies can barely imagine. The economic modernization and industrialization China needed could not be carried out on such a basis. A technologically oriented society cannot be built or operated simply by a few leaders and experts; it requires informed participation, at the very least, from a large proportion of the citizenry. An élite wishing to lead China into the twentieth century, to lead what is usually called a 'nationalist' revolution, could not succeed if it cut itself off from the masses in the way its predecessors had done. The question of just how far egalitarianism should be pushed has been a matter of intense dispute up to the present day, but there can be little doubt that Chinese society needed to become much more egalitarian than it was.

3

The Communist Party and the First United Front

For all the developments of the May Fourth era, the advocates of modernization and progress in China had found no way to apply their new ideas to their nation's political ills. Nationalist sentiments would be no more effective than the old xenophobia until the Chinese could find an organizational pattern to put them to political use. When such organizational techniques finally came they were packaged together with a radically egalitarian ideology, and they did not come from the countries which had most influenced China in the past century (Western Europe and to a lesser extent the United States). They came from Russia.

The CCP was officially founded, with some encouragement from the Soviet Union, in 1921. It remained fairly small at first, but soon a three-way alliance was formed between the CCP, the Russians, and Sun Yat-sen's Guomindang. With Russian advice and assistance, both the CCP and the Guomindang grew very rapidly, and by 1927 they controlled a considerable portion of China. At this point, however, the Guomindang turned against its erstwhile Communist allies, and the CCP was almost destroyed.

The coming of Communism

The Bolshevik Party, soon to be renamed the Communist Party, seized control of the Russian government in 1917. It advocated policies of class struggle, leading the poor to take control of the economy from the rich, and attempting to establish a socialist economic system. The Bolsheviks looked at revolution as a world-wide phenomenon, both out of a passionate belief that the benefits of socialism should be brought to all, and because they doubted that socialism could survive, much less reach its full potential, if it were restricted to a single country surrounded by enemies. Capitalist powers as far away as England and the United States had reacted with quick and violent hostility to the Bolshevik Revolution; the weakening or overthrow of such governments could only help the new regime in Russia. The Bolsheviks therefore established the Comintern (Communist International or Third International), a world-wide organization of revolutionary parties, with head-quarters in the Soviet Union. The Comintern took in some existing socialist parties, and helped to establish them in countries that had not had any.

Communist ideas found adherents in many countries. Lenin's techniques for organizing a tight, disciplined revolutionary party had proven a certain degree of effectiveness in the Russian Revolution, and infinitely greater successes were promised. The new ideology claimed the ability to solve virtually all of humanity's problems. In addition, the Comintern's hostility to the capitalist powers appealed strongly to people in countries like China, which had long been victims of European imperialism. In 1919 and 1920 the revolutionary regime in Russia offered, in striking contrast to the Western powers, to give up all the special privileges that the former Tsarist government had extracted from China. The Chinese were much impressed, though the Russians did not in the end carry out their pledge. Interest in Marxist and Bolshevik ideas spread among some Chinese intellectuals, especially in Beijing and Shanghai; the CCP was formally established in 1921. Advice and assistance from the Comintern were useful in getting the Party started, but they gave the Russians a considerable degree of control over CCP policy from 1921 up to about 1935. The results of this control, as we shall see, were not beneficial to the CCP.

In theory, Communism seemed a complete antithesis to traditional Chinese patterns of thought and behaviour. It was totally dedicated to the concept of progress, not only in the sense that the socialist society of the foreseeable future would be greatly superior to anything that exists today, but also that the civilizations of the present are far superior to those of past centuries. According to Chinese tradition, most of history had been characterized by a downward trend.

Communism was radically egalitarian. It argued that the proletariat – the class of people who owned little or nothing, and who lived by doing manual labour for wages – was destined to rule. Even Chinese who were dissatisfied with the steeply hierarchical nature of Chinese society often found this a bit hard to swallow.

The Communists advocated socialism – placing most of the wealth of society under collective ownership. One could find traces of such an idea in Chinese tradition, but in practice the Chinese people were so committed to the family as an economic unit that most observers felt it would be impossible for socialism really to be accepted.

The Communists believed that there existed one set of true ideas, and that all others were wrong. They advocated class struggle; they said that Chinese society contained major internal conflicts, and that these conflicts needed to be fought through to a conclusion, by violent means, rather than being settled by compromise. Confucianism preached harmony, generally inclined away from violence, and rejected fanaticism of any sort.

Communism was, in short, a foreign ideology totally alien to the Chinese tradition. The fact that it could gain any foothold at all in China shows the extent of the crisis China was facing, and the degree to which the old ideas had been discredited. However, it would have been naïve to expect that everyone who joined the Communist movement would actually abandon all of his or her old patterns of thought. Many individuals decided that the Communist Party as an organization offered a solution to China's problems, and therefore joined it, without actually discarding all their traditional patterns of thought and adopting the attitudes supposedly dictated by Communist doctrine.

The CCP remained very small – less than a thousand members – for several years after it was founded. Most of its members were educated people, which meant that they came from middle- and upper-class backgrounds. Many received their first exposure to Communist doctrine either in a modern school or from people they had come to know in school. The children of ordinary workers or peasants were seldom able to go to such schools. However, in accord with the Marxist ideas they were studying, these young intellectuals were soon trying to organize the proletariat – the industrial workers – as the main basis of the revolution. Chinese workers, like those in many countries just embarking on industrialization, suffered from long hours, low wages, and atrocious working conditions. Their dissatisfaction made a considerable proportion of them willing to listen to Communist labour organizers. When Hong Kong seamen went on strike in 1922, the CCP helped mobilize dock-workers to strike in sympathy, and block the recruitment of strike-breakers, in ports as far away as

Shanghai. In the end, the Hong Kong seamen won a wage increase. However, there were few such victories. The proletariat was still very small, and did not have the economic power to win many battles against the employers, much less to take over the Chinese government. The CCP supported a major strike by railroad workers in 1922, but it was bloodily suppressed by warlord troops. The proletariat could not provide Communist intellectuals with enough support to make them more than a fringe group in Chinese politics.

The First United Front

Negotiations lasting from 1922 to 1924 changed this situation by creating a three-way alliance of the Comintern, the CCP, and Sun Yat-sen's Guomindang. The Communists were invited to join the Guomindang, and in some cases to take top positions in it, while retaining their Communist Party membership. They worked within the Guomindang to build up a joint revolutionary force.

Not all participants in this united front were comfortable with it. On the Guomindang side, some leaders were afraid that the unity and discipline of their party, precarious at best, would be totally destroyed if a separate group with its own goals and organization were allowed to join it.

Some Communists also had doubts. The Guomindang's ideology was vague. Although Sun allowed his Three People's Principles – nationalism, democracy, and people's livelihood – to be interpreted to fit in with Communist goals ('people's livelihood' became socialism), the Guomindang as an organization had not in the past been inclined to radical class struggle, and did not seem likely to develop such an inclination. Most of its members and leaders, like those of the CCP, came from the upper levels of Chinese society, but unlike CCP members they had not been indoctrinated with radically egalitarian ideas, and they did not seem likely to carry out a revolutionary attack on their own class. However, Comintern advisers pointed out to their Chinese comrades the obvious fact that China was still too backward for a proletarian uprising to be practical. The creation of a unified, independent national government, and capitalist economic development, would be steps in the right direction and would bring closer the day when a genuine Communist revolution would be possible.

This reflected one of the fundamental theoretical dilemmas of Communism. Marxist doctrine had originally predicted that capitalist economic development would lead to a steady growth in the power of the proletariat, and that at about the time the capitalist class had gone as far as it could in developing industry, the proletariat would take over and establish a socialist system. Lenin had created the possibility of a very different path by developing the organizational techniques that enabled the Bolshevik Party to take control of Russia long before the capitalist class had completed the development of modern industry, indeed at a time when the proletariat was still quite small. Lenin's techniques later proved applicable to countries where modern industry hardly existed at all. A Communist Party active in a country at a low level of development, such as China, had to decide to what extent it would oppose the capitalist class in the name of class struggle, and to what extent it might support the capitalists against common enemies – foreign powers attempting to dominate the country, and remnants of pre-capitalist ('feudal') ruling classes. A Communist Party actually in power in such a country had to carry out tasks such as the establishment of national unity, mass literacy, and the initial stages of industrialization, which according to earlier Marxist theories should have been largely completed by the capitalist class before the revolution. In this context, it appeared not unreasonable for the Communist Party to join with the Guomindang to overthrow the warlords and establish an effective government for China, knowing that eventually it would probably come into conflict with some of the bourgeois and petit-bourgeois elements in the Guomindang.

In more practical terms, the alliance seemed to offer considerable benefits to all the parties involved. The Russians hoped that large portions of China would come under the control of the CCP, over which they had a great deal of power through the Comintern, or at least of the Guomindang with which they were now allied. In general, any strengthening of Chinese nationalism would weaken the European imperialist powers, which were enemies of the Soviet Union. The tiny CCP, which probably had less than a thousand members, gained the prestige of affiliation with the famous Sun Yat-sen, and the cooperation of Sun's organization (which while small in the scale of national politics was still much larger than the CCP). Sun gained new recruits from among the Communists, arms and funding from the Comintern, and the invaluable services of Comintern advisers to teach the Guomindang, barely more than a secret society at this time, how to run a political party and an army. By the time Comintern

3.1   Chiang Kai-shek, Commandant of the Huangpu Military Academy and later head of the Guomindang.

involvement reached its peak, in 1925 and 1926, there were about sixty Comintern military advisers attached to the Guomindang.

From 1924 to 1926 the activities of the coalition centred on the south coast city of Guangzhou (Canton). Both its political apparatus and its army developed very rapidly. The Huangpu (Whampoa) Military Academy in particular, whose instructors included Comintern advisers as well as Communist and non-Communist members of the Guomindang, trained military officers of a considerably higher quality than most of those found in the warlord armies to the north.

The Comintern advisers got along quite well with the Guomindang. They were tremendously useful, and they did not seem excessively preoccupied with making China a Communist country. They were, after all, in China largely as representatives of the Soviet Union, and Soviet interests might be served very well by a friendly but non-Communist government. The CCP, on the other hand, was deeply committed to making China a Communist country, and thus was more likely to come into conflict with non-Communist members of the Guomindang. Mikhail Borodin, the chief Comintern representative in China, was therefore allowed to exercise far more influence in the Guomindang than did any of the Chinese Communists who had joined the Guomindang. Sun Yat-sen, explaining in October 1924 why Guomindang leaders unfriendly to Russia would have to be excluded from a certain important committee, said: 'Henceforth our party must take Russia as its teacher in revolution, otherwise there will be no achievement by us.'

Sun Yat-sen died in March 1925. Tension between the various men hoping to succeed him was exacerbated when one of the most important Left-wing leaders in the Guomindang was assassinated by persons unknown in August 1925. None of the serious competitors for Sun's position was a Communist, but the apparent winner of the struggle, a long-time Guomindang member named Wang Jingwei (Wang Ching-wei), was friendly to the CCP, and appointed Communists to many important positions in the Guomindang. By this time CCP membership was expanding fantastically, due both to the advantages it had gained from its united front with the Guomindang, and to the role it played in the anti-foreign demonstrations and strikes that had begun in May 1925 (see below).

Both the rise of Wang Jingwei and the growth of the CCP, however, were essentially phenomena of civilian politics. Command of the Guomindang's armed forces lay with Chiang Kai-shek, a friend of Sun Yat-sen who as commandant of the Huangpu Military Academy had acquired great influence among the newly trained army officers. In March 1926, Chiang decided that it was time to start cutting down the power of the CCP and the Russian advisers. Claiming that a coup was being plotted against him, he arrested the advisers and some of the leading CCP cadres. He later released them, with apologies to the Russians. However,

3.2 Mikhail Borodin, the Comintern's representative in China.

from this point onward the activities of the Russian advisers were restricted, and most CCP cadres were removed from the armed forces. Having consolidated his control of the army, Chiang moved to take command of the party and government. Wang Jingwei, instead of fighting to retain his position, embarked on an extended trip abroad. By the middle of 1926, Chiang was the effective head of the Guomindang.

The Communist Party concerned itself mainly with the proletariat – factory workers, miners, railroad employees, and so on. Labour organizing activities often went together with nationalist

3.3 Mother and child during the Great Northwest Famine of the late 1920s.

agitation, since so many of the large enterprises in China were owned by foreigners. During 1925 the police in the foreign-controlled concessions, defending the interests of foreign factory owners, repeatedly fired upon crowds of Chinese workers. These incidents inspired waves of nationalist outrage, arousing students and businessmen to support worker protests. Strikes in the summer of 1925 involved hundreds of thousands; the CCP was heavily involved in these strikes.

Only a few Communists, of whom Mao Zedong would later become the most famous, were beginning to notice that by far the largest element of the population in China was the peasantry, and that the peasants could also be very responsive to Communist appeals for class struggle.

Many of the peasants were in truly desperate straits. Hunger was a normal part of life; a major crop failure could bring actual starvation. In Northwest China, with its uncertain rainfall, famines killed millions during the 1920s. Poor peasants struggled as best they could to earn more, to acquire land, and to acquire a position of some economic security for themselves and their children, but most failed. Indeed, the average man in China was significantly poorer than his father. The poorest men in China were seldom able to reproduce themselves; to raise children, or even just to marry, took more resources than they had. This meant that most of the poorest men of any particular generation could not be the children of people as poor as themselves, because people as poor as themselves did not have children. The poorest men of each generation were mostly the children of parents higher on the economic scale, victims of a systematic pattern of downward social mobility. The fact that most families tended to become poorer from one generation to the next was most conspicuous among families that were already fairly poor, but this tendency existed at all levels of the social scale. Any revolutionary movement which could convince the peasants that it could better their lives would be able to tap a tremendous reservoir of support.

The area in which the Communists happened to be operating, around Guangzhou, was not one of the poorest, and famine was not a normal part of existence as it was in the northwest. However, this was one of the most landlord-ridden areas of China. A tremendous proportion of the peasants were tenants, so their poverty and misery, even if not as acute as in other regions, could more easily be blamed on exploitation by the rich. Mao Zedong is only the most famous of a number of CCP agitators who went out to the countryside to organize peasant unions and whip up class struggle, especially in Guangdong and Hunan provinces. By February 1927 Mao, who ranked fairly high in the Communist Party but was not among its top leaders, had decided that the peasants rather than the industrial workers might become the primary basis for the revolution.

> In a very short time, several hundred million peasants in China's central, southern, and northern provinces will rise like a tornado or tempest – a force so extraordinarily swift and violent that no power, however great, will be able to suppress

it . . . They will send all imperialists, warlords, corrupt officials, local bullies, and evil gentry to their graves. All revolutionary parties and all revolutionary comrades will stand before them to be tested, to be accepted or rejected by them. To march at their head and lead them? To follow in the rear, gesticulating at them and criticizing them? To face them as opponents? Every Chinese is free to choose among the three, but circumstances demand that a quick choice be made . . .

To give credit where due, if we allot ten points to the accomplishments of the democratic revolution, then the achievements of the urban dwellers and the military rate only three points, while the remaining seven points should go to the peasants in their rural revolution . . .

These passages contain a certain degree of youthful exaggeration. Mao had not been in the business of peasant organization very long, and within a few years he would learn that it was not as easy as he had at first thought. In the short run, however, his most frustrating problem was probably his inability to convince his superiors in the Party of the importance of the peasants. Marxist doctrine was firmly committed to the primacy of the urban working class. The CCP did not formulate a coherent land policy, or assign a large proportion of its members to the tasks of peasant organization. Indeed Mao, who under the United Front was a member of both the CCP and the Guomindang, sometimes seemed to be doing his work with the peasants primarily in his capacity as a Guomindang member.

Despite its internal conflicts, the Guomindang grew rapidly. By late 1925 it controlled the southern provinces of Guangdong and Guangxi, and it was contemplating an attack on the warlords of the north. At this point a debate broke out; many people doubted that the Guomindang should risk attacking the large, if poorly trained, northern armies. The Russians in particular, who had begun to establish friendly relations with one of the northern warlords, were afraid that this connection would be jeopardized if a Russian-backed revolutionary force should begin aggressive expansion. Chiang Kai-shek, however, pushed very hard for a campaign to the north. Chiang won, and the Northern Expedition began in July 1926. The army itself was made up mostly of the non-Communist elements of the Guomindang. The Communists concentrated on political activity among the civilian population. They worked not only in areas already under the rule of the Communist–Guomindang United

Map 3. The Northern Expedition, 1926–1928.

∙─∙∙─ Province border

── ── Dotted line indicating that the island of Hainan is part of the province of Guangdong.

● City

HUNAN Province

↑ 3/27 Main routes of Guomindang advance, with dates 3/27 means March 1927

↑ The most important of the warlord armies that joined the Guomindang during the Northern Expedition

kilometres
0   200   500   1000
0   200   400   600
miles

Front, but in areas not yet reached by the northward advance, advertising the virtues of the Guomindang. When Chiang Kai-shek moved north into the Yangzi basin, his men behaved far better than the usual warlord armies, just as the Communists had promised the peasants they would. In particular, the Guomindang forces habitually paid for food supplies, instead of simply taking them at gunpoint. The peasants, as a result, were far more willing to supply food to the Guomindang than to its enemies; this was one of Chiang Kai-shek's major military advantages.

The Guomindang pushed rapidly north through Hunan in July 1926, and reached the Yangzi River in August. From this point onward it faced stiffer resistance; the conquest of Jiangxi took about two months of hard fighting. However, Chiang Kai-shek's forces grew stronger as the campaign went on, thanks to their capture of weapons and equipment from their opponents, and to the fact that an increasing number of warlord units were changing sides and allying themselves with the Guomindang.

Chiang fought an aggressive and mobile style of warfare. His warlord opponents had more heavy weaponry, but they were dependent on the railroads for transportation. Chiang's men, less burdened with heavy equipment and able to count on more cooperation from the peasants, could more easily move across country to bypass enemy units and threaten their rail communications from behind.

The Communist–Guomindang split

The non-Communist members of the Guomindang – both those who had been with the organization before the United Front with the Communists was established, and the much larger number who had joined later – seldom had much sympathy for Communist ideas of class struggle. Most of them came from well-to-do families, including landlords and capitalists. The idea of organizing the poor to struggle against the rich struck such people as at best unnatural, and at worst a direct attack on their own families. The potential conflict had been manageable during the earliest days of the United Front, when the Communists had not yet developed much interest in organizing the peasants, and in any case the alliance controlled so little territory that the question of how it should be ruled did not seem worth a quarrel. What was important was united action against the warlords. But as the Guomindang acquired more power and more territory, its member factions struggled increasingly for control. When the Northern Expedition conquered vast new areas, including the homes of many Guomindang officers from landlord families, the problem became acute. Chinese Communist Party organizers set up some peasant associations and labour unions ahead of Chiang's forces as they moved north. Even more important was the rapid growth of the peasant associations in many areas after the arrival of Guomindang armies. The CCP leadership, anxious to avoid rupturing the United Front, tried to restrain the extremes of peasant radicalism, but soon the landlords and gentry of many areas were under severe attack. In the cities, Communist-led labour unions were leading the workers in strikes for higher wages. Many Communists, furthermore, while they continued to support the Guomindang as an organization, were increasingly hostile to Chiang Kai-shek as an individual.

Open violence broke out when the Northern Expedition reached Shanghai, the richest commercial city in China, near the mouth of the Yangzi River. As Chiang's troops neared the city, Communist labour unions rose up to seize it from within. Chiang treated this not as part of a joint operation to take Shanghai in the quickest possible fashion, but as a power play designed to give the Communists the predominant voice in running the city. When his army arrived it treated the workers not as allies but as competitors, and slaughtered them by the thousands.

In April 1927, Guomindang leaders associated with Chiang Kai-shek, meeting in Nanjing, decreed the establishment of a national government and proscribed the CCP. Through the middle of 1927 there was a three-way struggle among the Communists, the centre and Right-wing elements of the Guomindang under Chiang Kai-shek, and non-Communist leftist elements in the Guomindang, headed by Wang Jingwei, which cooperated with the Communists against Chiang. The CCP, in this crisis, was crippled by its subservience to the Comintern. Joseph Stalin, who had by this time consolidated his control of the Soviet Union sufficiently to have a dominant voice in the formulation of Russian advice to the CCP, did not want to admit that the alliance with the Guomindang was not working out well. To have done so would have provided embarrassing ammunition for his competitors for power in Moscow, including Leon Trotsky. Even after the slaughter of the Communists in Shanghai, therefore, Stalin denied the seriousness of the conflict with Chiang, arguing that the Guomindang as an institution could continue to be an ally of the Communists despite Chiang's defection. He foisted upon the CCP a policy of complacency when the Party should have been trying to make military preparations for the impending struggle against an extremely powerful foe. At the same time, Stalin's visible assumption that the non-Communist leftists in the Guomindang were fools, people to be manipulated and exploited by the Communists, offended them and helped to drive them over to the anti-Communist side.

The CCP finally turned to armed struggle in August and September. The uprising of 1 August 1927, at Nanchang (the capital of Jiangxi province), was carried out mainly by military units whose officers were Communists or Communist sympathizers. Their strength was inadequate and they were able to hold the city for less than a week, but the units involved in this affair later provided many of the leaders of the Chinese Red Army.

Uprisings during the following months in Hunan, Hubei, and Guangdong provinces had even less chance of success. Party doctrine held that politics was primary and that one should have faith in the revolutionary strength of the masses. This meant in practice that the Party had not devoted much effort to acquiring military forces; it expected ordinary workers and peasants to carry out an armed uprising when the time came, defeating or winning over Guomindang armies. Mao Zedong, who was assigned responsibility for organizing the 'Autumn Harvest Uprising' in his native province of Hunan, argued desperately that in order to fight against soldiers one needed soldiers. The Communists had no real army of their own, but if they were going to start a revolt they should at least base it as much as possible on winning over Guomindang units. Mao was overruled, and when the rebellion came it was primarily a civilian affair. Most of the participants were peasant union members from the countryside around Changsha, in Hunan province. Guomindang troops, though initially caught by surprise, quickly defeated the rebels. The 'Canton Commune', a Communist-led uprising in the city of Guangzhou in December, was equally unsuccessful. Mao drew from these defeats a confirmation of the view he had already held, that real military forces would be necessary for any serious uprising to succeed, and also he became more dubious about efforts to take large cities like Changsha and Guangzhou. Survivors from these affairs, and some equally disastrous ones in other areas, withdrew into the hills.

The Communist Party had been virtually destroyed; its membership dropped to less than a fifth of the level attained just before the split with Chiang Kai-shek. What might logically have been expected, given the history of Marxist and Communist movements in other countries, was that the CCP would be reduced to the same sort of weak and essentially urban movement it had been up to 1923, with some of its leaders in exile and others working underground in the coastal cities of China. Few people supposed that the Communist leaders who had chosen to retreat to the countryside, and who indeed had found themselves forced to retreat to unusually backward sections of the countryside, would be able to accomplish much there. The success of Communist guerrillas in the countryside was so unexpected that it did not attract much attention for several years.

4

The Nanjing decade, 1927–1937

The central government of China, under Chiang Kai-shek, grew steadily stronger during the ten years from 1927 to 1937. However, it had serious internal problems which limited its success in spreading its control to outlying areas. In particular, while it repeatedly decimated the Communist organizations, it never actually managed to destroy Chinese Communism. Fighting between the CCP and the Guomindang continued until 1937, when Chiang finally had to join once again in a united front with the Communists for joint resistance against Japanese encroachments on China.

The Guomindang government at Nanjing

Once the Communists had been defeated, Chiang Kai-shek continued his task of unifying China. He already held the provinces along the lower Yangzi River, the richest and most developed area in China. His capital was at Nanjing, on the Yangzi between Shanghai and Wuhan. By 1928 his control reached north to the former capital of Beijing, which he renamed Beiping. His influence stretched even into Manchuria, where a local warlord nervous about Japanese domination looked to a restored national government for support. During the next ten years Chiang won confrontations with various warlords in more distant areas of China. He could defeat any warlord or likely combination of warlords in an open contest, but he did not have the power to move simultaneously on all fronts, to eliminate warlordism throughout China. He had absorbed warlord armies rather than destroyed them; by 1928 his army was made up mostly of warlord units, which allied themselves with the Guomindang without altering their internal structure to any great extent. Yan Xishan (Yen Hsi-shan), master of Shanxi province, typifies some of the problems Chiang faced. Yan had joined Chiang

4.1   Chiang Kai-shek with two North Chinese warlords, Feng Yuxiang (left) and Yan Xishan (right), in 1928. They had allied themselves with Chiang during the Northern Expedition, but in 1930 rebelled against him.

during the Northern Expedition, and in fact it had been his troops that completed the Northern Expedition by taking Beijing in 1928. Shortly thereafter, Yan and another major warlord rebelled against Chiang, and were suppressed only after a bloody war. Chiang, however, proved unable to impose effective Guomindang rule in Shanxi, and within a very short time Yan Xishan returned to power there, once more running the province as an autonomous satrapy.

Chiang could not count on the loyalty of his subordinates; generals tended to drift into warlordism if they got very far from the centre of his power. Guomindang generals in Guangdong province, which had been Chiang's headquarters at the beginning of 1926, slipped out of his control as soon as he moved north. One of them actually launched a war against Chiang in 1936. While Chiang created the closest thing to a national government that China had had since Yuan Shikai died in 1916, and nibbled away at warlord power whenever he could, there was much that remained outside his control.

In one sense, his power was concentrated in the lower Yangzi Valley. This was the richest and most populous portion of China, and the power base it provided him enabled him to overawe local leaders in some other areas, but he never even came close to controlling the whole nation. In 1936, the area that was under at least a loose form of Guomindang rule encompassed about two-thirds of the population, but only a quarter of the land area of China. The area where Chiang's control was strong enough so that he could actually compel provincial authorities to hand over to him the land taxes they collected was much smaller.

In another sense, his control was largely limited to the cities and main communication lines. Even in provinces where he had no major rivals, his government did not penetrate the villages very deeply. He had an accommodation with local leaders, somewhat like the Qing Dynasty during its declining years, rather than a genuinely strong rural administration.

In some respects he functioned as a modern-style nationalist leader. He maintained a respectable rate of industrial growth, and built some roads, telegraph lines, railways, and so on. He negotiated quite successfully with the Westerners, recovering control over China's Customs Service almost immediately after he came to power, recovering some of the foreign concessions (sections of Chinese cities under foreign administration), and beginning the negotiations that finally led (in the 1940s) to the elimination of extraterritoriality. In his political manoeuvring within China, however, it sometimes seemed that he was functioning as a warlord. He distrusted his subordinates, and tried to keep them from becoming too powerful even if this sometimes meant keeping them too weak to do their jobs. He had to tolerate, and negotiate alliances with, warlords in outlying provinces.

However, if he had not made China a nation-state he had at least created a nucleus, centring on Nanjing, from which a nation-state seemed to be growing.

While the Guomindang proclaimed democracy as a long-range goal, it said that the Chinese people were not yet ready for such a system, and would first have to undergo a period of 'tutelage' under a *de facto* dictatorship. Chiang, in fact, showed little sympathy for democratic ideas. His political style was partly Confucian, and he encouraged study of the Confucian classics. He was also influenced by Fascism; he used some German advisers in his army and accepted certain Fascist ideas, especially in regard to every nation's need for a single supreme leader. He once said: 'I believe that unless everyone has absolute trust in one man, we cannot reconstruct the nation and we cannot complete the revolution.' His 'Blueshirts' paralleled the Italian Blackshirts and German Brownshirts. He thought of a good citizen as one who gave loyal and unquestioning obedience to the government, rather than as one who thought independently about public affairs.

His crucial problem was that he had no strong tie of any sort – democratic, Confucian, or Fascist – to most of the Chinese people. He could not depend on the voluntary allegiance of the mass population, or even of the officials who made up his own government. Many members of the urban middle class thought of themselves as citizens, and thought of the nation as an entity naturally entitled to the loyalty of its people, but this group was too small to form an effective basis for government. The peasants, the bulk of the population, felt no identification with the government and might barely be aware of its existence. Chiang had no network of reliable cadres[1] spread out through the countryside to popularize his ideas and enforce his policies. In the early 1930s, the Guomindang had an organized party branch in less than one-fifth of the counties in China. The ruling class was preoccupied with struggles over power and personal wealth. The loyalty of many officials went more to cliques based on personal relationships than to the government as a whole.

Chiang Kai-shek was aware of the way the spirit of his organization had decayed after 1927. He commented in 1930 that 'not only is it impossible to find a single party headquarters which administers to and works for the welfare of the people, but all are stigmatized by the most reprehensible practices, such as corruption, bribery, and scrambling for power'. Both idealistic dedication and simple efficiency had declined very severely. The split between the Guomindang and the Communists had contributed to this. Of those members of the Guomindang who had been seriously concerned to organize the common people and improve their lot, a large fraction had been Communists; these people had been driven out of the Guomindang in 1927 and 1928. Most of the remainder came under suspicion of Communist sympathies, since a desire to organize the masses was identified as a Communist trait; they were discouraged from continuing such activities, and often purged from the organization. The Guomindang thus cut itself off from real contact with the mass of the population.

At the same time, the Guomindang was recruiting very indiscriminately in the newly conquered areas. A great variety of people, mostly from the upper classes, swarmed to join once it became apparent that the Guomindang was now to rule China. Administrators from the North Chinese warlord regimes, and some of the actual warlords, signed up and were given senior positions. Certainly Chiang Kai-shek could not have administered his new domains without recruiting many such people, but the lack of discrimination in recruitment, the lack of indoctrination of the new people, and the lack of any serious effort to supervise them and force them to adhere to some higher standard of political morality than that to which they had been accustomed during the warlord era, allowed them to bring their political style into the new regime almost without alteration. The result was a large administration, many of whose branches never seemed to accomplish much except for the enrichment of their own personnel.

In the past, the rise of a new dynasty had sometimes been accompanied by a break-up of large landholdings. This made tax-collection easier and also eased the lot of the ordinary peasant. No such thing happened when Chiang rose to power. The amount of land in the hands of very large landlords may even have increased, though not as much as many Chinese thought it was increasing. Many landlords had enough influence to evade taxation to a very

4.2   The Bund, Shanghai. One of the more modern and westernized parts of Shanghai in the 1930s.

considerable extent; both the government and the ordinary peasants suffered as a result.

The Jiangxi Soviet

The tattered little groups that followed various Communist leaders into the hills after the Communist defeats of 1927 did not at first pose much threat to the government; only after several years had passed did they begin to become conspicuous. They were not in a position to obtain significant aid, or even much guidance, from the Comintern or the top leaders of the Communist Party. They were not operating in areas containing many intellectuals or industrial workers, the two groups from which Communist Parties normally recruited their supporters. Local peasants distrusted the Communists at first; they could not see how a scruffy band of inadequately armed men could represent anything but trouble.

The writings of Mao Zedong describe some of the problems he faced at this time, operating in the countryside of southern China after the failure of his effort to take the city of Changsha in September 1927. Lacking a base of political support in the villages, and hunted (if not with great vigour) by the Guomindang, he was forced to build up his forces in any way he could. He absorbed local bandits into his 'Red Army', and the former bandit leaders became officers. (Some of these men, when times later became difficult, revealed the shallowness of their conversion by reverting to apolitical banditry.) Mao took in not only Guomindang soldiers who had decided to change sides and join the Communists, but some who had simply been captured in battle. For a while the former bandits and former Guomindang troops, between them, made up a majority of his army.

Somehow he kept control of this motley group; he made the bandits become Communists, instead of allowing the Communists to become bandits. He was operating in areas where the structure of government was weak; a small and not very well-armed band could establish a local administration and have its way, at least until provincial or national authorities could bestir themselves to send a superior force against it.

In 1928, Mao joined forces with Zhu De (Chu Teh), one of the few CCP members who had held a military command in the Guomindang in 1927. Zhu had participated in the Communist seizure of Nanchang in August 1927, and then in an effort to take an important town in eastern Guangdong. After this effort failed he had retreated into the hills. Soon Mao and Zhu acquired a substantial territory, lying mostly in the southern portion of Jiangxi province. Officially named the 'Chinese Soviet Republic' in 1931, it is generally known as the Jiangxi Soviet. (The term 'soviet' was used in China to describe any section of the countryside where the CCP had been able to establish a functioning government.) Zhu became Commander-in-chief of the armed forces of the Jiangxi Soviet, but Mao was in fact the senior partner in their relationship. Once they had acquired their initial territory, their task was to penetrate the villages – to win the loyalty of the peasants, and place the movement on a solid mass base.

This was a far more complex problem than some Communists had supposed. Marxist doctrines of class struggle teach that the rich and the poor are natural enemies. The Communist Party is supposed to lead the poor in a struggle, inevitably destined for eventual success, to overthrow their wealthy enemies. In a society like China's, the factors making for misery among the peasants appeared overwhelming. The fundamental poverty of the Chinese economy was exacerbated, in many areas, by the rapacity, brutality, or sheer callousness of the élite. In famines, food was sometimes shipped *out* of the areas of worst starvation to places where the situation was not so bad, because in the worst areas there was no longer anyone with the money to pay for it. The poor were quite naturally dissatisfied with the state of their lives; they would have had to be insane to be satisfied. China had in past centuries witnessed repeated rebellions fuelled by their discontent, the most recent having been the Taiping Rebellion. However, inexperienced Communists often made the mistake of assuming that the poor would see their situation in Marxist terms, would blame the wealthy, as a group, for their plight, and would join enthusiastically in a revolution based on class struggle as soon as they were presented the opportunity. This turned out not to be the case; not all the poor believed either that the existence of a class of wealthy landlords was inherently unjust, or that an attempt to abolish the landlord class would have the slightest chance of success.

The most important programme for winning the peasants was land reform. This consisted primarily of redistributing land from the rich to the poor, as private property. (A few early gestures towards the Marxist goal of collectivization were quickly abandoned; the peasants were not ready.) The CCP considered that any economic relationship in which one person enjoyed an income that came from labour done by some other person constituted exploitation; if the person who worked a plot of land had to pay rent to some other person who owned it, this was automatically considered to be exploitation, even if the rent were quite modest. The Party sorted the rural population into classes primarily on the basis of who was exploiting whom. The main categories were as follows:

- Landlords were people who did not do significant amounts of agricultural labour themselves, but lived by exploiting others. The most important form of exploitation they used was renting out land, but they also sometimes hired labourers to work their land, and made usurious loans.
- Rich peasants obtained a significant part of their incomes from exploitation, usually hiring labourers and lending money, but they also worked on the land themselves.
- Middle peasants were small farmers who lived primarily off their own labour. They might exploit others to a small extent (most frequently by hiring some supplementary labour at the harvesting season), but most of the work on their farms they did themselves.
- Poor peasants did not live so well. They were usually exploited by others; they had to rent land, borrow money at high interest, or work as hired hands on other people's farms for part of the year.
- Agricultural labourers were the poorest class; they were people who had been unable to get land even as tenants.

The 'Land Law of the Chinese Revolutionary Military Council', passed in 1930, said that the cultivated land was to be divided equally among all the agricultural population, except that landlords, reactionaries, etc., and their families, might be left with less land than the peasants or no land at all.

Carrying out land redistribution on this basis, the CCP was able to win a substantial peasant following, and by 1931 and 1932 Mao was getting peasants to enlist in his army, instead of the bandits and prisoners of war who had earlier been his main sources of recruits. However, he also found substantial numbers of landlords and rich peasants joining his organizations. When members of the village élite saw that the Communist Party had become the government of a given area, they naturally tried to fit themselves into the new power structure, just as their counterparts in other areas were swarming to join the Guomindang. When Communist Party organizers came into a village and looked for recruits, the people likely to step forward first were those with self-confidence, literacy, prestige, and enough wealth to be able to take time off from earning a living and work on political tasks – in other words people who came at least from the richest half of village society, and often actually from the landlord class. The poor peasants would *not* immediately tell Communist organizers from outside the village: 'Do not accept that man; he is a landlord.' For one thing, to do so and thus offend a powerful man would be very dangerous. For another, it took the peasants a considerable time to realize that an alternative to landlord rule existed – that village affairs might actually be placed in the hands of the poor. Even if the recruiters sent into the villages by the CCP realized that some of the people joining their organization were not poor peasants, they might not object. After all, many of the recruiters were (like Mao Zedong himself) intellectuals from well-to-do families.

This naturally affected the results of any effort at land reform. Late in 1930, Mao commented that in any given area, the first time land redistribution was attempted, the rich peasants and middle peasants played the leading role; the poor peasants had little power over the process. Naturally, this situation enabled the rich peasants to conceal some of their best land.

In June 1933, at a conference on problems of land redistribution, Mao described areas where the old village élite had been remarkably successful in adapting itself to life under a Communist regime:

> Here the landlords' and rich peasants' open counter-revolutionary struggle had already been crushed by the revolutionary masses during the first stage. After this, many of them quickly altered their appearance, taking off their counter-revolutionary masks and putting on revolutionary masks. They express approval of the revolution and of land redistribution. They claim that they are poor peasants, and are entitled to share in the distribution of land. They have been very active, relying on their historic advantages: 'They are the ones who can speak, and they are the ones who can write.' Therefore, during the first stage they were able to snatch the fruits of the land revolution. The facts from countless localities prove that they are controlling the provisional administrations, infiltrating local armed forces, manipulating revolutionary organizations, and [in land redistribution] receiving more land and better land than the poor peasants.

This was a problem that Communist Parties in Russia and Western Europe had never really faced. It is a truism that one does not find many poor peasants or industrial workers running a Communist Party. The leaders are generally intellectuals from middle-class backgrounds. But in the rather depersonalized atmosphere of a city, the main centre of action for previous Communist movements, this seldom caused direct personal conflicts of interest. Such people were rarely in the position of deciding the fate of their own families or even close friends. In the smaller and tighter environment of the village such things happen all the time. When the CCP obtained recruits who came from the upper classes it had to worry more than previous Communist Parties both about the possibility that those who had joined the revolution sincerely would become involved in conflicts of interest, and that some would have joined for reasons of self-interest rather than conviction.

The Communist base area that Zhu De and Mao were building up did not follow the previous patterns of Communist revolution. The most obvious innovation was the idea of basing the revolution on the peasants. Marxists had always thought of themselves as representing the most advanced, developed sectors of society. Their base of support was supposed to be the industrial workers, especially those in the largest factories. The peasants were uneducated and technologically primitive; with each family a separate economic unit, the peasant economy provided no natural basis for united political action. Few Marxists expected that the peasants could do more than become junior partners in the revolution, following the lead of the industrial workers. The Bolshevik Revolution in Russia had moved beyond this pattern to acquire a considerable degree of peasant support, but its real base remained in the cities. Mao wrote as if the proletariat were the leading force in the Chinese Revolution, and the Communist Party a party of the proletariat, but this was a verbal gesture towards doctrinal orthodoxy. His actual policies placed the main theatre of the revolution entirely in the countryside, and reduced the role of the proletariat to a negligible level.

Even more fundamental was the shift in the way the Communist Party appealed for support. The previous assumption had been that a Communist movement would spread propaganda among the people, and when enough had been converted there would be an uprising and the Communists would come to power. Communist movements had sought support by making promises.

Furthermore, the propagandists making the promises lacked genuine experience with the realities of economics or administration, so even if they were attempting to be honest they had no way of knowing which of the things they were promising could actually be delivered. Promotion within such a movement was not – could not be – based on actual ability to run a government, since the Party had no way of testing the abilities of its members. A talent for making idealistic speeches was likely to be at a premium.

This had been the pattern of revolution European Marxist parties had always expected to follow, and the Russian Revolution had indeed followed it for the most part. Lenin and the Bolshevik Party had had virtually no experience in running either a government or an economy when they suddenly became the rulers of Russia in the autumn of 1917. Some things they learned fairly fast once they were in power, but others took years. In March 1922, more than four years after the revolution, Lenin reported in despair that the Communist Party still was not capable of running the economy, and that if it did not learn to do so, very quickly, it could not expect to survive.

> And the greatest danger is that not everybody realises this . . .
> The time has passed when the job was to draft a programme
> and call upon the people to carry out this great programme.
> That time has passed. Today you must prove that you can give
> practical economic assistance to the workers and to the
> peasants under the present difficult conditions, and thus
> demonstrate to them that you have stood the test of
> competition . . .
>
> [Even] responsible and good Communists . . . do not know
> how to run the economy and, in that respect, are inferior to the
> ordinary capitalist salesmen, who have received their training
> in big factories and big firms . . . The responsible Communists,
> even the best of them, who are unquestionably honest and
> loyal, who in the old days suffered penal servitude and did not
> fear death, do not know how to trade, because they are not
> businessmen, they have not learnt to trade, do not want to
> learn and do not understand that they must start learning from
> the beginning.

Mao was following a very different path to power. He had taken control of a small area, and was recruiting followers from villages that either were already under Communist rule, or were close enough to Communist areas to have heard something about the situation there. The revolutionary struggle was being carried out mostly by people who had already experienced life under a revolutionary regime. The result was a far healthier process than that which had occurred in Russia. The Chinese Communist Party was appealing for peasant support not just on the basis of promises, but on the basis of an actual, demonstrated ability to run local administrations in such a way as to benefit the peasants. Furthermore, promotion within the Party could be based not only on 'revolutionary attitudes', but also on proven administrative ability. No Communist Party could ever hope to come to power with its personnel fully competent to handle all the problems of economics and administration. Still, Communists like Mao and Zhu De had begun facing some of the problems of rule, and promoting cadres at least partly on the basis of their ability to handle administrative and economic problems, as soon as they began establishing base areas in the back country in the late 1920s. This was fully twenty years before they became responsible for running China as a whole.

Mao's departure from Marxist tradition caused repeated conflicts with his superiors in the Party. During the Autumn Harvest Uprising in 1927, they had reproved him for lacking confidence in the masses when he tried to centre the uprising on army units, instead of relying on civilian mobs. After he and other similar leaders had built up significant armies over the next few years, the Party command urged that these armies come down out of the hills and try to take over towns and cities. Such efforts were utterly hopeless given the small size of the Communist forces, and caused them heavy losses; after 1930 the rural guerrilla leaders refused to try for the cities again.

Friction grew worse when top Party leaders began to arrive in the Jiangxi Soviet. For several years after the disaster of 1927, much of the Party leadership had operated outside China, especially in Moscow. This had seemed necessary simply to keep the organizational machinery safe from destruction by the Guomindang, but it both kept Party leaders out of touch with conditions in China, and increased the degree of Russian control. Joseph Stalin, who in the late 1920s had firmly established his control of the Soviet Union, also had considerable control over both policy formation and the selection of leaders in the Chinese Communist Party. By 1931 a group of young Chinese known as the '28 Bolsheviks', who had been of no great importance in the CCP before they went to the Soviet Union for training, had risen, with Stalin's backing, to control of the Party.

When they found that Mao and similar organizers in some other areas had brought significant sections of the Chinese countryside under Communist rule, they began filtering back to China. Since they were officially the top leaders of the Party, they were able to take over the Jiangxi Soviet.

Their policies were doctrinaire and inflexible, as one might expect given their background. They had won control of the CCP not in the turmoil of actual revolutionary struggle, in which the relative merits of different leaders could be judged by the actual results of their policies, but in Moscow where displaying a correct revolutionary attitude was the important thing.

Mao had been willing to compromise a little on class struggle in the countryside, in order to maintain agricultural production. He favoured redistributing wealth from the rich to the poor, but he did not want to reduce large numbers of people to absolute destitution; he felt most of the rich should be left enough land to make a living. In contrast to Mao's views the Land Law of the Chinese Soviet Republic, heavily influenced by the 28 Bolsheviks and passed in October 1931, said that the landlords should be stripped of all the land they had, and the rich peasants reduced to extreme poverty (reduced to below the average level of wealth in the countryside).

Mao also said that redistribution should not be carried out in too disruptive a fashion. The easiest way to equalize landholdings in a village would have been simply to pool all the land of each village, divide it into equal parcels, and assign one parcel to each peasant. Mao felt that this would cause too much confusion, shift peasants from plots whose exact characteristics they understood to plots they did not know, and undermine the morale of peasants who had an emotional attachment to a particular plot of land and would not be happy if shifted arbitrarily to another. He said that one should take the existing situation as a basis, and shift the ownership of as little land as possible, trimming down the landholdings of those who had more than their proper share of land by Communist standards, in order to give to those who had less. A rich peasant could more easily evade the land reform and retain excess land under Mao's policy than under a policy of simply redistributing all land in a village, but Mao thought this was a price worth paying in order to avoid disrupting production too much. He had noted that agricultural production in many of the areas under his rule was well below pre-revolutionary levels, and he did not want further decreases if he could avoid them. The 28 Bolsheviks, less concerned with the maintenance of agricultural production, attacked Mao for following a 'rich peasant line'. This was a very serious accusation at this time, when Stalin was waging all-out war against the rich peasants (kulaks) in the Soviet Union.

Even more important were conflicts over military strategy. The Guomindang had too many other problems to be able to keep up continual pressure on the Communists, but every so often provincial or national authorities would send a force, always far larger than the Red Army defending the Jiangxi Soviet, in an attempt to destroy the Communist base area. There were five major 'extermination campaigns' between 1930 and 1934. Mao's strategy for dealing with these attacks had been to fight only when he could win a quick, decisive victory. He did not defend the borders of the base area, trying to keep enemy troops out. Instead he would withdraw, avoiding contact while enemy armies advanced into Communist territory. Given the poor coordination that usually existed between Guomindang units in the field, Mao could expect that sooner or later the enemy units manoeuvring to surround him and force him to battle would become separated and he would be able to concentrate his full force on one section of the enemy force and destroy it. He was willing to retreat and wait for as long as necessary for such an opportunity to arise, despite the amount of harm the invading forces might be doing to Communist organizations, and to peasants who had sympathized with the Communists, in the countryside through which Mao was allowing them to pass. For one thing, he was always so outnumbered that if he tried to fight the whole enemy force, instead of just an isolated section of it, he would probably be obliterated. For another, he could not afford major battles which ended with the enemy retreating in defeat. He depended on capturing guns and ammunition to keep his army supplied, so he had to surround enemy units and destroy them in order to capture their equipment; this required that he wait until he could fight a battle in which he outnumbered the enemy locally. The 28 Bolsheviks considered this policy politically unsound and perhaps even cowardly. The Red Army should not retreat and allow Guomindang troops to enter the base area and abuse pro-Communist peasants, it should defend the borders.

This was not, as some people have supposed, a matter of Mao favouring guerrilla warfare and the 28 Bolsheviks favouring conventional warfare. Guerrilla warfare is a strategy in which much of the fighting is done either by peasant guerrillas, who spend most of their time farming but occasionally participate in raids or ambushes, or else by trained soldiers who operate in small groups, mixing with the population in such a way that it is very difficult for a regular army to find them. It is a matter of many very small battles, raids, and ambushes. But if we look at Mao's analysis of the policies he followed in the Jiangxi period, we will find little indication of fighting done by part-time peasant soldiers, or even by regular Red Army troops operating in units of less than 1,000 men. The fighting he describes is a matter of stand-up battles fought by very large units of the Red Army. He just wanted these units to operate as mobile forces rather than trying to defend fixed lines. As a matter of fact the 28 Bolsheviks, preoccupied with revolutionary purity and respect for the masses, may have attributed a greater importance to peasant militiamen than Mao did.

One interesting aspect of the difference was that Mao's ideas were more firmly rooted in Chinese tradition. The 28 Bolsheviks were trying to fit themselves to an image of revolutionary heroism forbidding retreat or compromise, which was largely European in origin. Mao's much more flexible tactics, and even some of the language he used to describe them, have parallels in Chinese documents going back more than 2,000 years to the Zhou period.

Mao had fought off three major attacks before the 28 Bolsheviks arrived in Jiangxi. A fourth was also beaten off in 1933. But the fifth, launched in 1934, was different. Chiang Kai-shek had observed the failures of poorly coordinated efforts in the past, and had decided that this one should be not only far stronger, but also more methodical. He slowly strangled the Jiangxi Soviet, by surrounding it with a cordon of blockhouses and fortified positions and then constricting the ring. Formerly, when Guomindang units had tried to move relatively fast, it had proven difficult or impossible to coordinate the movements of different units. Under the new strategy, Guomindang units moved so slowly that coordination was not a serious problem.

Mao later said, in line with the strategy he had been following for the past few years, that what the Red Army should have done was to concentrate its forces, break through the ring, and then take the attacking troops in the rear. They would then have been forced to choose between sitting in their fortified positions with the Communists astride their supply lines, or moving out of their positions and fighting in the open. This might not have worked, against a stronger and better equipped Guomindang force than Mao had ever fought before, but at least it would have had a chance. The strategy the 28 Bolsheviks followed had none. Arguing that it was the obligation of the Red Army to defend the population of the Soviet areas,

Map 4.   The rural soviets and the Long March.

Border of China

Province border

Communist base areas, 1934

Main route of the Long March

Secondary routes of the Long March

kilometres
0   200   500   1000

miles
0   200   400   600

they spread their troops out and tried to hold their borders. Heavily outnumbered, even more heavily outgunned, and following a strategy that gave it little chance to surprise or confuse the enemy, the Red Army soon found its position hopeless. It was forced to abandon the Jiangxi base area and flee.

The conflict pitting the 28 Bolsheviks' stress on correct revolutionary behaviour against Mao's desire to choose policies that worked was a conflict that would be repeated many times in the CCP; it is often described as a struggle of Red against Expert. Crises occurred in the years 1947–48, and again in 1966–76, when some Party leaders decided that the preservation of a correct revolutionary spirit was being neglected, and de-emphasized expertise in their efforts to restore a proper level of 'Redness'. Even during these periods, however, the Party had available plenty of people who had training and experience in running a government and an economy. Revolutionary spirit was not the only tool the Party had for maintaining its rule, as it very nearly had been for Lenin after the Russian Revolution.

The Long March

In October 1934, something of the order of 100,000 people broke through the Guomindang forces encircling the Jiangxi Soviet. At first they tried to take all the paraphernalia of a government – printing presses, files, and so on – but they soon tossed aside the excess baggage and ran for their lives. They moved westward, away from the centres of Guomindang power, and then turned north. This took them through mountainous and thinly settled areas, in some of which the population was not even ethnically Chinese. Casualties inflicted by the pursuing Guomindang forces, by local tribes which hated all Chinese, by disease, starvation, and the injuries inherent in forced marches through rough terrain, were heavy. The force that finally arrived in the northwestern province of Shaanxi (Shensi) in 1935, momentarily free of pursuers, was certainly less than a quarter – by some estimates less than a tenth – the size of the one that had set out from Jiangxi. However, this small group was the nucleus from which the Communist movement was reborn. The Party would be dominated by veterans of the Long March for the next thirty years.

It was during this march that Mao Zedong rose to command the Chinese Communist Party. At its outset he had not even been among the leaders of the Party; the 28 Bolsheviks had stripped him

4.3 At one point during the Long March, the Red Army was almost trapped and destroyed when enemy troops partially destroyed this bridge over the Dadu River. The Red forces could not repair it while their enemies held the far bank. Red soldiers crossed the section where the planking had been destroyed by swinging themselves hand-over-hand, dangling underneath the chains. Once a few men had reached the far side of the river in this fashion, it became possible to repair the bridge and bring the rest of the army across.

of his position and may have had him under arrest. But the defeats the Party had suffered under their guidance, defeats which would finally leave the CCP with its membership reduced from around 300,000 to around 40,000, made the demand for new leadership overwhelming. In January 1935, during the third month of the Long March, those CCP leaders making the march stopped to confer and made Mao the effective head of the party.

Mao did not, however, try to establish one-man domination. He was, rather, just the most important single individual in a group of very talented leaders, who managed to work together in remarkable harmony for many years. Those who became most important in the later history of Chinese Communism included the following.

- **Deng Xiaoping** (Teng Hsiao-p'ing) had first joined the CCP while in France in 1924. He played a major role in efforts to establish a Communist base area in Guangxi province in 1929 and 1930, but when this failed he marched east to Jiangxi. Deng worked in the Jiangxi Soviet (not getting along well with the 28 Bolsheviks) until the Long March.
- **Lin Biao** (Lin Piao), a brilliant general, had been trained at the Guomindang's Huangpu Military Academy in 1925 and 1926. He participated in the Northern Expedition of 1926–27 and won rapid promotion, becoming commander of a battalion before the age of twenty. When the CCP and the Guomindang split in 1927, Lin participated in the Nanchang uprising. The force in which he served, commanded by Zhu De, joined with Mao Zedong's group in early 1928. By the time of the Long March, Lin (in his mid twenties) commanded an army corps.
- **Liu Shaoqi** (Liu Shao-ch'i) had been one of the first Chinese Communists to receive training in Moscow; he joined the CCP while in Moscow in 1921. He specialized in labour organization and the operation of underground organizations in areas under enemy control. He was in the Jiangxi Soviet in 1934, and started out on the Long March, but he seems to have dropped out before the end of the march, in order to take up an underground assignment behind Guomindang lines in North China. He rejoined the other Communist leaders in the northwest in 1937.
- **Peng Dehuai** (P'eng Te-huai) had been an officer in the army of a Hunan warlord whose forces were amalgamated into those of the Guomindang in 1926. Peng led his men in rebellion against the Guomindang in 1928, and became one of the most important military commanders of the Jiangxi Soviet.
- **Zhou Enlai** (Chou En-lai) was the most cosmopolitan of the major CCP leaders. He had studied in Japan as a young man, and travelled to several European countries in the early 1920s. As Director of the Political Department of the Huangpu Military Academy (of which Chiang Kai-shek was Commandant) from 1925 to 1926, Zhou was one of the few Communists to have much influence in the Guomindang armed forces during the First United Front. He helped plan the Nanchang uprising in 1927, but he spent most of the next few years in Shanghai and Moscow, occupying high positions in the Party hierarchy, instead of going into the hills. He finally moved to the Jiangxi Soviet in 1931, and was near the top of the Party hierarchy at the time of the Long March. He was an excellent negotiator and

diplomat. He mediated disputes within the Party, and in his later years he played a very important role in handling the Communist Party's relations both with non-Communist Chinese and with foreign countries.
- **Zhu De**, Mao's partner since 1928, was officially Commander-in-Chief of the entire Chinese Red Army.

The CCP became a more nationalist organization under Mao. In part this was a simple matter of reduced foreign influence. The 28 Bolsheviks had been trained in the Soviet Union, had risen to the top largely through Stalin's backing, and had been highly responsive to Russian ideas and advice. Mao had never been outside of China and had frequently disagreed with Russian advice. Stalin probably would have blocked his promotion if he had been consulted, and indeed would quite possibly have ordered his death had Mao been so unwise as to visit Moscow during the next few years. But beyond the question of sheer independence, there was a more general sense in which Mao was more of a nationalist than the 28 Bolsheviks. He placed a great emphasis on issues such as economic development and effective administration, which concerned Chinese of all political persuasions. The 28 Bolsheviks, while of course supporting such things, were primarily interested in issues of class struggle, which were specifically Communist policies. Under Mao the CCP struggled for nationalist goals more vigorously and more competently than the 'Nationalist Party', the Guomindang. Had it not done so it certainly would not have risen to control the nation as fast as it did, and might not have done so at all.

The relationship between the two types of goals – strengthening the nation as a whole, and promoting the interests of the poor against those of the rich – was not a simple one. Certainly the two could reinforce one another. In its first twenty years under Mao's leadership, combining the two types of activity, the CCP accomplished far more in the way of class struggle than it had under the 28 Bolsheviks. At the same time it was a more effective nationalist instrument than the Guomindang, which had tried to achieve nationalist goals without class struggle. However, there were also conflicts between the two, eventually very acute conflicts. By the last years of his life Mao, who had done more than any other man to make the CCP a nationalist organization, would find himself engaged in a desperate struggle against Party leaders who put their main emphasis on nationalist goals and were losing interest in class-centred issues.

The Japanese threat

China had been subject to various forms of outside interference for decades. There were foreign troops in Beiping and foreign warships on the Yangzi River; portions of Shanghai and Tianjin were under actual foreign rule. By the 1930s most of the Western nations were becoming less threatening; once Chiang Kai-shek had unified large portions of China and built something approaching a national government, he was able to persuade the British, French, and Americans to cease further encroachments on Chinese sovereignty and even abandon some of what they had acquired in the past. Japan, however, reacted differently; it refused to tolerate any threat to its position in China.

The Japanese had begun moving into Manchuria – the north-eastern section of China – in the 1890s. By the late 1920s they controlled the tip of the Liaodong Peninsula on the south coast of Manchuria, which included the two major seaports of Dalian and Port Arthur. They also had the South Manchurian Railway running north from Dalian through most of the major cities of Manchuria. They had substantial investments in branch railway lines, mines, factories, and so on. Japanese troops guarded these possessions. Chinese resentment of such threats to their independence was growing; during and after the First World War there had been repeated anti-Japanese demonstrations, and boycotts of Japanese goods, protesting at Japanese encroachment in Manchuria, Shandong, and elsewhere. These protests did not as yet seriously threaten the Japanese sphere of influence, but the Japanese wished to avoid the rise of any strong authority in China, and especially in Manchuria.

They had for many years coexisted with a Chinese warlord based in Manchuria, named Zhang Zuolin (Chang Tso-lin). While powerful as warlords went, he had not been a threat to their position. However, the northward expansion of the Guomindang in 1928 created the prospect that Zhang and the Guomindang together might be able seriously to oppose Japanese domination of Manchuria. Some Japanese officers assassinated Zhang Zuolin, expecting that his dissolute, drug-addicted son Zhang Xueliang (Chang Hsueh-liang) would be easier to control. They were mistaken; once the 'Young Marshal' had inherited his father's position he reformed his personal life, affiliated himself with the new Guomindang government in Nanjing, and finally became a serious opponent of Japan.

By the early 1930s Japan was beginning to fall under the domination of militarist fanatics. Both dreams of national glory and the economic pressures of the Depression pushed them to the idea of foreign conquest. Young, relatively junior officers of the army were the leaders. The high command, and the civilian politicians in the Cabinet, provided only weak opposition to the plans of the young officers. In 1931 the forces in Manchuria, defying the policies of the Japanese government, staged an incident (a supposed Chinese attack on the South Manchurian Railway), which they used as an excuse to conquer all of Manchuria. The civilians in the Cabinet opposed this action but did nothing effective to halt or reverse it, and within a few years the militarists took control of the government.

In Manchuria the Japanese established a puppet state, nominally independent, called Manzhouguo (Manchukuo), or 'land of the Manchus'. Its 'ruler' was the last Emperor of the Qing Dynasty, the man who had been overthrown by the Revolution of 1911. Behind this façade the Japanese ran Manchuria. They accelerated their efforts to develop its minerals, timber, and other resources. However, this was only the beginning of their ambitions. They began pushing southward almost immediately, and by 1936 Beiping (the traditional capital of China) existed in a sort of no man's land between Chinese and Japanese control. There seemed a real possibility that Japan would conquer all of China.

Chiang Kai-shek did his best to postpone a direct confrontation. When the open seizure of Manchuria began in 1931, he ordered Zhang Xueliang to withdraw without serious resistance. He wanted to have all of China united behind him before he fought a strong foreign foe. However, what this amounted to was that he wanted to continue fighting his Chinese enemies while leaving the Japanese unopposed. He was quoted as saying that the Japanese were only a disease of the skin, while the Communists were a disease of the heart. People who agitated too vigorously for Chinese resistance against Japan's encroachments were arrested. Indeed, the Guomindang was so eager to conciliate Japan that when a Chinese magazine published an article stating that the Emperor of Japan was basically a figurehead rather than a real ruler (fairly accurate, but profoundly insulting to Japanese sensibilities), a Guomindang court sentenced the editor to fourteen months' imprisonment. As the Japanese threat became more acute, even anti-Communist Chinese began to question the wisdom of such a stand.

The Second United Front

The Communist Party had been saying for several years that all good Chinese should unite to defend the nation. In the Jiangxi period this had been a purely verbal stance, but the Long March had brought the Party much closer to the areas under an immediate Japanese threat. The Party did not at first include Chiang Kai-shek among those being invited to join the Second United Front, whether because it doubted he wanted to fight Japan, or because he would have had to be the senior partner in any coalition. In December 1935 the CCP Central Committee resolved:

> All people, all parties, all armed forces and all classes, in so far as they are opposed to Japanese imperialism and the traitor Chiang Kai-shek, should unite and wage the sacred national revolutionary war . . . Only by establishing the broadest anti-Japanese national united front (embracing the lower and upper strata) can we defeat Japanese imperialism and its running dog, Chiang Kai-shek.

The CCP was willing, however, to negotiate with Chiang's generals. Chiang had assigned two men to command the forces attacking the new Communist base area in Shaanxi: an ex-bandit and Shaanxi warlord named Yang Hucheng (Yang Hu-ch'eng), and the 'Young Marshal' Zhang Xueliang, who had been driven out of Manchuria by the Japanese in 1931. Both men listened to Communist appeals that it was foolish for Chinese to fight one another when the nation was being invaded. Zhang Xueliang, who wanted revenge for his murdered father and lost territory, had special reasons to be receptive. In the summer of 1936, Zhang and Yang reached a covert accommodation with the Communists, and from then on their forces staged only mock battles with the Red Army. This did not lead to total peace, since some troops not under the command of the two generals continued to make genuine attacks on Communist territory, but it reduced the pressure on the Communists to a low level while the CCP and the two generals considered their next moves.

In December 1936 Chiang Kai-shek, suspicious of the lack of progress in this phony war, flew up to Shaanxi to urge on the two generals; they responded by taking him prisoner. They then had to decide, in consultation with the Communists and the Russian government, what to do with him. In the end everyone involved agreed that China needed Chiang. If he were executed the country would be left with no true national leader, and the resulting struggles for power would be disastrous. If there were to be any effective resistance to Japan, Chiang would have to lead it. While Chiang did not humiliate himself by offering public concessions in return for his release, an implicit accommodation was worked out, Chiang was allowed to return to Nanjing, and a few months later the Communist Party formally joined in a new united front with the Guomindang. The Soviet Union also briefly resumed military aid to Chiang Kai-shek at this time.

In form, the CCP recognized the Guomindang as the legitimate government of China, while Chiang recognized the Communists as local authorities with a certain degree of autonomy. The main body of the Red Army, in the northwest, was renamed the Eighth Route Army, placed nominally under Chiang's authority, and granted a subsidy. Smaller Communist forces in East-central China were gathered together as the New Fourth Army. In fact, both sides well remembered that the First United Front between the CCP and the Guomindang had ended in the bloody conflicts of 1927, and both understood that the same thing was likely to happen again once the Japanese threat had abated.

Notes

1. In standard English usage, a 'cadre' is a group of people who perform a leadership role in an organization or movement. In writings on Asia, especially on China and Vietnam, the term is used in a variant sense; a 'cadre' is a single individual who provides ideological and organizational leadership. The cadre does not necessarily hold a high rank in the organization in which he or she functions as a cadre.

5

World war and Communist victory

The Second World War provided the CCP with its great opportunity. Japan's invasion of China disrupted and demoralized the Guomindang, and at the same time provided the CCP with a cause by means of which it could rally millions of supporters to itself. By 1945 the Communist Party was not only larger and stronger than it had ever been before, it was also more unified internally. Its relations with the population of the area it ruled were excellent. Meanwhile the Guomindang, never the world's model of efficient and honest government, had sunk to a level of corruption and decay that could hardly have been predicted in 1937. A relatively short civil war, from 1946 to 1949, sufficed for the CCP to expel the Guomindang from the Chinese mainland and establish a Communist regime.

The war begins

War between China and Japan broke out in July 1937. The shooting started over a minor incident, when a Japanese Army unit on manoeuvres near Beiping was refused entry at the gate of a walled town, but it quickly escalated into a full-scale invasion of China. At first the Japanese seemed unstoppable. They pushed south from Manchuria, and also made landings on the coast. The heartland of Chiang's power, the developed areas near the mouth of the Yangzi, were highly vulnerable to Japanese attack. The Guomindang armies fought bravely for these areas, but overwhelming Japanese superiority in leadership and in armaments prevailed. Furthermore, the weaknesses of the Guomindang forces in command, coordination, and communications made it very difficult for them to conduct an orderly retreat when Japanese pressure became too much for them, and they suffered very severely. Chiang lost

Shanghai in November 1937, his capital of Nanjing in December, and Wuhan in October 1938. He was forced back into the interior of China, behind the mountain barriers of Sichuan province, where he established a wartime capital at Chongqing (Chungking).

Morale in Chongqing was initially high. Millions of Chinese had been wanting for years to make some effective resistance to Japanese incursions. Most of them remained enthusiastic despite the defeats of the opening months of the war, and the bombing raids to which Chongqing was soon subjected.

The Japanese found themselves in a quandary. They had been able to defeat the Guomindang armies even at their strongest, and by 1939 the Guomindang had lost most of its industry and many of its best troops. The Japanese could take any particular place on which they set their sights. They had supposed this meant that they could end the war by defeating the enemy and taking his capital city. The Chinese, however, when they lost a capital simply withdrew and established another one. Japan was a small country attacking a large one; it did not have the manpower to occupy the whole of China. Once the Japanese had occupied all the major cities on or near the coast, the key communication lines between them, and some of the surrounding countryside, they had taken on nearly as much as they could handle. This left a large hinterland in which their Chinese opponents could continue to operate.

The Japanese could perhaps have found enough Chinese collaborators to make up for their own numerical weakness. China's lack of internal unity offered fertile ground for such a strategy. Japan recruited a considerable number of Chinese auxiliary troops, and eventually set up a puppet regime in China headed by Wang Jingwei (who had at one point seemed to be Sun Yat-sen's heir as head of the Guomindang). However, the extent of the collaboration they received was limited. Partly this was because, like the German troops who invaded the Soviet Union a few years later, they alienated potential supporters by their extraordinary brutality. They had raped and looted, and had killed large numbers of non-combatants, starting quite early in the war. Some units actually elaborated this into a slogan of the 'Three Alls': kill all, burn all, destroy all. Chinese were naturally reluctant to collaborate with such an occupier. Also, the Japanese were not really very generous with collaborators; they wanted so much out of China for themselves that there was not much left as a reward for Chinese

5.1   A sector of Shanghai after a Japanese attack in 1937.

who supported them. The result was that they got much less cooperation from the Chinese than they might have, less than the Manchus had received while conquering the country 300 years before. It is a measure of China's decay that they received as much as they did.

The numerical weakness of the Japanese offered opportunities to both the Guomindang and the CCP, but the response of the two parties was very different. Chiang Kai-shek's was essentially defensive; after putting up a stubborn fight for the lower Yangzi Valley, he retreated to the southwest beyond the reach of the enemy. Some modern institutions came with him. Whole factories were dismantled and moved up the Yangzi to Sichuan, with the workers carrying their machines. Universities moved, with the professors and students carrying their books. But these were mainly independent initiatives; the government provided little aid or leadership, and the amount that reached the interior was tiny compared to what had been needed. Cut off from the relatively westernized areas and the industry on which it had depended, Chiang's government was also cut off from the kind of environment in which it knew how to take constructive action. A disastrous inflation wracked the economy. Chiang was not even able to eliminate warlordism in the province of Sichuan, where his new capital was located. His government decayed, both in the sense that corruption ran rampant, and in the sense that many officials were struggling for personal power more than for national goals.

The Communists interpreted Japanese weakness not as an opportunity to avoid battle, but as an invitation to expand their territory very aggressively. The Fascist rulers of Japan were intensely anti-Communist, and had made propaganda claims that they were invading China in order to save it from the Communists, but in fact they almost ignored the small Communist Party for several years. The far larger and better equipped armies of the Guomindang seemed the main obstacles to their ambitions, so instead of moving west against the Communist base area in Shaanxi, they drove southward trying to destroy Chiang Kai-shek. This opened a fabulous opportunity for the Communists in the North China countryside. The Japanese had first driven away the Guomindang forces which formerly held most of this area, and then moved on themselves in pursuit of the Guomindang. Behind their advance the Japanese left a power vacuum, in which large areas were almost empty of armed forces. The Communist Party moved into such areas and began to organize the peasants. By 1940, without even having had to do a great deal of fighting, the CCP had made itself the ruler of perhaps 100 million people scattered across the North China Plain. At this point it began causing real trouble for the Japanese, attacking garrisons and communication lines in many areas. The Japanese brought in reinforcements and counter-attacked, but they had waited too long and allowed the CCP to become too firmly entrenched. Despite extensive fighting, which caused heavy casualties among both the Communist troops and the Chinese peasants, the Japanese were unable to reduce the areas under Communist control below a level of about 50,000,000 people.

This is the period when the CCP really came into its own. The Shaanxi–Gansu–Ningxia base area, centring on Yanan (Yenan) in Shaanxi province, was the first area where the CCP had ever been able to establish a reasonably secure and stable government. The Party's relations with the peasants were good, and it was not troubled by serious internal conflict. A significant number of students and intellectuals, when the Japanese threatened the cities along the coast, went to Yanan instead of Chongqing; their education and skills proved very valuable to the CCP. There were no ostentatious personal luxuries, even for the top leaders; unselfish dedication to the cause seemed the general rule. The period when the CCP had its capital at Yanan, from 1937 to 1947, came to seem a sort of golden age; the 'Yanan spirit and style' remained a byword of revolutionary virtue for decades after.

Yanan, in the northwest, was for the CCP a secure base out of the way of major fighting. Most of the Eighth Route Army was further east, behind Japanese lines, spreading across the countryside in small bands. Peasant militiamen, who were farmers most of the time and only fought if the Japanese came into their immediate area, provided local support for the regular troops. The Japanese found themselves trying to destroy forces that they simply could not find.

Special tactics were part of the reason the Eighth Route Army could evade the Japanese. There was a trick called 'the segmented worm', which could be used if a guerrilla unit were being tracked by the Japanese. The guerrillas marched as a group, but every so often two men dropped out of the column and hid. The result was a nice clear trail, left by the main body of guerrillas, but this trail was left by fewer and fewer men until it finally faded into nothingness. If the Japanese unit were large, this would be the end of the matter. If it were small, the guerrillas scattered behind the Japanese unit might even reassemble and try to ambush it on its way home.

Such tricks, however, were much less important to Communist success than effective organization of the peasants. The Eighth Route Army tried to build itself a base of support in every village. Troops operated under strict discipline, and were forbidden to abuse the population. Local militias and underground organizations kept the Eighth Route Army informed about enemy activities, while denying information to the Japanese. The peasants dug extensive networks of tunnels under and around many villages, in which both peasants and guerrillas could hide when necessary. In the 'liberated areas', local governments under a greater or lesser degree of Communist leadership helped guarantee material support. They enabled the Eighth Route Army to support itself through taxes collected within each village by organizations within the village, rather than having to take things from villagers on the impromptu basis, closely resembling looting, by which most Chinese armies supplemented formal taxes.

Most important was the inadequate size of the Japanese Army. Man for man the Japanese were far more formidable than the Guomindang forces the CCP had previously fought, but Japan did not have enough men to garrison every area simultaneously; most villages were free of Japanese troops at any given time. Communist-ruled villages were vulnerable to patrols or raids from Japanese units, but cooperation between the Eighth Route Army forces and local guerrillas made such raids risky for small Japanese forces, and tied down enough Japanese troops guarding vital installations to make it hard for the Japanese to mount many large offensive operations into the liberated areas. Peasants could afford to flee their villages and go into the hills for a brief period, in the face of such raids, provided they did not have to do so too often. This was quite different from the situation the Communists had faced during the Jiangxi period. Then the Guomindang Army had been large enough, relative to the size of the CCP base areas, so that it could seriously have contemplated garrisoning every village. Furthermore, inhabitants of the villages were much closer to being unanimous in opposition to the Japanese than they had been in earlier struggles against the Guomindang.

What developed in North China was a classic case of guerrilla warfare. Japanese posts and communication lines were harassed both by raids of the Eighth Route Army and by local guerrillas. The Communists, whether operating as individuals in villages under Japanese control or as units in areas under Communist control, were very hard to find. Widespread popular support ensured that they had recruits, supplies, information, and relative secrecy in their own movements.

Communism, nationalism, and the 'New Democracy'

The CCP was determined to drive out the Japanese. Besides direct military struggle, this required great effort devoted to administrative construction, building up the economy, and so on in order to support the military effort. None of these matters were specifically Communist programmes. The Party was functioning very much as a nationalist organization; indeed it was struggling for nationalist goals more vigorously and more competently than the Guomindang.

Traditional Marxism had treated the initial modernization of society as a task of the capitalist class. Bourgeois leaders were supposed to overthrow feudalism and establish nation–states with strong central governments, effective communications, modern industry, and a large class of industrial workers. Only then would it be time for the working class, under Marxist leadership, to carry out a socialist revolution. When a Marxist revolution actually came, however, it was in the rather primitive society of Russia where the bourgeoisie had not yet got very far with this process of development. Lenin and his followers had therefore had to develop a variant theory, according to which the bourgeoisie of some societies was too weak and inept to carry out the role which traditional Marxism had assigned to it. The Communist Party would have to carry out the actual tasks of what it called the 'bourgeois', 'bourgeois-democratic', or 'national-democratic' revolution. These are tasks which non-Marxists usually describe as 'nationalist'.

The CCP, by 1940, had carried this shift in ideas even further than the Russian Communists. Tasks traditionally regarded as part of the 'bourgeois-democratic' revolution – national independence, strong government, and the abolition of 'feudalism' – had become its central preoccupations. Mao said: 'Today, whoever can lead the people in driving out Japanese imperialism and introducing democratic government will be the saviours of the people. History has proved that the Chinese bourgeoisie cannot fulfil this responsibility.'

'The proletariat', or in practical terms the Communist Party which theoretically represented the proletariat, would have to take the lead. The CCP said that China needed a 'New Democratic Revolution'. Its two great tasks would be to beat off the foreign

invaders and to abolish the 'feudal' structure of landlord rule in the
countryside, distributing land to the tillers. It would also have to
undertake more general tasks of national development – economic
growth, education, and so on. The weakness and vacillation of the
bourgeoisie required that the proletariat take the lead, but there was
nothing specifically proletarian about the goals of the New
Democratic Revolution as Mao defined them, and in any case the
Chinese proletariat was far too small to accomplish them alone. The
revolution, therefore, would be a joint action by four classes: the
proletariat, the peasantry, the petite bourgeoisie (intellectuals,
white-collar workers, shopkeepers, etc.), and the 'national
bourgeoisie' (those among the capitalists who were not considered
to have tainted themselves too badly by close association with the
foreigners or the landlords). The statement that the revolution
would be 'democratic' did not mean that individuals would have the
right to oppose its policies, only that members of the four
'revolutionary classes' listed above would have the right to help
shape the policies of the revolution. Private property would be the
norm under the New Democracy; only at a later stage, when China
had reached a far higher economic level, would the establishment of
a socialist economy become appropriate.

At the time he wrote this, Mao was in fact compromising the
class struggle even more than was required by his theory. The
anti-Japanese resistance required the participation of all Chinese
who could be persuaded to join, including not only people who
carried out forms of 'exploitation' which the Communists
considered fairly respectable, like capitalists who used wage-labour
in their factories, but even the 'feudal' landlords. Mao's writings on
the New Democracy included the slogan of 'land to the tillers', but
for the duration of the war, landlords who opposed the Japanese
were confirmed in the ownership of their land, and tenants were
supposed to go on paying rent. The CCP enforced reduction of rent
and of the interest rate on debts, but it did not reduce either rent or
interest to negligible levels. Landlords and rich peasants could serve
in local administrations, especially after the 'three-thirds' system
was introduced in 1940. This was a policy under which the
Communist Party limited itself to about one-third of the positions in
local administrations. This was enough to let Party members
dominate these organizations, but only if they could apply effective
persuasion; they could not simply occupy all top posts and give
orders. Landlords and rich peasants even joined the Communist
Party in significant numbers.

Such practices raised the obvious question of whether the CCP was transforming itself from a Communist Party, an instrument for class struggle, into a simple nationalist movement. Consideration of the actual progress of the class struggle, both before and after the formation of the Second United Front, will show that this was not the case. Certainly the Party had become more nationalist than before, but the real cost to the class struggle had been rather small. When the Eighth Route Army arrived in a North China village, it did not truly have the option of immediately overthrowing the landlords and rich peasants, distributing their land to the peasants, and placing the village under the political control of the poor. Experience had shown that involving the broad mass of the peasants in class struggle, and really freeing them from landlord and rich peasant control, took years to accomplish. In the Jiangxi period the landlords and rich peasants had often been able to infiltrate the Party and block or distort the effects of land reform for a considerable time, despite the best efforts of the CCP. An attempt quickly and radically to restructure North China villages in 1938 would have been dubious not only on the grounds that it would have forced the Party to put resources into the class struggle which were desperately needed in the struggle against Japan, but also on the grounds that the attempt would have failed.

After a few years in power in a given area the Party was in a much better position to lead a genuine class struggle. Its military control was firmer. It had a more extensive knowledge of local society. It could draw on the services of some poor peasants who had been mobilized politically, who could identify landlord and rich peasant elements within the Party and within local administrations, and could become replacements for these elements if the leadership decided to carry out a purge. Had the Party, in this situation, still remained as lax in the class struggle as it had seemed in the beginning, then one could really conclude that it had, temporarily or permanently, abandoned its commitment to class struggle.

Such was not the case. As the war progressed, some of the landlords and rich peasants within the Party were weeded out. Rent reduction laws, once loosely enforced, not only became more effective but were applied retroactively. Landlords who had not reduced rents when the laws were first announced were made to cough up the surplus rent they had collected. The laws themselves were stiffened; in some areas the limitation of rents to 37.5 per cent of the crop, set early in the war, was reduced to 30 per cent and then to 22.5 per cent before its end. Landlords and rich peasants, long in the habit of shifting the tax burden on to the poor, had to pay graduated land taxes, plus retroactive payments for taxes evaded in the past. Without an overt land reform, the Party had weakened the economic position of the landlords and rich peasants very drastically. Many of them had to sell part of their land, for considerably less than its real value, in order to make the payments demanded of them. Land was also confiscated from those accused of collaboration with the enemy.

If one looked only at Party rhetoric, one might think that the CCP had made, temporarily, a drastic shift in its nature when it entered the Second United Front in 1937. In actual fact, however, it was continuing to carry out egalitarian reforms which constituted a large fraction of what it would have been able to accomplish if not involved in a united front. If one considers in addition that a certain amount of class compromise was vital if the Party were to expand its territorial base rapidly, one will note that the United Front was enabling the Party to implement mildly egalitarian policies in areas where it would not otherwise have been doing anything at all. United front and egalitarian reform were not incompatible at this time.

Chiang and the United States

Japan had originally envisaged a fairly short and simple campaign. However, the Guomindang proved unwilling to surrender, even after repeated defeats. Furthermore, there were increasing problems with third countries. Japan was attempting to displace the major Western powers from the spheres of influence they had long enjoyed in China. Britain and France were too preoccupied with their impending war against Germany to offer direct opposition, but they allowed supplies to move through their respective colonies, Burma and Vietnam, to reach the beleaguered government of Chiang Kai-shek. Japan began moving into Southeast Asia, partly in an effort to choke off some of these supply routes.

The United States had likewise been distressed by the Japanese invasion of China, was more distressed by Japanese penetration of Southeast Asia, and unlike the preoccupied European powers, had the ability to make its displeasure felt. Despite the generally isolationist temper of the country, President Roosevelt favoured resistance against German and Japanese aggression. By 1940 his administration was providing Chiang Kai-shek with significant material aid. In 1941, the US Army even began unofficially supplying pilots to fight in Chiang's forces. These men became known as the 'Flying Tigers'.

More important, by 1940 the USA was beginning to reduce its trade with Japan. This forced Tokyo to choose between retreating and expanding the war. The Japanese economy could not survive without imported raw materials, much of which had been coming from the USA. Persuading the USA to continue or resume trade in petroleum and other vital goods would require Japan to abandon its effort to conquer China; Japan's military rulers could not have remained in power after such a humiliation. The alternative was to obtain another source, by conquering sections of Southeast Asia in which many vital raw materials, especially rubber and petroleum, could be found. Once the decision had been taken to go forward rather than back, the logical consequence was war between Japan and the USA, which began at Pearl Harbor in December 1941. In the following months the Japanese were astonishingly successful, taking the Philippines, Malaya, Indonesia, and Burma. This not only won them the petroleum, rubber, and other raw materials they needed, it cut the last land route for US aid coming into China. For the time being the only supplies that could reach China were those flown over 'the Hump', an air route across the Himalayas which was tremendously dangerous and expensive for the relatively low-flying aircraft of this period.

As soon as the United States entered the war it sent General Joseph Stilwell to coordinate aid to Chiang Kai-shek, and US military activities in the area of China. He quickly found himself on very hostile terms with Chiang. Stilwell, an aggressive military commander, felt that his mission was to make the Chinese as effective as possible in the war against Japan. This required drastic improvements in the Chinese Army, whose men were not adequately armed, trained, paid, clothed, or fed, and whose officers were often incompetent and corrupt. It also required that Chiang Kai-shek use his forces aggressively, especially to expel the Japanese from Burma and reopen a transport route by which large amounts of US supplies could reach China.

Chiang showed no enthusiasm for any of this. During his rise to power in the 1920s he had been willing to take risks, but years of struggle to defend his position against external opponents and disloyal subordinates had given him a miser's attitude to power. He hoarded guns, ammunition, and troops. He knew he would be fighting for many years – against the Japanese, perhaps against competing non-Communist leaders within China, and surely

5.2   Madam Chiang Kai-shek stands arm-in-arm between her husband (left) and General Joseph Stilwell (right). Chiang Kai-shek and Stilwell despised one another, but had to maintain a public pretence of friendship and cooperation.

against the Communists. The United States was going to defeat Japan regardless of what he did; why should he launch vigorous campaigns against the Japanese now, which would use up supplies he might need desperately in some future war?

The idea of letting Stilwell train his officer corps seemed equally undesirable. Like many emperors of previous centuries, Chiang felt that it was better to be poorly served by weak subordinates than to be overthrown by strong ones. He was not likely to forget how two of his generals had taken him prisoner and almost executed him in 1936. If Stilwell had been able to train and select officers he would have increased the effectiveness of the Guomindang Army tremendously, but he also would have replaced a venal and passive group, which Chiang could control, with just the sort of alert young men who have carried out innumerable military coups, in Asia, Africa, and Latin America, during the past half-century. Chiang preferred to listen to the advocates of air power. General Claire Chennault (commander of the Flying Tigers before Pearl Harbor, commander of the US Army's 14th Air Force in China from 1942 onward) offered the hope that bombing planes could do most of the fighting against Japan, without the need for dangerous reforms in the army.

Stilwell quickly came to dislike Chiang and eventually to hate him. It has often been said that Chiang was concerned with the long-range problem of fighting the Communists, and that Stilwell objected because he wanted to concentrate on the immediate problem of the Japanese. This is true only in part. If Chiang had followed a rational policy of strengthening his army as much as possible for a future war against the Communists, and this had prevented him from doing much against the Japanese, Stilwell would certainly have objected, but it is not likely that he would have come to despise Chiang so totally. In fact much of Chiang's miserliness made no sense in terms of *any* military objective. His chances of defeating the Communists would have been higher – much higher – if he had fought the Japanese vigorously, accepting Stilwell's advice, instead of acting the way he did. By abandoning the idea of vigorous resistance to the Japanese he was throwing away the morale of his army and his prestige among the population, both of which had been fairly high in 1937 when he had seemed a symbol of nationalist resistance. If he had distributed equipment and supplies to his troops more freely this would not have been mere expenditure, it would have been investment, enabling the army to hold or retake territory the possession of which would have strengthened Chiang considerably. This was most conspicuous in regard to Burma. The expense of expelling the Japanese from Burma, when Chiang finally (with great reluctance) was persuaded to participate in a Burmese campaign, was far more than compensated for by the great increase in the amount of supplies that could be brought into China once a Burmese route was opened. Chiang did not really think in such terms. Stockpiles containing thousands of tons of ammunition and supplies, brought over 'the Hump' at great cost in money and lives, were destroyed when Chinese troops, who had not been issued adequate ammunition, were unable to defend the stockpiles against Japanese advances.

At first, when all Chiang had against Stilwell was that he was a brash and insufficiently respectful foreigner with dubious ideas, cooperation had been difficult. Eventually, the mutual hatred of the two men made it impossible. Stilwell wrote poetry referring to Chiang as 'the little bastard' and 'the Peanut'. He even got to the point of drafting some preliminary plans for a military coup against Chiang, although he never developed a serious plot. Chiang might tolerate the presence of such a man for the supplies he provided, but at all costs would prevent him from becoming too influential in the Chinese officer corps. Stilwell continuously tried to use American aid as a source of leverage, to persuade Washington to make such aid contingent on Chiang's willingness to reform his army or even place it under Stilwell's command, and sometimes he seemed to be succeeding. In the end, however, President Roosevelt decided that if Stilwell and Chiang could not work together it was Stilwell who would have to go. Stilwell's successor, General Wedemeyer, developed a better relationship with Chiang and accomplished more.

The 'Dixie Mission'

As the war went on, the Americans grew interested in another Chinese group: the Communists. They knew that the CCP was conducting some kind of resistance against the Japanese in northern China, and wanted, at the very least, to have the Communist forces rescue American fliers shot down in the area. Some Americans suggested going much further, to engage in joint operations and supply the CCP with US arms and ammunition. This was not as startling a proposal at the time as it would have appeared a few years later. In the European theatre of the war the USA was supplying the Soviet Union, and Tito's Communist partisans in Yugoslavia. In the struggle against Japan, the USA cooperated to some extent with Ho Chi Minh's organization in Vietnam, the Viet Minh. However in Vietnam, and even more in China, the USA had to deal with important allies who opposed aid to local Communists. Chiang Kai-shek was able to prevent US aid from being given to the CCP, and not much US equipment was given to the Viet Minh.

Mao was eager to develop a cooperative relationship. In the short run, he had many men but few modern weapons; even a very modest quantity of US equipment would have strengthened his army tremendously. Looking a little further ahead he could see that the Civil War between Communists and Guomindang was likely to resume before long, and he wished to avoid having the US support the Guomindang if and when such a thing occurred. He also wished to avoid excessive dependence on the Soviet Union. His past experiences with Stalin had not been pleasant, and in any case the Soviet Union had been too devastated by the war to be capable of helping much in the reconstruction of China. A friendly relationship with the USA seemed overwhelmingly desirable, and the main thing the USA was likely to demand in return for any aid it provided – vigorous action against the Japanese – was something the CCP was doing anyway.

The USA finally defied Chiang to the extent of sending some diplomats and officers to Mao Zedong's headquarters in Yanan. The US Observer Group (sometimes referred to as the 'Dixie Mission' because it was going into rebel territory), commanded by Colonel David Barrett, arrived there in July 1944. Most of the Americans were favourably impressed. The CCP seemed less corrupt, more unified, and more vigorous in its resistance to Japan than the Guomindang. United States fliers shot down over North China, and smuggled across hundreds of miles of territory where the Communists either ruled outright or operated as guerrillas, confirmed to their superiors that the CCP was both strong and popular over a broad area.

In the end, the contacts that the USA developed with the CCP led to very little. Allying with the CCP would have been tantamount to abandoning Chiang Kai-shek, and for a whole range of reasons the USA could not do this. Turning against what it recognized as the legitimate government of China, the government it had come to aid, would have seemed dubious on moral grounds. In practical terms, Chiang Kai-shek had an army that was far larger and better equipped than Mao's, so for all its problems this army seemed likely to be the more useful as an ally against Japan. Finally there were political considerations. Both Chiang and his American-educated wife were extremely popular in the USA. Wartime propaganda usually tends to exaggerate the merits of an ally. Chiang had been built up in the American press as a strong and popular ruler, leading a vigorous resistance against the Japanese invaders. Reports by American diplomats in China, showing the real situation, were not available to the general public. Some of the diplomats in question would later see their careers destroyed as punishment for their having questioned Chiang's virtue.

The Japanese surrender

The end of the war caught everyone by surprise. On 6 August 1945, the United States used an atomic bomb to obliterate Hiroshima, one

5.3   A twelve-year old Chinese soldier. Children such as this one frequently
did sentry duty at the gates of Communist-ruled villages in North China,
checking the identity of everyone entering and leaving. The use of civilians
for such duties freed Communist troops for the battle front.

of the few Japanese cities that had not already been destroyed by conventional explosives. On 8 August, in accord with promises made at the Yalta Conference six months before, the Soviet Union declared war on Japan and invaded Manchuria. On 9 August a second atomic bomb fell on Nagasaki. Japan capitulated within a few days. This led to an immediate and drastic intensification of the competition between the CCP and the Guomindang. Japanese troops would be surrendering; which side would obtain their weapons? Which side would take over the cities Japan had held, which included almost all of China's industries?

General George C. Marshall went to China in December 1945, as President Truman's personal representative, with instructions to prevent civil war and achieve the 'unification of China by peaceful, democratic methods'. President Truman (like President Roosevelt before him) wanted a strong China, allied with the USA, to form the linchpin of post-war US policy for Asia. A war between the Guomindang and the CCP would weaken China and therefore had to be prevented. Roosevelt and Truman tried to make the wartime United Front permanent; to make the Guomindang and the CCP compromise their differences peacefully. Neither the CCP nor the Guomindang expected this to work, but neither side wanted the onus of starting a new war, so for about a year they manoeuvred for advantage, while the USA tried to keep them from one another's throats and arrange for a coalition government.

Unfortunately for Marshall, US policy was fundamentally inconsistent. He was supposed to mediate between Chiang Kai-shek and the Communists, to help them settle their differences without civil war. His success in this role depended on convincing both sides that the USA was strictly impartial in this dispute. At the same time the USA was treating the Republic of China (in other words Chiang Kai-shek) as a US ally, and providing it with very important military assistance. The United States tried to prevent Japanese troops from surrendering to the Communist forces; the USA told the Japanese to keep their weapons until Guomindang forces could come up from the southwest to accept their surrender. It provided sea and air transport for Guomindang forces to come up from the distant southwest to take over the cities of North and Central China. This helped to overcome the advantage of the Communists, who had a much shorter distance to travel but had to move on foot. United States Marines landed at some key points in North China to hold them against the Communists until the Guomindang forces could arrive. By the time Marshall reached

China at the end of 1945, the US role in Chiang's manoeuvring against the CCP was no longer quite so massive as it had been in the first months after the Japanese surrender, but it was still substantial. The Marines were still in North China, US advisers were assisting the Guomindang armed forces in a variety of ways, and US equipment continued to arrive. In this light, Marshall's attempts to convince CCP negotiators of his impartiality in the developing conflict appear rather naïve.

The Russians formed a complicating factor. Earlier in 1945, before the USA was sure that the atomic bomb would really work, it had asked the Soviet Union for a promise that Russian troops would help in the final stage of the war against Japan. The Soviet Union declared war on Japan on 8 August. This was approximately the date that had been agreed between Stalin and the Americans, but by this time the atomic bomb, first used two days before, had reduced the need for Russian troops. Instead of facing a difficult and bloody battle to subdue a fanatical enemy, the Russian troops were able to conquer Manchuria, the most industrialized area of China, quickly and without much loss.

This was a boon to the CCP, but not an unlimited one. The Russian troops allowed their Chinese comrades into Manchuria, and CCP forces under General Lin Biao spread over the Manchurian countryside and began to propagandize and recruit among the villages. Stalin, however, was far more interested in his own welfare than in that of non-Russian Communists. Manchuria was important to him mainly as a source of industrial equipment, which could be hauled back and used in the reconstruction of the war-ravaged Soviet Union, and as a bargaining chip for the extraction of concessions from the Guomindang government. He was willing to aid the Chinese Communists to a certain extent, allowing them to operate in Manchuria and giving them a portion of the equipment taken from surrendering Japanese forces. However, he did not expect them to take control of China in the immediate future, so he did not feel the need to win their goodwill by really generous aid; on the contrary the CCP was long to remember the way the Soviet forces looted the factories of Manchuria during the winter of 1945/46.

On 14 August 1945 the Soviet Union signed a set of agreements with Chiang Kai-shek, including a Treaty of Friendship and Alliance. Chiang gave Stalin the naval base at Port Arthur, at the tip of the Liaodong Peninsula in southern Manchuria, and partial control (which soon became in practice full control) of the adjacent commercial port of Dalian. The Soviet Union also got partial control of major rail lines in Manchuria. In return Stalin recognized Chiang's government as the government of China, and promised that Russian aid and support would go to Chiang and to no one else.

Within a few months after the Japanese surrender, the first stage of the contest between the Guomindang and the CCP had been completed. It did not involve much violence; it was mainly a matter of which side reached and occupied any given area first. The rich provinces along the Yangzi River went mostly to the Guomindang, which took not only the major cities and communication lines, but much of the countryside in between. In the North China Plain, especially north of the Yellow River, the Guomindang got some of the cities but the Communists got most of the countryside. Finally, in Manchuria the Russians held the cities and the CCP the countryside. Here the Guomindang and the CCP manoeuvred to determine which would be able to occupy the cities when the Russians withdrew. Each side obtained some Japanese arms and even got some Japanese soldiers to join its forces.

The Soviet Union had originally promised to withdraw from all of Manchuria by 3 December 1945. However, Chiang found the Russians not cooperative about letting Guomindang armies into Russian-held areas before Russian withdrawals, so they would be in position to take over as the Russians moved out. By the time the Guomindang could arrive in evacuated positions, it often found them in the hands of the CCP. Stalin offered to postpone his withdrawal if Chiang asked him to do so, to give the Guomindang time to organize itself so it would at least be ready to move into evacuated positions immediately after the Russians left them. Chiang did indeed ask for postponements of the Russian evacuation, first to 3 January 1946, and then to 1 February.

Chiang clearly felt that the presence of Russian troops in Manchurian cities would hinder rather than aid the efforts of the CCP to take these cities. Chiang assumed, and seems to have been correct in assuming, that CCP forces would not be able to get into key positions until the Russians left them. Furthermore, he thought there was a reasonable chance that when the Russians withdrew they would do so in such a fashion that Guomindang forces would be able to replace them before the CCP could occupy the positions being evacuated. This reveals an extraordinary awareness, on Chiang's part and that of the Americans who were advising him, of the differences that could exist between Russian and Chinese Communists. This was a period when Communism was often

5.4   General Zhou Enlai (left) and General George Marshall (right) watch as the representative of the Nationalist Government of China, Governor Zhang Qun, signs a cease-fire order at Chongqing on 10 January 1946.

regarded as a monolithic world-wide movement, and historians have taken too little note of the way Chiang Kai-shek, in 1945, treated the Russian and Chinese Communist parties as separate organizations with divergent interests.

The Russians did not, in the end, prove as cooperative as Chiang had hoped. They eventually allowed Guomindang units to enter some key Russian-held cities before the Russian troops pulled out, but not on the scale that Chiang needed, and to the delays in evacuation which Chiang had requested they added further delays of their own. The pull-out of Russian troops was not completed until 3 May 1946, and it was handled in such a manner that the CCP was able to reach many important positions before the Guomindang. The departure of Soviet forces, except for their continued presence in Port Arthur and Dalian, left no significant armed force separating the Guomindang and the CCP.

A truce existed, but it was never very firm. Aside from an

absence of genuine goodwill on either side, the truce suffered from
the tension between two principles. It was supposed to protect the
territory held by the CCP from efforts at armed seizure by the
Guomindang. At the same time it recognized Chiang Kai-shek's
government as the legal government of China, and forbade CCP
interference with Guomindang communication routes. Even given
far more goodwill than actually existed, it would have been difficult
to avoid trouble over Chiang's desire to open communication routes
through the Communist territory which often separated the
Guomindang-held cities.

Both the CCP and the Guomindang sometimes made promises,
to please General Marshall, which they had no intention of keeping.
Thus in late February of 1946 the two sides signed an agreement on
mutual reduction of armed forces, under which the Guomindang
Army was to be reduced to ninety divisions of not more than 14,000
men each, while the Communist forces would be cut to eighteen
divisions. This would have been tremendously advantageous to
Chiang, and not simply because the numbers were loaded in his
favour. Many of the units nominally under his command were in
fact so unreliable that if, with American backing, he managed to
disband them, his position would be strengthened rather than
weakened. The CCP, on the other hand, really needed all the forces
it had and was vigorously expanding them. It signed the agreement,
but thereafter did not make even the most preliminary gestures
towards implementing it.

The Guomindang, on the other hand, took just as cavalier an
attitude to the cease-fire agreement it signed in January 1946. The
implementation of this agreement was supposed to be supervised in
the field by joint teams of US, Guomindang, and CCP representatives. The Guomindang signed, but then simply refused for an
extended period to allow any joint teams to enter Manchuria, the
area of greatest conflict. The problem in this case was that peace
seemed likely to be far more beneficial to the CCP than to the
Guomindang. The Japanese surrender had allowed the CCP to take
over an area out of proportion to its military strength. Given a few
years, Communist cadres would win the allegiance of the peasants,
reform village politics on revolutionary lines, and build for themselves a tremendously powerful organizational base. The longer
Chiang waited before attacking the Communists in these areas, the
stronger the opposition he would face when he finally did so. In the
areas that had recently come under Guomindang rule, on the other
hand, Chiang's government was utterly incapable of carrying out

programmes analogous to those of the Communists, to win the allegiance of the mass population. It could not expect its strength to grow spectacularly with the passage of time. In July 1947 the US Ambassador commented on the rapacity of the men who had come up from the south to represent Chiang in Manchuria, and the hatred that had grown up between them and the people they were trying to rule:

> Nationalist southern military forces and civil administrators conduct themselves in Manchuria as conquerors, not as fellow countrymen, and have imposed a 'carpet-bag' regime of unbridled exploitation upon areas under their control. If military and civil authorities of local origin were in control, they too would probably exploit the populace, but experience has shown that Chinese authorities of local origin, in general, never quite strangle a goose laying golden eggs, and furthermore, it is a human trait to be less resentful toward exploitation by one's own than toward that by outsiders. The result of this is that the countryside is so antagonistic toward outsiders as to affect the morale of non-Manchurian troops and at the same time arouse vindictiveness in southern military officers and civil administrators.

The Communist forces under Lin Biao had of course also been outsiders when they entered Manchuria in 1945, but they had established good relations with the people, and by 1947 local recruits made up a large proportion of their troops there.

The result of this difference in situations was that while both sides expected war, and probably both sides wanted war, it was to Chiang's advantage to hasten it, and to the advantage of the CCP to postpone it. There were serious violations of the truce on both sides, but the Guomindang was the side which launched such systematic and such massive offensives as to give the impression that it had no desire for a peaceful settlement.

The spring and summer of 1946 saw repeated armed clashes, after which American mediators had increasing difficulty restoring even a temporary truce. Finally, in November 1946, negotiations broke down completely. The pattern of the fighting at first seemed similar to that which had followed Japan's attack on China in 1937, but this time it was the Guomindang that spread along the roads and railroads. It took most major cities, but it did not have the troops to spread over the whole of the countryside as it advanced through North China and Manchuria. Chiang's men took the Communist capital at Yanan in February 1947, but the Communist leaders simply evacuated it and managed their war from mobile bases.

Some Guomindang leaders said they expected to destroy the CCP within a few months; most Americans expected a long and inconclusive struggle. However, CCP strength and Guomindang weakness soon began to show. On paper Chiang's army was perhaps three times as large as that of the Communists, and better armed, but much of this army was either of very low quality or not available for actual use. Chiang had to play off his various generals against one another, and many of the troops nominally under his control were either commanded by men he did not trust, or needed for the task of watching men he did not trust, far from the areas of combat against the Communists. Chiang no longer had anything like the advantage he had enjoyed against the Jiangxi Soviet; he could not even occupy all of the cities and major transportation lines. His troops pushing up the South Manchurian Railway were stopped before they had taken all the important cities along the line. At the same time, the low quality of the Guomindang troops guaranteed that the Communists would be able to capture considerable quantities of weapons to equip their new recruits.

In late 1946 and early 1947 Chiang Kai-shek stretched his forces to the limit, whether because he wanted to knock out the Communists before they got any stronger, or simply because he wanted to take as much territory, and especially as many of the relatively industrialized cities, as he could. He put hundreds of thousands of his best troops into Manchuria. His armies in the north, far from their bases of supply, were threatened by steadily growing Communist armies in the countryside around them.

The United States found it difficult to work out a clear policy. Chiang Kai-shek had been a US ally for several years, and was popular with the American public. The USA was also distrustful, to say the least, of any Communist Party. However, American policy-makers were reluctant to get involved in a civil war which Chiang had started against American advice, and which he was conducting in a manner very unlikely to lead to victory. Chiang was launching over-optimistic offensives against a powerful enemy, while American advisers were pleading with him to make the kind of reforms that could give him a really firm grip on the territory he already held. The USA was reluctant to give him much aid as long as he ignored this advice, and was determined not to allow aid to escalate to the point where it would imply a guarantee to preserve Chiang's government.

In August 1946, wanting to disengage the US a little further from the growing conflict, General Marshall instituted an embargo on the sale of US weapons to Chiang, which lasted for about ten months. He also withdrew US military advisers from some Guomindang units actually involved in conflict against the Communists. However, the effect of these steps was blurred by the continuation of several forms of US aid to Chiang Kai-shek. Military advisers remained in some sections of the Guomindang armed forces. The US Marines remained in North China until well into 1947, and while they were not actually in combat against the Communists, they maintained security in crucial territory, thus freeing Guomindang troops for combat. Finally, the embargo on military material only applied to sales; it did not stop the Marines from *giving* the Guomindang large quantities of surplus ammunition when they finally began to withdraw in the spring of 1947. The USA, despite Marshall's wishes, was involved.

The return to land reform

At the same time it resumed civil war against the Guomindang, the CCP also resumed violent class struggle against the landlords and rich peasants. This was a gradual and unplanned development. Party leaders were not sure how radical they were going to become, and indeed they did not always define their policies of the moment very clearly.

As has been remarked above, the CCP had not abandoned the class struggle totally during the war against Japan. Rent reduction, graduated taxation, and the promotion of some peasants to leadership positions in the villages had weakened the traditional élite considerably. However, this élite was far from having been destroyed. Many landlords and rich peasants retained most of their land, and retained either general prestige or actual positions of leadership in their villages. In the second half of 1945, and in 1946, the CCP made increasingly radical attacks on these people. The Party first directed the peasants against people who had supported the Japanese, but then turned the attack against those guilty only of collecting rent or making high-interest loans. Before the end of 1946 there were many areas in which all conspicuously large landholdings had been eliminated.

The land reform campaign soon became very radical indeed. It led to attacks on middle peasants who did not really have much more than an average amount of wealth, and even on some people whose wealth was average or a shade below average. It also led to damaging purges within the Communist Party. There are a variety of reasons for these excesses, which the Party later realized to have been mistakes. One was that the Party had unrealistic expectations of what land reform could accomplish. The Party liked to blame the exploitation of the landlords for all or almost all of the peasants' problems. It was far too quick to assume that the peasants could all have a decent life if only the landlords' wealth were properly distributed. Chinese Communist Party publications often stated that the landlords and rich peasants, who together amounted to not more than 10 per cent of the rural population, owned 70 to 80 per cent of the land in China. Unfortunately for the CCP, the actual landholdings of the landlords and rich peasants were nowhere near this level. Landlord and rich peasant holdings were particularly small in North and Northwest China. Redistribution of wealth could at best partially alleviate the peasants' problems in these provinces; the real problem was that there was not enough wealth to go around.

When the landlords' wealth had been divided and many peasants were still unpleasantly close to the edge of starvation, the Party began spreading its nets further and further to find additional people from whom land and other wealth could be confiscated. The victims included rich peasants, and then middle peasants who owned more than the average amount of land and farm equipment, and finally some people who were actually at or below the average level of wealth, but whose parents or grandparents had been landlords or rich peasants, so it could be claimed that their inherited land and goods had come originally from their ancestors' exploitation of the poor.

Party leaders became increasingly suspicious of their own village-level organizations. If redistribution of wealth had not resolved the plight of the poor, suspicion naturally fell on those who had managed the programme. The suspicion was partially justified. Some cadres had taken for themselves part of the wealth confiscated from the rich. Some had protected landlords or rich peasants from full redistribution of their property. But Party leaders, who had exaggerated ideas of what a full and correct redistribution could have done for the poor, thought the village cadres must be far worse than they actually were.

By the second half of 1947 the Party was pushing a remarkably extremist policy in the villages of northern China, to bring the poor peasants and agricultural labourers up to full equality with all the other elements in society. Landholdings were to be equalized in each area, and there was also to be significant redistribution of agricultural tools, draft animals, seed grain, money, and other forms of wealth. Landlords and rich peasants were in theory to be cut down to equality with the poor; in practice many landlords were stripped of everything they had, and some were killed. More startlingly, the ordinary poor peasants were also promoted relative to the veteran cadres of the Communist Party. Top leaders decided that local cadres had been abusing their positions to the detriment of the Party. They invited the poor peasants to stand in judgement over the cadres and Party members, to take from them any excess land and goods which might have stuck to their fingers during previous redistribution of wealth, and to criticize and punish them if they had been arrogant or abusive to those below them.

The ensuing turmoil involved the collision of two very different views of the nature of society and politics. Traditional China had been a very hierarchical society. All understood that some members of society were wealthy, powerful, and could do almost as they pleased, while others were poor and weak. Many peasants who had risen to positions of village leadership in the early stages of the revolution assumed as a matter of course that they would enjoy what they regarded as the normal perquisites of leadership – the rights to make decisions and command obedience. They were the ones who had made possible the redistribution of landlord wealth; to many of them, and to many of the ordinary peasants, it seemed only fair that they should be rewarded by being given an extra share in the distribution. Some of them had acquired valuable objects simply by default. Everyone knew that if the Communist Party were ever defeated, peasants who had taken large and valuable objects would be in danger of their lives. If landlord property were distributed while the village was still not sure which way the civil war was going, a revolutionary cadre could sometimes get a wagon or a team of mules simply by being the only person who dared accept them. For such reasons, peasants who had led in the early stages of the revolution in any particular village were likely to have profited from it more than their neighbours.

To Party leaders, on the other hand, such phenomena represented serious corruption. Communism was supposed to be an egalitarian doctrine, and real egalitarianism required a total break with the hierarchical traditions of Chinese society. The Party decided that infiltration by the traditional élite, and the tendency of peasants who rose to positions of leadership to differentiate themselves from the people, enrich themselves beyond the level of the common peasants, and take on the arrogance and self-importance of the traditional élite, threatened the very soul of the revolution.

Given such a climate of opinion, Party leaders exaggerated the magnitude of the problem they faced. As has been mentioned above, they exaggerated the extent to which redistribution of landlord wealth could improve the lives of the peasants, so when they saw the peasants still in difficulties they thought that some very large proportion of the wealth formerly held by the landlords must have failed to reach the hands of the peasants. When they saw veteran cadres at the village level guilty of arrogance, minor corruption, or simply giving orders to the peasants instead of explaining programmes to them in such a fashion as to win voluntary cooperation, they reacted with a degree of shock and horror which implied not only that this behaviour was undesirable, but that it reflected an astonishing failure to meet normal and reasonable standards of behaviour. In fact, most of the cadres in question had adhered to a standard considerably higher than what they had grown up thinking of as normal élite behaviour. If Party leaders wanted to set a still higher standard, they should have understood that they would need to conduct a long, slow educational campaign among the cadres.

In the early months of 1948, the Party relaxed the extremes of its drive for egalitarianism. It had always been hesitant about trying to achieve total equalization of landholdings, since this would require taking land from anyone who owned even a little more than the average amount. Complete equalization attacked the interests of well-to-do middle peasants who were not to any serious extent exploiters, who were not hated by their neighbours, and who did not own enough for their expropriation to bring all that great a benefit to the poor. It appeared threatening even to poor peasants, whose ambition after the land reform was to work hard on the land they had just acquired, save, and make themselves well-to-do middle peasants. China could not afford for the poor to think that if they worked hard and enriched themselves they would only be expropriated.

In the political sphere the extremes of anti-élitism were similarly relaxed. Those who investigated village cadres and village Party branches stopped assuming that they were likely to find massive corruption, landlord infiltration, and abuses of power. The Party stopped being so determined to get all the poor peasants involved equally in village politics; it would settle for having all of the poor involved to some extent, and those of the poor peasants who seemed to have a talent for leadership moving to the top positions.

However, one must remember that while this might be more moderate than what had been happening in the autumn of 1947, the Communist Party was still carrying out a remarkably radical programme by any other standard. In villages where a Communist apparatus existed, local Party members and cadres continued to be called to account if there were solid evidence that they had been guilty of arrogant abuses of their powers, or that they had used their positions to enrich themselves. In newly 'liberated' areas the Party did not act quite so hastily as before, but it was still determined that the destruction of the traditional village élite should be completed within two or three years. Landlords lost most of their wealth, and rich peasants lost a significant amount. Landlords continued to be imprisoned or executed, even if in smaller numbers than in earlier years. Their prestige, and their control of village affairs, were destroyed as completely as the Communist Party could manage. In their place a new ruling structure was recruited from among the peasants. Where village reforms were carried out in accord with Party policy, the bulk of the peasants not only acquired considerable wealth from the expropriation of the landlords, they acquired a significant voice in village affairs. Even where local officials carried out the reforms in a hasty and slipshod manner, the degree of equality in village society was greater than it had ever been before.

The very radical line followed in the villages during the winter of 1947/48 provides interesting parallels, and contrasts, to the radicalism of the Cultural Revolution in the 1960s. In both cases the Party developed policies of extreme egalitarianism, which were later repudiated on the grounds that they had harmed both the Party itself, and elements of the mass population. However, from the Communist viewpoint the damage done by leftist excesses in the land reform of the late 1940s was limited, and the errors were corrected quite fast. Some of the reasons will be discussed in Chapter 6, but it is worth mentioning here that in the 1940s policy discussions were still being conducted on a rational basis. The Party was describing what it believed the situation to be, and the policies it was developing to deal with that situation, in clear, simple, and rational language. This made it relatively easy for people to notice if the description failed to match the actual situation (as with wild exaggerations of the number of landlord infiltrators in the Party), or if the arguments justifying a particular policy seemed weak (as with the expropriation of land from well-to-do middle peasants). In the Cultural Revolution, public debate was conducted in such stereotyped and inflated rhetoric as to hamper rational decision-making.

The final Communist victory

Meanwhile, the Civil War was approaching an end. Chiang had sent his best military units into North China and Manchuria. They pushed northward as far as they could go, taking the CCP capital at Yanan, and moving up the rail lines into the interior of Manchuria. They strung themselves out over long and tenuous communication lines, surrounded by Communist-held villages, until they needed to devote most of their efforts just to defending their positions and their supply lines against the harassment of CCP guerrillas. By the middle of 1947 they were losing the initiative, and starting to huddle into their garrisons. Their advantage in numbers and weapons was still great, but not as great as in the past; the CCP had been recruiting vigorously, and had acquired a considerable amount of Japanese equipment, some captured directly and some handed over by the Russians before they left Manchuria in 1946. The Guomindang forces, suffering from incompetence, corruption, and disunity, were losing such offensive spirit as they had previously had.

Civil society in the Guomindang zone was also in a state of decay. Rampant inflation undermined the economic position of the middle class. The corruption of the Guomindang administration remained a conspicuous embarrassment.

Chiang Kai-shek, who could remember when the Guomindang had been a dynamic and aggressive party, bent on a revolutionary transformation of Chinese society, was well aware of how low it had sunk (though he may not have realized the extent of his own responsibility for the decline). Desperately trying to shame his subordinates into some effort at reform, he commented: 'To tell the truth, never, in China or abroad, has there been a revolutionary party as decrepit and degenerate as we [the Guomindang] are today; nor one as lacking spirit, lacking discipline, and even more, lacking standards of right and wrong as we are today.' Officers neither trained their men properly in combat skills, nor gave them adequate food, clothing, or medical care; 'since the officers treat the men in this way it must be considered very good if the men do not mutiny or desert'. Loyalty to the cause was minimal; 'Everyone nourishes the evil habit of caring only for himself and is concerned only for the advantage of his own unit; towards the perils and difficulties of other troops, or the success or failure of the whole campaign, they give almost no thought.'

By the autumn of 1947 the Communist forces, which had adopted the name 'People's Liberation Army' (PLA) in 1946, had definitely gained the initiative. They controlled almost all of the countryside not only in Manchuria, but also in the section of the North China Plain lying north of the Yellow River. By the first half of 1948 increasing numbers of Guomindang troops were defecting to the CCP. The Guomindang positions in Manchuria were shrinking islands in the sea of the Communist countryside, having steadily less contact with one another. The Communists could probably have begun eliminating these islands considerably sooner than they did, but instead they chose to push south of the Yellow River, until the pattern of isolated Guomindang positions surrounded by Communist countryside reached down halfway to the Yangzi. In this fashion Mao and his generals ensured that the Guomindang armies in North China and Manchuria would not be able to escape southward when the final push came. Also, by leaving Guomindang armies surrounded in their garrisons for months, the CCP ensured that they would be too demoralized to put up any effective resistance when the decisive attack finally came. Chiang Kai-shek's refusal to extract his armies from this trap ensured the success of CCP strategy.

Once it became apparent that the CCP could not only isolate Guomindang garrisons from one another, but actually bring strong enough forces against individual garrisons to destroy them, the end came very quickly. Normally, a victorious army uses up supplies and equipment in the course of its advance, stretches its supply lines, and has to garrison conquered territory. The effective strength available at the front will therefore tend to shrink as the advance goes on. The Communists in North and Northeast China, however, were clearing out Guomindang bases from between Communist bases. With each victory they captured large quantities of equipment and ammunition, their supply lines became shorter with the removal of an obstacle around which they had formerly had to detour, and the forces that could be concentrated against the next target became larger.

As late as 15 September 1948, just before the collapse began, the Guomindang armies still had substantially more total manpower than the CCP. Their superiority in arms and equipment was even greater, and for the most part they had adequate ammunition.

However, it was a case of the sheep outnumbering the wolves. The Guomindang forces in North China and Manchuria were scattered in garrisons far enough from one another to make supply very difficult. Chiang Kai-shek, in his determination to hold important cities, kept his men in exposed positions far to the north rather than pull them south while there was time to do so. If asked to come to one another's assistance they generally moved slowly and hesitantly or not at all, so the Communists could concentrate overwhelming force against one, and then move on to the next. Finally, when the attack began against any particular city, some units immediately surrendered or went over to the Communist side, opening up great gaps in the defensive line, with the result that troops who were willing to make a last-ditch resistance were unable to do so in any effective manner. Thus the Guomindang armies, first in Manchuria and then in North China, ceased to exist in a remarkably short period. The Communist forces not only suffered few losses, they actually expanded during the campaign through the absorption of troops who switched sides.

The destruction of the Guomindang forces in Manchuria, in October and November of 1948, made an eventual Communist victory certain. The destruction of Guomindang forces on the North China Plain, culminating in the Huai-Hai campaign of November 1948 to January 1949, ended the possibility that the Guomindang would even be able to mount a decent rearguard action. It had lost over a million men, including almost all of what passed in its decrepit forces for élite units, in four and a half months. It had not even imposed significant casualties on the enemy. From this point onward the PLA swept southward against minimal resistance.

On 21 January 1949, Chiang Kai-shek officially resigned as President of the Republic of China; Vice-president Li Zongren (Li Tsung-jen) theoretically took Chiang's place. Chiang thus escaped the embarrassment of presiding officially over the collapse of his government. However, he kept real power in his own hands; he continued to issue orders to his generals and other high officials just as if he were still President. As his military position on the mainland of China became hopeless, he withdrew as many of his troops as possible to the island of Taiwan. On 1 March 1950, on Taiwan, he once more took the title of President of the Republic of China.

The PLA crossed the Yangzi River in April 1949, and reached Guangzhou on the south coast in October. At this point the Civil War seemed effectively over. Before the end of 1950 the PLA had even reached Tibet in the southwest, which had been shown as part

5.5   Mao Zedong arrives in Beiping (soon to be restored to its old name of Beijing), March 1949. The Guomindang had about 200,000 troops in and around the city, but the general commanding this force had surrendered his men, and their weapons, without a serious fight. He was rewarded by being made Minister of Water Conservancy in the new Communist government of China.

of China on maps, but where no Chinese government had exercised any real power for almost forty years. The only Chinese territory they did not hold was Taiwan. On 1 October 1949, in the old imperial capital of Beijing (now restored to its traditional name, after having been called Beiping for twenty-one years under the Guomindang), the nation's new rulers proclaimed the establishment of the People's Republic of China (PRC).

6

The People's Republic of China, 1949–1957

The new regime seemed at first to be in the mainstream of Communist development. The PRC, like other Communist states, was ruled by two parallel hierarchies. Each one ran from the capital in Beijing down to the village level. One was the formal government, with Mao Zedong as Chief of State and Zhou Enlai as Premier. It embraced both a structure of territorial units running from 'greater administrative regions' down through provinces and counties to village administrations, and also functional units such as the ministries of trade, justice, etc. Ultimate power, however, lay with the Communist Party apparatus, which paralleled and penetrated that of the government at every level. The relationship of Party members to non-members was not one of simple command; there were many Party members in the government whose immediate superiors, in the governmental chain of command, were non-members of the Party. However, the Party as an institution provided the leading core of the government. The Party was tightly centralized; Party members accepted the decisions of the Central Committee, which in turn accepted the authority of a few top leaders who belonged to the Politburo.

Roles in this system were not highly specialized. For the first few years the PLA played a major role in most government operations. Even after the military as an organization was separated from the civilian government, almost everyone of real importance held more than one position, and it was not unusual for a single individual to hold simultaneous positions in the civil administration, the PLA, and the Party.

The very rapid advances of 1948 and 1949 had given the CCP control of very extensive areas where it had no real organizational base. Great cities like Shanghai and Wuhan were a serious challenge for a party most of whose past experience had been in the countryside, and indeed in the more primitive and backward parts of the countryside.

The CCP did not have deep roots even in all of the countryside. It had operated mainly north of the Yangzi for the past fifteen years; most of its activities in the south had been restricted to a few guerrilla zones. It did not have a great many members who spoke the southern dialects. Under such conditions plans for the rapid collectivization of agriculture, or the replacement of private ownership by socialist control in industry, would have been absurd. The Party might 'control' the newly conquered areas, in the sense that the PLA had driven out the Guomindang forces, but it had to do a great deal of work just to establish an effective administration in central and southern China, much less carry out its long-term goals of social transformation.

The Communist Party's policy was strictly pragmatic in the early years. It needed to maintain public services, maintain or establish law and order, and get an administration running. It did not have half the number of ideologically reliable people it would have needed to do these jobs, so it quite calmly set about recruiting thousands and thousands of unreliable ones. Before long standards would be raised, and these people would either have to be reindoctrinated in a satisfactory fashion or lose their positions, but for the moment the main priority was seeing that necessary tasks got done. The CCP did not merely ask technical personnel like railway maintenance men and power plant supervisors to stay on their jobs; it did the same with many of the people who had staffed the tax-collection bureaux, police agencies, and criminal courts of the old regime.

This was a remarkable demonstration of self-confidence, in a situation where many Communists might have felt that their power and their revolutionary purity were at risk. The Party knew that it was taking on people, in politically sensitive jobs, many of whom had no understanding of Communism and some of whom actively disliked it. It had seen how the opportunists had swarmed into the Guomindang after 1927, and had helped to convert a revolutionary movement into a corrupt and stagnant bureaucracy. However, the CCP had no doubt that it could guide and supervise its own new recruits, so they could neither take over the new government and subvert its revolutionary goals, nor conspire against it and overthrow it.

Reform in the countryside

In the villages of southern China, the first years of Communist rule were a period of continual turmoil and change. The CCP wanted to destroy the existing rural élite, and break up concentrations of wealth in the countryside. There were precedents for such a policy in Chinese tradition, both in ancient documents and in the actual policies of past dynasties. The founding of a dynasty in pre-modern China had usually been accompanied by an effort to break up at least some large landholdings, since large landholders tended to take for themselves the share of the land's production that might otherwise have gone to the government through taxation. However, the egalitarian policies of the CCP went far beyond those of past dynasties.

The Party aimed at two main goals. One was to destroy the traditional ruling order in the countryside, which meant stripping the old élite of its power, its prestige, and most of its wealth. The continued existence of the landlord class was intolerable to the CCP, not only from the viewpoint of Marxist doctrine but also as a practical matter. Redistribution of landlord wealth was the only rapid means by which the CCP could make substantial improvements in the lives of the poor peasants. Politically the landlords were deeply anti-Communist, and even in the unlikely event that they could be persuaded to give up open hostility, their control over the peasants would have been a barrier separating the CCP from the bulk of the population of China.

Furthermore, the attack on them had to be carried out by very drastic methods if it were to have any chance of success. The landlords' influence was far too deeply ingrained in village culture for Communist cadres simply to tell the peasants they did not have to serve and obey the landlords any more; the only way to eliminate the landlords' control was to destroy them as a class.

The other major goal was to build up a new power structure, which would be more satisfactory both to the peasants and to the CCP leadership in Beijing than the traditional élite had been. Part of the new structure was introduced from outside the villages: organizational networks made up of veteran Communists, and new recruits coming mostly from the educated population of the cities, spread out into the countryside from province capitals and county seats. Part grew up from the base level, as village peasant associations began to produce people with a talent for leadership, who could become village leaders and then move up to higher levels.

In each village the transformation was supervised, on a sporadic basis, by travelling work teams usually sent out by authorities in the county seat. Every few months a team would come, and stay for a few days or weeks. It might have some specific job to do, such as tax-collection, or it might have come simply to supervise social transformation, but in either case it would propangandize the poor peasants, to persuade them both to support the new government and to rise up to defend their own interests against the rich and take control of village society. The work teams sponsored the organization of peasant associations, and the most active and enthusiastic peasants became the new leaders of the villages.

In the early months the class struggle occurred mainly in connection with tax-collection and rent reduction. Every government must support itself, and the PRC came to the villages to collect taxes just as any other government would have had to do. The PRC tax-collectors, however, were supposed to win the voluntary cooperation of the peasants in a way their Guomindang counterparts had not. The peasants were invited to help ensure that taxes were really collected in a graduated fashion, with the rich carrying the heaviest share of the burden. The same cadres who collected taxes were also supposed to enforce rent reduction, so they could argue that the tenants had a moral obligation to pay their fair share of taxes to a government which was, in return, increasing the tenants' share of the crop quite substantially. Tenants were asked to pay the tax owed by their landlords directly to the government, rather than paying their rent to the landlords and leaving the government with the task of collecting a portion of it as tax.

There were a hundred things that could go wrong in the attempted transformation of the villages. Few members of the travelling work teams were experienced revolutionaries. A good many were intellectuals from the towns, from middle-class or even upper-class backgrounds. Some could not conceive of poor peasants really learning to run village affairs; others simply did not think they had the time to find and train peasant activists. All government personnel at this time had more work to do than time to do it in, and the tradition of élitism and bureaucracy in Chinese culture was so strong that it took newly recruited functionaries long enough just to learn that the new regime wanted them to politicize the poor at all; it took longer to persuade them that politicizing the poor could take precedence over other tasks. The idea that the government might use some criterion other than the successful collection of taxes, when judging tax-collectors and considering them for promotion to more important jobs, was especially startling.

The poor peasants did not automatically join in the revolution against the landlords; the idea of the poor overthrowing the rich was as alien to many peasants as it was to urban intellectuals. Some peasants felt they had been reasonably treated under the old order; they were grateful to have been able to rent land, rather than angry that part of the crop had gone to the landlord. Some simply did not believe that a group of strange people from the city, who were not even planning to remain in the village for very long, could really succeed in arranging the overthrow of the class that had ruled the village for time beyond memory. They feared that when the dust settled the landlords would still be in control, and that anyone who had been so foolish as to join in the attack on them would be in very serious trouble. Some peasants were bound to the landlords by kinship or clan ties. For any or all of these reasons, when the travelling work teams had recruited peasants into a peasant association, the peasants might still show little enthusiasm for a vigorous attack on the landlords. They might remain silent or even agree quite vocally when a landlord lied about his status, and passed himself off to the work team as a middle or poor peasant.

In many areas there were active feuds between rival villages or clans, and the 'us against them' in the peasants' minds was peasants and landlords of their own village fighting against peasants and landlords of the neighbouring village. They could not easily be brought to believe that the peasants of both villages should unite against the landlords.

The work teams could sometimes be caught up in such local rivalries. There was one village in Guangdong which before the revolution had been split by rivalry between two major landlords, Li Mingquan and Li Caixiong. Mingquan had controlled the village government; most of the peasants who lived in his immediate neighbourhood had been aligned with him against Caixiong. Then the revolution arrived, in the form of the PLA, which passed through the area but saw little reason to pay much attention to this particular village. Caixiong saw his chance. He mobilized those peasants who did not have personal ties with Mingquan, who formed a majority of the population, into a peasant association which overthrew Mingquan. Caixiong was then able to run the village through this peasant association. When the district author-ities heard about the situation they sent in a work team to mobilize peasants against this new landlord ruler of the village. But the peasants who were easiest to mobilize against Caixiong were the ones he was discriminating against, namely those with ties to Mingquan. The impression conveyed was that the Communist Party was siding with Mingquan's faction, and Mingquan was much less popular in the village than Caixiong. This situation took a considerable time to straighten out.

Even if power could be placed in the hands of genuine peasant activists, properly independent of the landlords and rich peasants, there was no guarantee that these activists would be the kind of leaders the CCP was looking for. Being a poor peasant did not necessarily cause one to treat other poor peasants with respect and consideration. In traditional village society, people of power and influence had been able to use their positions to command obedience from those below them, reward their friends and relatives, harass their enemies, and enrich themselves. Many poor and middle peasants now rising to positions of leadership felt entitled to behave in the same fashion, to a greater or lesser extent.

The work teams and county governments, trying to supervise villages where they were strangers, could be deceived and manipulated. Landlords and rich peasants could pass themselves off as middle or poor peasants. There was one village where a peasant association under genuine peasant leadership was set up and gained a fair degree of power. The landlords then organized every peasant they could still control, and flooded the county authorities with charges that the peasant association leaders in this village were corrupt. The county authorities were taken in, and removed the peasant association leadership; the landlords were then able to regain control of the village.

In the early stages of the transformation most landlords did not suffer too badly. The rents they collected were reduced and their taxes increased. Some debts the peasants owed them were cancelled, and the interest on others was reduced. But even where such policies were thoroughly enforced (which in many areas they were not), the typical landlord was left with a substantial income, and none of his property was confiscated outright. Only a few known as 'local despots', who were charged with exceptional crimes against the peasants, were put on trial, and had the bulk of their property confiscated.

After a year or two of these campaigns, each village had a core of peasant activists, with some leadership experience. A much larger number of peasants had achieved at least some degree of politicization through the peasant associations, and had attained enough benefits through the reduction of rents and the interest rate on debts, and refund of some rent recently collected by the landlords, to be convinced that class struggle really could be worth while. A couple of 'local despots' might have been tried before 'people's tribunals', raising the confidence of the peasants that they could actually win in a confrontation with a landlord. Once this ground-work had been laid, a full-scale land reform campaign, involving an attack on the whole landlord class and to some extent on the rich peasants, became practical.

The land reform was more thorough and more drastic than previous campaigns. Everyone classified as a landlord was sub-jected to expropriation; they were only allowed to keep an amount of land equivalent to what was being given to the poor peasants. This meant that they were being reduced to below the average level of wealth in the countryside, since the redistribution of their land usually left the poor peasants still owning less land than the average for the rural population as a whole. Significant amounts of money, grain stocks, tools, draught animals, and sometimes housing were also taken from the landlords. However, if they were involved in commercial or industrial enterprises these enterprises were at least partially protected from confiscation. A significant fraction of the landlords, charged with crimes more serious than mere economic exploitation, were imprisoned or executed.

The CCP was not trying to achieve total equalization of wealth in the countryside. To have taken away the surplus wealth of every-one who owned even a little more than the average would have made the Communist Party far too many enemies from a political viewpoint. It would have disrupted production in the short run by attacking the most efficient farmers, and in the long run by giving people the feeling that if they worked hard and saved to improve their position, they might end up losing everything to some future wave of redistribution. The CCP therefore gave absolute protection to middle peasants (people whose incomes came primarily from their own labour, with little or none coming from exploiting the labour of others), and partial protection to rich peasants (those whose land was worked to a substantial extent by tenants or hired labourers, but who still did a serious amount of agricultural labour themselves). The rich peasants had been among the more produc-tive farmers; they had better tools and could sometimes use more sophisticated farming techniques than the poor. To maintain pro-duction, especially in the areas immediately around major cities which kept the urban markets supplied, rich peasants were allowed to keep all the land they worked by their own labour and hired labour, and even some of what they rented out. This left them substantially better off than the average peasant.

The CCP was well aware of the difficulties facing outsiders coming into a village and trying to rebuild its whole political and economic structure. Even the work teams supervising land reform, which stayed in any given village longer than previous teams and had the assistance of peasant activists trained and recruited by previous teams, might have been lied to, been hasty or careless, or simply had the bad luck to rely on activists who looked good at the time but would later become corrupt or dictatorial in the way they ran village affairs. The Party therefore waited several months after the departure of the land reform work team from each village. During this time, if anything had gone seriously wrong, the fact usually became apparent to the peasants of the village in question. Then another team of cadres came to investigate. Only after this final team had given its seal of approval did the changes wrought during land reform become final.

Spreading the transformation out in stages like this had two great advantages. One was that the cadres of successive work teams were unlikely to make exactly the same mistakes; if a landlord trying to pass himself off as a middle peasant were able to deceive one team, he would probably be caught by the next. The other advantage was that this procedure increased the role of local peasants. If the CCP had tried to destroy the old élite in a single massive campaign (as the Vietnamese Communists tried to do in large areas of North Vietnam in 1955 and 1956), there would not have been time for local peasant activists to acquire experience and play a genuine leadership role. By handling things the way it did, the CCP ensured that when the land reform work team reached a village it found a considerable number of peasants who not only had been trained by previous teams, but had then acquired experience and self-confidence by running village affairs for several months on their own, without outside cadres watching over their shoulders. This made a great difference in the way land reform actually worked.

Leaders of the CCP had little trouble deciding how to manage class struggle in the villages, from 1950 to 1953, because their egalitarian ideology meshed so well with their own self-interest. When they handed landlord land over to the peasants, they were creating a tremendous reservoir of peasant gratitude and loyalty. (Fifteen years later, peasants who had no understanding of Mao Zedong's current policies still venerated him as the person who had given them the land.)

Land reform strengthened the national economy, since the landlords had been for the most part a parasitic class, whose involvement in the rural economy had inhibited the development of production. When the CCP destroyed the traditional élite in its capacity as an élite, and elevated poor peasants to political power in the villages, it was removing a serious political threat. When Party leaders tried to ensure that a really large proportion of the peasants became politicized – that the new village political structure had some genuinely democratic characteristics, and was not simply a matter of a few peasant activists rising to the top and ruling over their neighbours as arbitrarily as the landlords had formerly done – they were not simply satisfying their ideals. They were also reducing the likelihood that the new village leadership would concentrate so much wealth and power into its hands that it would be able to follow its own interests in defiance of the central authorities.

After the land reform things would seldom be so simple. The CCP would find, more and more, that it had to choose between its egalitarian ideals on the one hand, and its pragmatic economic and political interests on the other.

Into the cities

Chinese Communism had been born in the cities, but it had been essentially a rural movement since 1927. The Party that marched into Beijing, Shanghai, Wuhan, and Guangzhou in 1949 found itself in an essentially alien environment. If the CCP leaders were to run the urban economy, and then expand and develop it, they would have to gain the support not only of workers, but also of people with vital skills – technicians, managers, and administrators – and at the same time acquire some of those skills themselves.

This challenged the Communists, as Communists, in a way the problem of transforming the countryside had not. Few members of the traditional rural élite had skills vital to the economy; indeed many of them had constituted an actual impediment to a more efficient agricultural economy. There were only a few manager-landlords, and so on; they could be given special treatment, so their skills would not be lost to the economy, without compromising the overall pattern of the class struggle. But in the cities most of the élite

6.1   A crowded street in Shanghai.

made some genuine contribution to society. There were educated people of all sorts, desperately needed in a country as backward as China. There were technicians and skilled workers. There were industrial capitalists, who might be classed as exploiters but who had managerial expertise without which the country would be crippled. Even the merchants, treated as parasites by both Marxist and Confucian theory because they did not create goods, but made a profit simply by moving them about, would be indispensable until socialist networks of distribution could be organized.

In the short run, the Party had to prevent any breakdown in urban society; to maintain services and production. In the long run it was determined to expand and improve the industrial sector very drastically, to make China a modern nation. A class struggle of the intensity of the land reform could not even be considered; it would disrupt both short- and long-run goals too badly.

The CCP made no secret of its intention to establish a socialist system, but it offered people with valuable skills the opportunity to preserve their élite status if they supported the new regime. In 1949 Liu Shaoqi, then one of the top leaders of the CCP, is quoted as having put this offer in very attractive terms to a capitalist in Tianjin.

> Now you own only one factory, but in the future you can own one, two, three . . . or even eight. When socialism is at hand and the state issues an order, you hand them over or the state purchases them from you . . . Then the state will place these factories back under your management. You will remain the manager, but the factories will be state-owned. We may increase the number of factories under your supervision to sixteen, for you are a capable manager. Your salary will increase instead of being slashed. But you have to do a very good job. If that happens, will you say yes to the offer?
>   Mr Song replied: 'I will, of course!'
>   Therefore, I believe that in the future when everyone is called to a meeting to discuss how to move into socialism, no one is going to knit his eyebrows and there will be smiling faces all around.

As the new regime moved into the cities, it of course took over immediately those enterprises that had been owned by the previous government, and those owned by 'bureaucratic capitalists' (capitalists who held important positions in the Guomindang, or were closely affiliated with it). These enterprises, plus new ones established by government investment after 1949, added up to a substantial state sector in commerce and manufacturing by the mid 1950s. Key sections of the economy, such as transportation and heavy industry, were almost entirely under state control. State trading networks were established to replace private merchants in the distribution of certain commodities. However, there remained a private sector owned by the 'national bourgeoisie' (those among the capitalists who had not done anything to attract the hostility of the CCP). At first, the CCP simply tried to keep this private sector operating, and offered it the prospect of fairly liberal conditions for a considerable period. However, as the Party's reserves of qualified personnel became larger and its grip became stronger, it moved to impose tighter control.

The 'Five-Anti' campaign of 1952, nominally directed against bribery, tax evasion, theft of state assets, cheating on labour and materials, and stealing state economic intelligence, was in fact used to reduce the overall autonomy of the bourgeoisie. Almost every enterprise was vulnerable to this campaign. For one thing, Chinese businessmen had never been very amenable to government regulation; most of them had engaged in knowing violations of the law, and the fact could be proven. For another, the campaign penalized many people for perfectly normal business practices. Every businessman had tried to keep track of government decisions that could affect his supplies of raw materials and the market for his products, but this information was now included in the category of state economic secrets, and its possession could be treated as a crime. A high rate of profit, especially if acquired in commerce rather than manufacturing, was in itself considered evidence of criminal behaviour.

In a procedure somewhat analagous to the land reform, cadres went into each enterprise and mobilized the employees to investigate and criticize their employer. In the end few were actually imprisoned, but the great majority were harassed, intimidated, and forced to confess to various misdeeds. Their cash reserves were drained off in penalties. Their managerial autonomy was very severely reduced; both the state and the unions organized among their employees continued to supervise them rather closely after the campaign was over. The private sector clearly existed only on sufferance.

The transition to socialism

By 1955 and 1956 the CCP was ready to move from private property to socialist ownership as a basis for the economy. The change was made with remarkable speed; it was effectively over, both in industry and in agriculture, by the end of 1956.

In the countryside peasant farms were grouped, by stages, into agricultural producers' cooperatives equivalent to the kolkhoz (collective farm) of the Soviet Union. First perhaps half a dozen families got together in a mutual aid team, in which they helped work one another's land, but each family still owned its own fields and owned the crops grown on those fields. Next would come a semi-socialist cooperative, which might contain twenty families, who pooled their land together and worked it collectively. They kept records of 'work points' – tallies, kept on a day-to-day basis, of how much work each family had done in the fields. At harvest time the crop would be divided, with the share of each family depending partly on how many work points it had earned, and partly on how much land, tools, and other capital it had contributed when the cooperative was formed. Finally would come a fully socialist cooperative, which might contain 100 or more families, and in which the crop would be divided strictly according to the amount of work done by each family. Delays were permitted in areas inhabited by non-Chinese minorities, but the great majority of the ethnically Chinese peasants were not only in cooperatives but in fully socialist cooperatives by the end of 1956.

In the cities capitalist businesses were either taken over outright, or converted to the status of state–private joint enterprises, in which the state had the final say in all decisions. The former owners were paid dividends for several more years, and in many cases were kept on as managers, but they had lost control. This transition was mainly completed during the winter of 1955/56.

Most Party leaders had not expected the transition to come this soon, and some disapproved of hasty changes, but once the Party had consolidated its position enough to be capable of collectivizing the major sectors of the economy, which it had by 1955, Mao Zedong saw little reason to wait. The imminent abolition of the private economy was having an inhibiting effect on production, especially in the cities. The capitalists knew that their factories were probably going to be nationalized before long. This expectation could produce ghastly results, as with the man who did not bother to lubricate valuable machinery, because he was sure that by the time it collapsed under this abuse it would no longer be his. The capitalists' access to scarce raw materials often depended on Communist cadres who thought of capitalist enterprise as something being given a last few years of toleration, and were unlikely to treat it with great favour. The information they needed to plan their operations adequately was likely to be included in the category of 'state economic secrets'; its possession had brought severe penalties under the Five-Anti campaign. Very high levels of profits became, in themselves, grounds for suspicion. In general, the operation of capitalist business under a Communist government involved such tensions that many of the capitalists themselves felt relieved when nationalization finally came.

In the countryside there had been a tendency towards economic differentiation after land reform which bothered Communist leaders. Some peasants were gaining in wealth. There were rich peasants who still had the advantages of better tools, better land, and more draught animals than most of their neighbours, and former middle or poor peasants who were working their way up into the category of 'new rich peasants'. On the other hand, bad luck, bad management, or simply an acute land shortage in some villages, which had made it difficult to give viable farms to every poor peasant, had left some individuals in a position where they had to borrow at high interest rates, or even sell off some of their newly acquired land. This was, in principle, disturbing to a Party with the CCP's egalitarian doctrines. It also posed a practical threat to the development of socialism in the countryside. The Party wished to persuade the peasants to join cooperatives on a reasonably voluntary basis. A certain amount of pressure might be applied, but the PRC could not even consider the brute-force approach that had been used in the Soviet Union. Stalin had not concealed the fact that collectivization would reduce quite severely the incomes of the rich peasants (kulaks) in the Soviet countryside. The resulting kulak resistance, and the execution or deportation of kulaks and people accused of being kulaks, led to the deaths of many of Russia's most skilled farmers, and the destruction of tremendous amounts of livestock and other property in the late 1920s and early 1930s.

China could hope to avoid this, and persuade the peasants to join cooperatives on a voluntary or near-voluntary basis, only if it could promise that nobody's income would suffer very badly. This required that the peasants who joined cooperatives did so on something approaching an equal basis. In 1955, the differences in wealth in the countryside were small enough so that the CCP could say, even to people with more than the average land and capital, that if they joined in a cooperative with people slightly less wealthy than themselves, the efficiency of large-scale production, plus improved access to government loans and fertilizer supplies, would enable their share of the cooperative's income to match what they had had as individual farmers. Some well-to-do middle peasants believed this claim and others did not, but at least the claim was not transparently absurd. If the process of economic differentiation had been allowed to go on for another decade in the countryside, the prospects for voluntary collectivization would have worsened noticeably. When collectivization actually occurred it indeed avoided most of the costs that had accompanied it in the Soviet Union. Destruction of property, by people who felt that what was theirs would belong to themselves or to nobody, was relatively rare. Some people were shoved into cooperatives against their will, but there was hardly any outright violence.

To say that the transition to socialism was fast and smooth does not imply that there were no problems in the new socialist enterprises. In agriculture especially, once the land and tools were no longer the property of individual families, it was not easy to divide up responsibilities in such a way that necessary work, including maintenance of equipment, would get done. Some tools rusted in the fields, because nobody had been assigned the job of taking care of them, and there was no single individual who cared enough about them to look after them without being told. Much hard work and experience were required to deal with such problems, but the basic pattern of the Chinese economy seemed to be set.

There was one major question still facing the Party: how fast should it try to go in altering the psychological basis of the economic system? Could it expect people to work hard out of a sense of moral obligation to their neighbours and to society, or would it have to give material rewards for good work? Offering material rewards to those who did more work, or whose work required more training and skill, seemed necessary to keep the economy functioning smoothly. On the other hand, some CCP leaders feared that the use of such rewards would amount to institutionalizing inequality, and would perpetuate the individualistic attitudes already so deeply ingrained in Chinese culture. In the past, every man had been concerned primarily with his own interests and those of his family. Could one expect people to change their attitudes, and concern themselves with the interests of society as a whole, in a system which used the prospect of individual rewards as its major method for persuading them to work hard?

In the mid 1950s the CCP offered a substantial degree of material incentives, through wages, work points, and so on. There were even some spheres in which individuals or families still functioned as separate units in the economy. The most important of these was the private production which continued to occur in the countryside even after the peasants were grouped into cooperatives. Most households were assigned small private plots of land. They did not actually own these plots, but they could use them for whatever crops they wished. Many grew vegetables for sale in urban markets, and thus attained far greater profits than were available from grain crops. The peasants could also raise pigs or poultry. They could plant trees, the wood from which would belong to them as individuals. The extent to which such remnants of private enterprise should be tolerated has remained a subject of controversy ever since, but until the 1980s the peasants were seldom allowed to devote enough land or enough time to them to interfere seriously with the collective economy.

Chinese economic policy, in the mid 1950s, was following the pattern set by the USSR. The chief goal was to develop heavy industry – steel, machinery, and so forth – as quickly as possible. Russian technicians helped design and build large plants in many areas. Light industry and agriculture took second place, though they were not neglected to the extent they had been in the early stages of Stalinist industrialization in the Soviet Union. The people, especially the peasants, were expected to tolerate relatively slow growth in levels of living, so the government could put its main efforts into investment rather than into production of consumer goods.

Central economic planning really began to take effect in 1955. Yearly production targets for individual enterprises, and five-year plans establishing goals for investment and production increases in each sector of the economy, were set by the government in Beijing. The system was cumbersome, and inherently biased towards large enterprises because they were so much easier for central planners to keep track of than small ones, but it produced quite respectable rates of industrial growth during the First Five-Year Plan. (This plan ran nominally from 1953 to 1957, but the government did not actually finish writing it until 1955.)

The demands placed on the new socialist system were great. China was desperately poor, and faced all the problems typical of backward nations trying to develop themselves. The industrial sector was small, and its technical level was low. Most of the people lived in the countryside, trying to scrape out a living from inadequate plots of land without the chemical fertilizer, insecticides, or power machinery which might have enabled them to raise yields and compensate to some extent for the land shortage. All of the factors that could contribute to an alleviation of this situation were in short supply. Raising agricultural production to its full potential would require great quantities of industrial products, which the industrial sector was not yet capable of supplying. Rapid construction of new industry would require that a substantial portion of total output be used for investment rather than consumption, in a situation where the standard of living would have been miserably low even if the total output of the economy had been going into consumer goods. Out of China's tiny pool of technically trained personnel, some were unavailable for economic construction because they were busy training new technicians.

China's leaders took a fairly rational approach to the majority of such problems; but one they were reluctant to face: overpopulation. China had by this time over 600 million people, and was acquiring more every day. This was too many for the available resources, especially land, to support decently with the available technology. However, the CCP was for a variety of reasons reluctant to accept the idea that the population needed to be limited. Marxian economics, based on the labour theory of value, did not lead easily or naturally to an understanding of the dangers of having too large a labour force. Also, arguing that poverty was caused by overpopulation carried the implication that it should be blamed on the poor, with their tendency to have too many children. This seemed a gross insult to the egalitarian doctrines of the CCP. Mao commented in 1949:

> It is a very good thing that China has a big population. Even if China's population multiplies many times, she is fully capable of finding a solution; the solution is production. The absurd argument of Western bourgeois economists like Malthus that increases in food cannot keep pace with increases in population was not only thoroughly refuted in theory by Marxists long ago, but has also been completely exploded by the realities in the Soviet Union and the Liberated Areas of China after their revolutions . . .
>
> Of all things in the world, people are the most precious. Under the leadership of the Communist Party, as long as there are people, every kind of miracle can be performed.

Within a few years, however, the CCP began to realize the dreadful economic costs that rapid population growth could impose, and it began to advocate limitations on birth. However, even then the Party did not use the fundamental problem of over-population as the rationale for its policy. Instead, it stressed the short-term problems that would be posed by having too many children: the expense of educating them, the burdens on the mothers of large families, and so on. For a while, the world was presented with the odd spectacle of a Chinese government which enforced on its own people a birth-control programme unusually vigorous by world standards of the time, but which at the same time did not accept in theory the idea that excessively large populations could represent a problem for developing countries.

Ideological remoulding and the 'Hundred Flowers'

A large part of the revolution the CCP was trying to bring about had to take place within the minds of the Chinese people. The effort to achieve this has been variously described, according to who was talking, as 'criticism and self-criticism', 'thought reform', or 'brainwashing'. There was of course intensive indoctrination in loyalty to the Communist system. Everyone was urged to admire the Party, Chairman Mao, the Soviet Union, etc. But beyond such inculcation of loyalty, there was an important social content in the thought-reform campaigns. The Party was trying to build an egalitarian and collectivist society in a culture whose traditions were extremely hierarchical, and where individuals and families had long been accustomed to looking first to their own economic interests. The Party wanted the Chinese people to start thinking more about the interests of society. Most important, members of the élite had to be cured, at least partially, of the arrogance and selfishness that had formerly been hallmarks of élite status. For selfishness and contempt for the common people to have attained the same levels among the élite of the new regime as they had in Guomindang China would have destroyed the revolution.

Formal study of Marxist tracts was an important part of ideological reform. Some people were also immersed in an environment likely to alter their attitudes and perceptions, as when urban intellectuals were assigned to work on land reform as part of their re-education. But over the long run the central method of reform was 'criticism and self-criticism'. People had to present long analyses of their own past behaviour and attitudes, both written and verbal, which laid out their faults and errors. They also had to criticize the faults of those around them. Their peers, and the cadres supervising the process, pointed out any omissions or defects in their self-analyses. This was a very traumatic process; having one's faults exposed publicly, and laying bare the faults of friends and relatives, were extraordinary violations of traditional social norms. The sincerity of criticism and self-criticism varied, but it at least had a powerful effect in shaping public behaviour.

In 1956 Chairman Mao began to feel it was time to take some of the restrictions off public expression. He was becoming disturbed by the arrogance and inflexibility of some Communist bureaucrats, and he hoped that allowing the intellectuals to criticize such people might help to improve their behaviour. He seems to have expected that the criticism could be kept constructive, within the overall framework of the Communist system and Communist values. He assumed that ideological remoulding, plus the tremendous successes of the Communist Party in the past two decades, had made most intellectuals into genuine supporters of the system. Under the slogan 'Let a hundred flowers bloom, a hundred schools of thought contend' (a reference to the 'Hundred Schools' of the Zhou period), he invited them to express their true opinions.

It took a while for this invitation to be treated seriously, but in the spring of 1957 the intellectuals responded. Mao was shocked. Where he had hoped for criticism directed mainly against people who violated Communist norms, a great deal of what he got was directed against the system itself. The viewpoint was anti-revolutionary, 'bourgeois'. Mao seems to have allowed this to run on for a few weeks unchecked, to find out just how extreme the attacks would become and who would make them, but then the crackdown came in the form of an 'Anti-Rightist' campaign. Many of the people who had spoken out ended up under arrest, or were shipped out to the countryside to reform themselves through agricultural labour. All were subjected to a severe dose of criticism and self-criticism. Many reached the conclusion (reasonable but probably mistaken) that Mao had been lying from the beginning, and had never intended that the Hundred Flowers be anything but a trap to catch the unwary.

Beyond this, the Anti-Rightist campaign of 1957–58 tried to eradicate, even among those who had not spoken out during the Hundred Flowers, the kind of anti-Communist attitudes which that episode had revealed. Educated people in general, including many who were playing a significant role in managing the economy, came under a very suspicious scrutiny.

One problem the intellectuals faced was that many of them

came from class backgrounds the CCP considered undesirable; very few children of ordinary workers and peasants had been able to attain the level of education that qualified one for intellectual status. In the 1940s, the CCP had treated class status as a fairly flexible thing, and had recognized that changes in the economic circumstances of a person or family could change the class status of that family. By the mid 1950s, however, class labels were virtually frozen. People who had been labelled landlords, rich peasants, bourgeois, or petit bourgeois when class demarcation had been carried out in the late 1940s and early 1950s had virtually no chance of attaining a change in class status, no matter what their present means of earning a living might be. Their children inherited their class labels.

The international position of the PRC

The Guomindang had not been able actually to administer all of the territory that was marked on maps of Asia as 'China' (though its claims to almost all this territory had been accepted in principle by the world). When the CCP came to power, it was able to impose effective administration over the outlying areas inhabited mostly by ethnic minority groups. The PRC did not control as large an area as the Manchus had in 1911 – Outer Mongolia had been lost during the warlord era – but it controlled a larger area than any ethnically Chinese government in previous history. Its sheer size guaranteed it a considerable importance in international affairs.

The Communists came to power in China just as the Cold War was reaching its worst phase. The United States and the Soviet Union, together with their respective allies, confronted each other in hostility and fear. The PRC committed itself clearly to the Soviet side in this conflict, signing a treaty of alliance with the USSR in February 1950. Soon it was so deeply embroiled that the Western nations treated China as a worse enemy than the Soviet Union.

There had been a certain amount of friendly contact between the USA and the CCP in 1944 and 1945, but this had withered as the USA supported Chiang Kai-shek in the ensuing Civil War. Even so, it seemed in 1949 that the USA might at least establish the sort of guarded relationship it maintained with Moscow and the East European satellite states, in which formal diplomatic relations and a certain amount of trade continued despite mutual suspicion. In 1949, Mao Zedong and Zhou Enlai indicated a desire to establish diplomatic and trade relations with the United States, though Liu

Shaoqi was less enthusiastic. In June of that year, Mao and Zhou invited John Leighton Stuart, US Ambassador to China (which at that time meant Ambassador to the Guomindang government), to visit Beijing. They seemed rather bitter when, after seeming responsive at first, he rejected the invitation on orders from Washington.

The intense hostility between the United States and the Communist world made normalization of US–China relations difficult; the Korean War of 1950–53 made it impossible. After the Second World War Korea had been divided like Germany. By 1950 there was a Communist government in the North and an anti-Communist one in the South. The southern regime had a larger population, and made bellicose statements about forcible reunification, but the North was in fact stronger. In June 1950 the North, with the apparent connivance of the Soviet Union, invaded the South. The United States had not up to this time considered South Korea an area which the USA would have to defend if it were attacked. However, as North Korea pushed back the South Korean Army and the small American forces in Korea, taking almost all of South Korea in a matter of weeks, President Truman decided that Communist conquest of South Korea could not be permitted. The United Nations (UN), where US influence was far greater then than it is today, backed Truman's action. An American army under General Douglas MacArthur was officially designated a UN force, and was supplemented by units from Britain and several other countries. MacArthur's counter-attack was launched in September 1950, and enjoyed the same overwhelming superiority over the North Koreans that the North had enjoyed over the South. Soon it was North Korea which was on the brink of defeat.

The Chinese, who had not participated in the original North Korean attack on the South, became involved at this point. They feared to let a great capitalist power gain control of northern Korea; the last one that had done so, Japan, had used it as a stepping-stone for an invasion of China. The Chinese tried to warn the USA verbally that they would not permit an American conquest of North Korea. They sent several thousand Chinese troops into Korea, put them into combat for long enough to be sure the Americans would know they had been fighting Chinese forces, and then pulled them back to let the Americans reconsider. The US forces took no notice, but continued to advance, and by November were approaching the Chinese border. It is a measure of American over-confidence that at this point, when the Chinese Army attacked in force, it achieved complete surprise.

Chinese troops under Peng Dehuai pushed down the length of North Korea and a short distance into the South before they were stopped. Two more years of fighting resulted in only moderate US advances, and finally led to a peace settlement in 1953 which gave South Korea slightly more territory than it had held when the war began in 1950.

The war gave China no reason to love the USSR. On the contrary, the Russians had been far more involved than the Chinese in North Korea's decision to start the war, but when things went wrong the Russians stayed out and left China to fight the US. The Soviet Union was not even very generous with equipment and financial aid. For the Chinese, whose economy was in ghastly shape after the almost continuous warfare of the 1940s, this was a disaster. But at the same time, the war increased China's need for whatever aid the USSR was willing to give, and reduced China's prospects for friendly contact with non-Communist countries. The Chinese had already allied themselves voluntarily with the USSR, in February 1950, but the Korean War made them more dependent on their ally than they would have liked.

The war confirmed the United States in its hostility to the new government of China, and persuaded the USA to renew its backing for Chiang Kai-shek. Chiang had lost the mainland of China, but he managed to retain control of the island of Taiwan (also known as Formosa). This island had been part of China under the Qing Dynasty, until it was taken by Japan in 1895. It had been handed back to China when Japan surrendered in 1945. The Guomindang was not popular on Taiwan, since the generals Chiang sent there in 1945 had been interested in it mainly as a source of loot, but in 1949 Chiang brought to Taiwan his government, many of his supporters, and as much of his army as he could get off the mainland. The numerous and well-armed mainlanders had no trouble controlling the Taiwanese population. This government in semi-exile continued to claim authority over the whole of China. It said that the 'Communist bandits' had temporarily occupied a part of the country (admittedly a large part, with 98 per cent of the population and over 99 per cent of the land area), but that the real government, with its capital now at Taibei (Taipei) on the island of Taiwan, still controlled a portion of the country and would someday return to reconquer the mainland.

The USA was not at first inclined to support the Guomindang's pretensions too strongly. Even during the Civil War American diplomats had been alienated by the corruption and incompetence of

Chiang Kai-shek's regime, its inability to make the kind of reforms that might have given it a chance for survival, and the fact that arms and equipment given to it tended to end up in the hands of the Communists. These factors had kept US aid down to a fairly low level between 1946 and 1949; they seemed to argue for termination of aid once Chiang had completely lost the Civil War. The Communists were not at the moment capable of crossing the 110 miles of the Taiwan Strait to attack the Guomindang on Taiwan, and the Taiwanese themselves were helpless against the army Chiang had brought over from the mainland, so Chiang was not in any immediate danger. However, he did not look very valuable as an ally.

The USA did not like the new government in Beijing either. It was a Communist regime publicly allied with the Soviet Union; it permitted Russian participation in the development of Manchuria and Xinjiang, and the existence of a Russian naval base at Port Arthur at the tip of the Liaodong Peninsula, in southern Manchuria; it had arrested some US diplomats in northern China on charges of espionage; it was issuing rather shrill denunciations of American imperialism. Many American officials regarded it as a puppet government of the USSR, on a par with the Soviet satellites in Eastern Europe. Secretary of State Acheson said: 'The Communist leaders have forsworn their Chinese heritage and have publicly announced their subservience to a foreign power, Russia.' Still, the existence of this government was a fact which could be dealt with. The USA, after all, maintained diplomatic relations with countries that really were totally dominated by the Soviet Union; a mistaken belief that China was under such domination did not automatically preclude diplomatic relations.

The Korean War, and an intense burst of anti-Communism in American domestic politics, altered the situation. Shortly after the war broke out, even before China became involved, the USA announced that it would defend Taiwan against any effort at conquest from the mainland. Chiang was soon restored to his status of a few years before, as a valued ally.

The United States had long regarded China as a friendly nation; Americans felt a sense of shock and betrayal when a Communist government came to power there. A group of people friendly to Chiang Kai-shek, generally known as the 'China Lobby', persuaded much of the American public that the Communist revolution had succeeded in China only because it had been assisted by pro-Communist elements within the United States government, who had prevented China's great and virtuous national leader Chiang

Kai-shek from getting the aid he needed to hold his country. Many China experts in the US Diplomatic Corps had filed reports, in the 1940s, warning that the Guomindang government's weakness, corruption, and unpopularity imperiled its survival. Events had confirmed all they said, but in the 1950s some of the most important of them were dismissed in disgrace on the logic that if they had criticized Chiang Kai-shek they must be pro-Communist. Lack of respect for Chiang, or any suggestion that diplomatic relations with the People's Republic would be either useful or morally permissible for the USA, came to be considered subversive.

Chiang, who had been a hopeless failure trying to rule China, was able to do very well at the more modest task of ruling Taiwan. The USA gave him enough aid not only to make him secure on Taiwan, but to let him hold small islands within a few miles of the Chinese coast, and occasionally raid the mainland itself. His government was a dictatorship, in which the native Taiwanese were allowed only a limited role. To advocate that the Taiwanese be given political control of Taiwan was to court imprisonment. The government was unabashed in its lack of respect for individual freedom, as was illustrated by the case of an opposition politician who found concealed microphones in his house, smashed them, and was then arrested and gaoled for destroying government property. However, police brutality no longer occurred on any large scale. In the old days on the mainland it had been carried out both by police organizations actually working to defend Chiang's rule against real or imagined threats, and (perhaps even more frequently) by organizations nominally under the Guomindang but actually pursuing their own interests. Chiang's hold on Taiwan was too firm to require much use of such methods, and his hold on his own government had become strong enough to prevent massive police abuses from occurring against his wishes.

The economy flourished. Taiwan had been richer than the mainland even in 1949, and its continued development since that time has been one of the great success stories of modern Asia. When Chiang Kai-shek finally died in 1975, his son Jiang Jingguo (Chiang Ching-kuo) inherited a stable government and a thriving economy.

The United States recognized the Guomindang government on Taiwan as the legal government of all China, and refused to have anything to do with the Communist regime. It pressured other governments to do likewise. The Guomindang continued to represent China in the United Nations for more than twenty years. The US attitude was symbolized by the way it called Beijing by its

1928–49 name of Beiping (Peiping); in Chinese Beijing means 'Northern Capital', and the US did not admit that this city was the capital of any genuine government. Assistant Secretary of State Dean Rusk said in 1951: 'We do not recognize the authorities in Peiping for what they pretend to be. The Peiping regime may be a colonial Russian government . . . It is not the government of China. It does not pass the first test. It is not Chinese.' United States Foreign Service officers who had an extensive knowledge of China, who were capable of recognizing the utter absurdity of statements like this, had either been silenced or dismissed in disgrace.

More important than denial of diplomatic relations, and UN membership, was an American-organized trade embargo. To deny the Chinese access to dollars, the USA made it illegal for American citizens to buy anything whatever from China. There was also a long list of things that could not be sold to China. This list was theoretically based on the principle of denying the Chinese access to goods of strategic military importance, but in fact stretched far beyond this, to the point that many things which could be sold to the USSR could not be sold to China. A report of the US Congress explained the

6.2   John Foster Dulles, US Secretary of State, meeting Chiang Kai-shek, with (centre) the Nationalist Chinese Ambassador to the US, George Yeh.

6.3   Zhou Enlai at the Geneva Conference, 1954.

inclusion of plastic haircombs on the list of restricted items on the grounds that having such combs would strengthen the Chinese government, because it could use them as 'incentive goods'. (A proposal to include women's brassières on the list was rejected.) The USA had considerable success in persuading other nations to join it in imposing similar restrictions on trade.

Finally, there were actual armed attacks. The Guomindang used some of its US military assistance to conduct raids into China both across the Taiwan Strait and from northern Burma, where some Guomindang armies had established bases after they were driven out of southwestern China in 1949 and 1950. The US Central Intelligence Agency (CIA) trained and armed anti-Communists from Tibet, and sent them back into Tibet to start guerrilla warfare against the Chinese government. This operation was highly successful; Chinese rule was widely resented in Tibet, and the uprising soon spread far beyond the small group of men the CIA had trained. The PLA finally moved into Tibet with massive force, in 1959, to put it down.

Few countries, however, were as hostile to China as was the USA. Some states not allied with either side in the Cold War, of which the most important was India, got on quite well with China in the early to mid 1950s. China was able to participate despite US displeasure at the Geneva Conference of 1954, which ended the First Indo-China War. The PRC was even more successful at the April 1955 Conference of Asian and African Nations, held at the city of Bandung in Indonesia. The twenty-nine nations present included all of China's major non-Communist neighbours; some such as Japan and the Philippines had close ties with the USA. The fact that the PRC was invited to attend, and participated very successfully despite suspicion on the part of some of the others there, was a striking diplomatic triumph.

Even major US allies maintained a certain degree of contact with China, and were reluctant to impose as strict a trade embargo as the USA. Britain had established formal diplomatic relations with the PRC early in 1950, and did not break them off when the Korean War began. In May 1957 Britain decided, despite US pressure, to relax its controls on exports to China to the point that they were no more stringent than controls on exports to the USSR. Most other Western powers quickly followed suit, although some of the differential treatment seems to have been restored for a while at a later date.

7

The Great Leap and the great split

Up to 1957, China's policies in both domestic and international affairs seemed to fall within the normal limits of Communist behaviour. China's habit of carrying out 'mass campaigns' like the Five-Anti campaign, in which a particular policy was given tremendous emphasis for a limited period, made policy more of an on-and-off thing than in most other Communist states. The Hundred Flowers represented an extraordinary, if brief, adventure in freedom of expression. These things, however, could be considered idiosyncrasies rather than major differences setting China off from the rest of the socialist camp. In the next few years everything changed; China abandoned both its alliance with the Soviet Union and its adherence to the Russian pattern of economic development. The shift in economic policies came first, starting in 1957 and becoming really extreme in the second half of 1958.

The Great Leap Forward

In the period immediately following the conversion to a socialist economy, China achieved respectable levels of industrial growth but very little increase in agricultural production. Mao Zedong decided that by taking adequate advantage of the economies of large-scale production, and especially by liberating the creative energies and enthusiasm of the masses instead of working through a bureaucratic planning structure, China could do much better. Experiments with units much larger than the existing cooperatives began in the countryside during 1958. In August the Central Committee endorsed 'People's Communes', which grouped together 2,000 or more households in an organization combining economic, political, and militia functions. Soon the whole of the Chinese countryside was organized into about 26,000 communes,

7.1 A team of workers on a Chinese commune.

containing an average of almost 5,000 households each. These units tried to use all the advantages of large-scale operation. They established communal mess-halls, so the number of people who had to spend time cooking meals could be reduced, and the extra hands freed for work in the fields. Many children were put in boarding-schools to free their parents for labour. Small fields were amalgamated into much larger ones. A commune contained enough people so that the limited percentage of its manpower that could be spared from the regular routine of production, at any given time, amounted to a large enough number in absolute terms to permit large construction projects: clearing waste land and bringing it under production, digging canals, and opening industrial enterprises of various sorts.

The ultimate goal of the Communist movement is a communist (small letter c) society, in which there will be no connection between the labour people do and the incomes they receive. Everyone will work because that is their obligation as members of society, and everyone will get food, clothing, housing, etc. because that is their right as members of society. 'From each according to his ability, to each according to his needs.' During the Great Leap, most communes attempted to move a considerable distance towards this goal, though there was great variation between one commune and another. Most of the peasants' private plots were abolished. Most peasants were expected to do at least some work for which they were not paid. On the other hand, many communes simply gave food free to commune members, without regard to how much work each family had done to earn that food. The Chinese later described this equal sharing of food, without regard to how much labour each family had done, as 'eating out of a big pot'.

By late 1958 and early 1959 China had adopted an approach to economic life very different from that of the First Five-Year Plan announced in 1955. The communes were only a part of this new approach. Mao was trying to achieve economic miracles by whipping people into a fever of enthusiasm. Everyone was supposed to work very long hours, under difficult conditions, to achieve in a short time an economic transformation that would normally have taken years. Growth targets of 30 per cent per year were rejected as too modest; it was claimed that food production for 1958 would be double that of 1957, and that a similar rate of growth could be expected to continue in 1959. Chairman Mao even suggested to some peasants that perhaps they should de-emphasize food production, since their production seemed to be going beyond China's needs. The orderly processes of economic planning were discarded.

Mao was trying to industrialize the countryside. The Soviet model for growth had emphasized heavy industry, and large plants in general. This necessarily implied a clear distinction between industrial and agricultural sectors of the economy. But when the organization of the communes made it possible to detach some of the peasants from the regular round of agricultural production for greater or lesser periods of time, they were not put only into projects for expansion of the agricultural infrastructure; many of them began to set up small industrial plants of various sorts. Perhaps the most extreme examples were the 'backyard steel mills', little furnaces capable of turning out a few tons of low-grade steel, which were set up not only in towns but even in villages scattered all over China.

The Great Leap began with a certain amount of genuine popular enthusiasm, and with some genuinely spectacular results. In the first eight months of 1958, agricultural production was running well above the levels of 1957, and the average monthly level of steel production was 50 per cent higher than in 1957. At this point, instead of consolidating the gains that had been achieved, Mao and other Party leaders lost all sense of reality and began demanding even higher rates of economic growth. They said, for instance, that the monthly rate of steel production in the last four months of 1958 should be double the monthly rate for the first eight months. A dangerously high proportion of the agricultural labour force was diverted into steel production and other industrial projects.

The situation soon began to deteriorate. Reports of tremendous success became obligatory, and soon everyone was making them regardless of reality. The disorganization in the systems for planning and data collection allowed these inflated figures to be accepted for a while; they were not just lies intended for public consumption, they were actually believed, and used as a basis for planning. Many low-level officials persuaded themselves that their units were doing better than was actually the case, so planning not only at the national level but even at the commune level was sometimes based on excessive expectations. (Inaccurate reporting of production figures was not just a temporary phenomenon. The habit of honest reporting, once lost, was not easy to restore, and the effects would be felt for the next twenty years.)

The total grain crop for 1957 had been about 195 million tons. In 1958, the total actually increased to about 200 million tons. The weather was excellent, and the increase could have been still greater if part of the autumn crop had not been lost when the diversion of agricultural labour into industry left some villages without enough peasants to harvest the fields properly. At the time, however, it was officially proclaimed that the crop had been 260 million tons. The exaggerated estimate led dining-halls in some communes to offer very generous meals, and use up most of their food stocks before the 1959 harvest began coming in.

In 1959, the Great Leap began to become a disaster. Sheer fatigue was taking its toll; people were no longer capable of the fantastic exertions of late 1958, especially without material incentives. The shortage of agricultural labour was so acute that the total acreage planted in food crops was significantly below the level of 1957. Peasants all over China were urged to plough the land very deeply and then plant seeds very close together in order to increase production; these practices were grossly inappropriate to conditions in many areas. Most important, the weather was disastrous. The

1959 harvest amounted to only about 170 million tons. It seemed for a time that the policies of the Great Leap were being abandoned (see below), but they were reaffirmed in the second half of the year, and carried on into 1960. Hunger became widespread, and some people began to starve; others went on the roads as beggars. At the time, however, the harvest for 1959 was glowingly reported as 282 million tons.

In 1957, the last year before the Great Leap, 1.08 per cent of the Chinese population, or about 7,130,000 people, had died from one cause or another. This was a relatively low death-rate for a country as poor as China. No definite figures are available for 1958, but the death-rate was probably about the same as in 1957. Then, however, came the crop failure of 1959. Some people literally starved to death. Others died of diseases from which they would have been able to recover, or which they might not have caught at all, if their bodies had not been weakened by malnutrition. About 1.46 per cent of the population, or 9,640,000 people, died during that year. This does not seem very bad if it is compared with pre-revolutionary conditions – probably there was no year when China was under Guomindang control when the death-rate was as *low* as 1.46 per cent – but what seems more relevant is the comparison with the period immediately before the Great Leap. The number of 'excess deaths' – the people who would not have died if it had not been for the food shortages and other problems of 1959 – was about 2,500,000.

In 1960, the policies of the Great Leap were combined with a second consecutive year of disastrous weather, and together these factors reduced the harvest to only about 144 million tons, 26 per cent below the level of 1957. Real famine returned to China for the first time since 1949. Sun Yefang, a senior Chinese economist, recently revealed that the death-rate reached 2.54 per cent in 1960. In other words, almost 17 million people died in China during that year. More than 9 million of these were people who would not have died if it had not been for the food shortage of that year. The policies of the Great Leap were finally abandoned late in 1960, and the situation improved substantially in 1961, but the crisis did not end completely; the death-rate for that year was about 1.7 per cent. During the 'three bitter years' of 1959–61, the total number of deaths seems to have been at least 16 million more than it would have been in three years of normal food supply; some Western analysts give even higher figures. The standard of living remained below pre-Great Leap levels until about 1965.

However, while bad decisions on the part of the CCP had

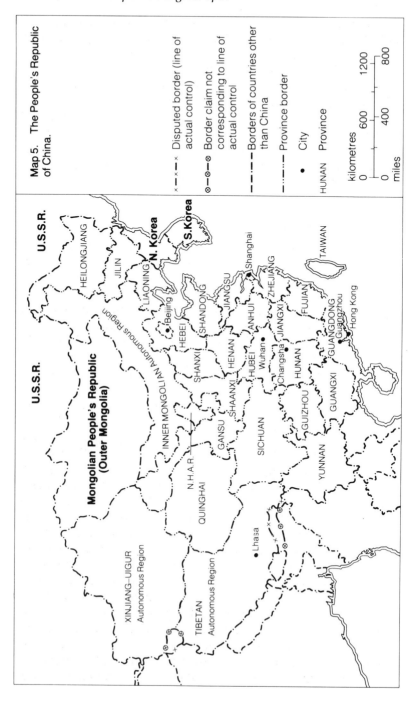

Map 5. The People's Republic of China.

× – × – ×   Disputed border (line of actual control)

⊗ – ⊗ – ⊗   Border claim not corresponding to line of actual control

– – – –   Borders of countries other than China

– · – · –   Province border

●   City

HUNAN   Province

kilometres
0   600   1200
0   400   800
miles

U.S.S.R.

HEILONGJIANG

JILIN

LIAONING   N. Korea

S. Korea

SHANDONG

JIANGSU

●Shanghai

ZHEJIANG

ANHUI

●Beijing

HEBEI

SHANXI

HENAN

SHAANXI

HUBEI

Wuhan●

JIANGXI

FUJIAN

TAIWAN

GUANGDONG

Guangzhou●

Hong Kong

Changsha●

HUNAN

GUIZHOU

GUANGXI

SICHUAN

YUNNAN

GANSU

N.H.A.R.

QUINGHAI

●Lhasa

TIBETAN
Autonomous Region

XINJIANG–UIGUR
Autonomous Region

INNER MONGOLIAN Autonomous Region

U.S.S.R.

Mongolian People's Republic
(Outer Mongolia)

helped create a worse crop failure than atrocious weather by itself could have caused, the way the country got through the crisis showed some of the merits of the revolution. The central government had a far better command of the resources of China than any in the previous century, and could allocate considerable amounts of food where they were needed. One may doubt whether members of the Central Committee missed many meals, but the hunger was still shared between masses and élite to a far greater extent than could have occurred under any previous government. If the same degree of crop failure had occurred twenty-five or fifty years earlier, the death-toll would probably have been much worse.

The Sino-Soviet split

The alliance between China and the Soviet Union, apparently so firm in 1950, was cracking by 1960. Among the important reasons for the split were increasing Chinese self-confidence which made China less willing to accept a subordinate role in the Communist bloc, increasing Chinese demands on its ally, and doctrinal shifts in both China and the Soviet Union which eroded ideological unity.

The first source of public disagreement was de-Stalinization in the Soviet Union. When Stalin died in 1953 it was not clear who would succeed him, but all of his potential heirs agreed that the Stalinist system needed some degree of reform. By 1956 Nikita Khrushchev, who wanted really substantial reform of the Soviet system, was emerging as the new leader in Moscow. He decided that undoing Stalin's works required destroying Stalin's godlike image. At the Twentieth Congress of the Communist Party of the Soviet Union, in February 1956, Khrushchev delivered a speech denouncing Stalin. He did not describe the full extent of Stalin's crimes; he had been, after all, one of Stalin's lieutenants. But he said enough, about everything from the killing of innocent people in the purges to Stalin's gross incompetence at the beginning of the Second World War, to establish the psychological foundation for major reforms. Millions of prisoners were released from the forced labour camps. Some of the cruder aspects of centralized economic management were reformed and rationalized. Some of the limits on free expression were even relaxed, though they were by no means eliminated. (The Soviet Union has been troubled ever since by conflict between dissidents trying to maintain or expand the permitted range of free speech, and officials trying to narrow it.)

To Khrushchev the myth of Stalin, as the infinitely wise and benevolent leader of International Communism, was a prop maintaining a dangerously inefficient economic system, and a political structure under which top Communist Party leaders lived in fear for their lives. Reform of the system was vital, and the destruction of the myth a necessary prerequisite for reform. To the CCP leaders, however, the Stalin myth was a very useful thing. They had not loved Stalin – he had given them bad advice and little aid – but they had been out from under his thumb, and immune to his worst excesses, for twenty years. He had been a rather distant figure. They had been able quite safely to accept the myths ground out by the Soviet propaganda apparatus, and pass them on to the Chinese people to encourage friendship for the USSR and belief in International Communism.

The shock of Khrushchev's attack on Stalin was considerable in the CCP; it was even greater in some Communist parties that had been more under Stalin's control, such as those of Hungary, Britain, and the United States. The Chinese were outraged that Khrushchev had done this without consulting or even warning them in advance.

Aside from criticizing Stalin as an individual, Khrushchev was dismantling some of Stalin's policies. The Soviet Union became somewhat less overbearing in its treatment of other Communist countries. The Chinese benefited from this in a direct fashion; the Russians withdrew voluntarily from their naval base at Port Arthur (in southern Manchuria), and from various other operations on the fringes of China that had to some extent compromised Chinese sovereignty. However, when the apparatus of Russian domination was relaxed in Eastern Europe, the results seemed less attractive: the Hungarians tried to break free of Soviet domination completely, and indeed seemed to be abandoning Communism. It took a direct invasion by the Soviet Red Army, in November 1956, to restore Hungary to the Soviet bloc. To the Chinese this seemed evidence of abominable Soviet incompetence. The Russians, on the other hand, resented Chinese presumption in trying to tell the Soviet Union how to run Eastern Europe.

Probably the most bitter controversy was that over peaceful coexistence. Khrushchev felt it was time to put relations with the Western democracies on a more reasonable basis, to increase trade, and reduce the threat of war. Obviously, this would be easier if he stopped advocating the violent overthrow of the governments with which he was trying to negotiate. On the other hand, he did not wish to give up the doctrine that the whole world would one day be

Communist. He therefore argued that the further expansion of Communism in the world would be by peaceful political means, rather than by war. Thermonuclear war could benefit nobody.

From the Russian viewpoint this made excellent sense. The Western countries were ready to accept some relaxation of tensions, and the potential benefits to the Soviet Union were considerable. In any case, the area of greatest interest in Russian foreign policy was Europe, and here the doctrine that Communists should choose a peaceful route to power was simple realism. A West European Communist Party that tried to take power by violent means would have been quickly obliterated by the armies of the North Atlantic Treaty Organization (NATO) powers. If the Soviet Union had tried to intervene it would have been even more quickly obliterated by the United States, which had a substantial edge in nuclear arms at this time. On the other hand, several countries of Western Europe had strong Communist Parties, which were permitted to run candidates in free elections, and had genuine grounds to hope that they could someday take power through the ballot box. Under these conditions, it must have seemed to Khrushchev that only a mental defective would choose violence as the road to power.

China, on the other hand, was more interested in Southeast Asia. Here conditions were very different. South Vietnam, for instance, had a government which seemed unlikely ever to permit the local Communists to participate in peaceful political processes; Communist activities were punishable by imprisonment or death. The army supporting this government, however, was extremely weak. Violent means could offer a reasonable hope for success, and eventually they did in fact succeed in making South Vietnam Communist. Mao Zedong must have felt that, given these circumstances, only a mental defective would expect a Communist Party to come to power by peaceful means.

The debate between China and the Soviet Union over this subject was a remarkably futile one, because both sides spent much of their time talking about how Communist Parties in general should act, in the world as a whole. The Chinese made incidental remarks to the effect that a peaceful road to power would be desirable if possible, while the Russians said that they approved of the national liberation movements in Africa and Asia, but both sides spent most of their time talking about the things that really interested them, and failing to notice that these were not the things their opponents were discussing. The result was that the Russians decided the Chinese were dangerously insane (which would have been reasonable if the Chinese policy line had been designed to apply to Europe), while the Chinese decided the Russians were cowards who were abandoning the idea of revolution (which would have been reasonable if the Russian policy line had been designed to apply to Southeast Asia).

The Chinese had the better of this argument in a purely doctrinal sense. They could muster a great deal of evidence for their charge that Khrushchev was abandoning traditional Communist theory and becoming a 'revisionist'. The Russians, however, had the greatest success in winning the sympathy of third parties. Chinese statements about not fearing war, even a war involving nuclear weapons (which China did not possess), created the image that the Chinese might be willing to provoke such a war.

Chinese annoyance over Russian policy was increased by the fact that the Russians seemed to be making not a general peace between the two great world blocs, but a separate peace between the Soviet Union and the United States, which left the USA free to continue its hostility to the PRC. By the late 1950s the Western powers had stopped infiltrating guerrillas and saboteurs into Eastern Europe, but similar activities directed against China were causing even more trouble than in the early 1950s. When tensions between the PRC and the Guomindang flared up in the Taiwan Straits in 1958, Russian support for the PRC did not match US support for Chiang Kai-shek. In 1959 the USSR began to cut back its military aid to China, and in particular reneged on an earlier agreement to help China acquire atomic weapons. The Chinese felt they were being left to bear the hostility of the capitalists alone. The Russians, on the other hand, feared that Chinese recklessness might drag the Soviet Union into a war with the United States. By 1960 tension over such issues was becoming a matter of public dispute.

Soviet leaders had never liked the Great Leap Forward, based as it was on rejection of the Russian model of economic development. They felt that the abandonment of orderly planning procedures was leading to a great deal of waste in the use of foreign aid. Also, the Chinese seemed to be upstaging the Russians with their claims of miraculous social and economic transformation. After other aspects of the Sino-Soviet relationship had also deteriorated, all Soviet technical advisers in China were called home in 1960. They took the blueprints of many half-completed plants with them. Construction of these plants, in the sectors of the Chinese economy with the highest levels of technology and planning, ground to a halt just as the more impromptu enterprises established in the Great Leap were also encountering difficulties.

Border problems

A border dispute between China and India helped to exacerbate the Sino-Soviet dispute. In the late 1940s, when India became independent of Britain and the CCP took power in China, there were considerable areas where the border between them had never been settled by any formal treaty, and where the maps used by the two sides differed substantially. Some of the areas potentially in dispute were uninhabited. Others were occupied by groups that were not really, in an ethnic sense, either Chinese or Indian, and would constitute minority groups in whichever country finally won control. In short, there not only was not any clearly agreed border between the two countries, there was not any clearly defined *de facto* border. Neither China nor India seems to have realized the danger implicit in this situation.

In 1957, the Indians discovered that the Chinese had for several years been operating a highway cutting across territory that was marked part of India on Indian maps. India protested, and discussions began between the two powers. There were two areas of significant size in dispute. At the eastern end of the Sino-Indian border was an area of over 35,000 square miles, loosely administered by India, called the North-East Frontier Agency (NEFA). During the Guomindang era it had been shown as part of China on Chinese maps, and sometimes on maps published in the West, but none of it had ever been under direct Chinese administration. Part of it had been administered by Tibet, but this had been before the PRC brought Tibet under full Chinese control. At the western end of the border was a block of about 14,000 square miles, consisting mostly of the deserts of the Aksai Chin Plateau, but stretching south and west into some thinly settled areas under Indian influence. The part of the Aksai Chin across which the Chinese highway ran had been shown as part of British India on maps of the colonial era, but had never been administered by Britain, or by India after the granting of independence in 1947. Prime Minister Nehru explained to the Indian Parliament that India had not attempted actually to administer this area because it was uninhabited and uninhabitable.

The Chinese attitude was that the border had never been formally defined, and would have to be negotiated. China seemed to be aiming at a compromise settlement that would basically ratify the existing situation on the ground. This would give to China the Aksai Chin Plateau, which was of value to China but not to India and had never been controlled by India. It would give to India the NEFA, which was of value to India but not to China and had never been controlled by China. The remainder of the areas in dispute were fairly small, and were of no genuine importance to either side, so a settlement should have been possible. The Chinese signed a very generous border settlement with Burma at about this time.

The Indians regarded any compromise settlement as an offence against national pride. Also, on large portions of the border they rejected the Chinese assertion that the border had never been formally defined, apparently fearing that if they admitted that their own claim was less than ironclad, the Chinese would then demand the whole of the disputed area. The Indian Army began pushing forward, and Indian government leaders hinted (despite the overwhelming military superiority of China) that they might eventually evict the Chinese from the whole of the disputed area by force. By the autumn of 1962 Chinese and Indian troops confronted one another at close range on the western end of the border, while on the northern edge of the NEFA the Indian government was ordering its troops to attack Chinese positions that even according to Indian maps lay in Chinese territory.

The Chinese reacted with overwhelming force to these rather minor Indian advances. In a few weeks of campaigning, the Chinese expelled the Indians from the whole of the disputed area, but were careful not to venture beyond the area which China had claimed. China then handed back to India the NEFA, plus all prisoners and weapons taken in the campaign. The result was to impose roughly the compromise that China had been offering before, giving India somewhat more than two-thirds of the disputed area. Sino-Indian relations remained extremely hostile for about twenty years. Negotiations over the border dispute finally resumed in 1981, but produced no quick resolution.

The war seriously harmed China's international image. China was already known to be attacking the doctrine of 'peaceful coexistence' in its dispute with the Soviet Union, while India had a good reputation as the largest and most prestigious of the countries maintaining neutrality in the Cold War. Much of the international community accepted the Indian claim that the war had been unprovoked Chinese aggression. Many accounts published in the West contained blatant errors, such as: that the Indians had simply claimed the territory which had been under the *de facto* control of the

British colonial government at the time India became independent, that the Chinese advance of 1962 had gone beyond the disputed zone into areas China had not claimed, that the Chinese retained after the war more than 10,000 square miles of the territory they had conquered in the war, and that the Chinese retained after the war all the territory they had claimed before it. Such errors created an exaggerated image of Chinese aggressiveness.

The Sino-Indian conflict exacerbated the Sino-Soviet dispute; China's already low opinion of the Soviet Union was confirmed when the Russians maintained a neutral attitude in this war, fought between a Communist and a non-Communist power. By the middle and late 1960s, the dispute between China and the Soviet Union had hardened into savage hostility, with massive troop build-ups along the border between the two countries. There were even armed clashes along the border, though not on a very large scale

The existence of border disputes between China and the Soviet Union has been more a result than a cause of the hostility between the two countries. The areas actually in dispute are small, and of no genuine importance to either side. A typical example is the island that the Russians call Damansky and the Chinese call Chenbao. It lies in the middle of the Ussuri River, which forms part of the boundary between Heilongjiang province and the Soviet Union. The channel of the river shifts from time to time, and this has created disputes as to the proper ownership of the island. With reasonable goodwill the question could have been negotiated or simply ignored, but such goodwill was conspicuously lacking by the mid 1960s. There were bloody clashes over this island in March 1969, involving not only infantry but armoured vehicles and artillery.

Negotiations over the details of the border have been hampered by disagreement as to its overall status. It was produced by a series of treaties imposed on the Manchus by the Tsars at a time when the Russian Empire was stronger than China; these treaties handed over significant amounts of previously Chinese territory to Russia. When the Sino-Soviet dispute emerged in the 1960s, it was natural for the Chinese to point out, publicly, that large amounts of territory now in the hands of the Soviet Union had in the past been taken from China by dubious methods. China never actually demanded that the Soviet Union return the land in question, and eventually stated publicly that no such demand had been or would be made. However, the Russians interpreted statements that large areas of the Soviet Union had once belonged to China, and that they had been taken from China illegitimately, as equivalent to declarations

that China intended to reclaim this land. This angered Soviet negotiators and made them reluctant to show any flexibility in their claim
that the old treaties were legitimate and binding. The Chinese, on
the other hand, while they basically accepted the border that the old
treaties had created, rejected the idea that the old treaties constituted a legal foundation for that border.

The level of hatred that existed from the mid 1960s onward was
out of proportion to the actual conflicts of interest between China
and the Soviet Union. It seems to have been motivated mainly by
emotional factors: racially based hostilities, and the sense of shock
and betrayal felt by each side over the way the other, a Communist
country that had been expected to be a political and doctrinal ally,
had inexplicably turned hostile.

Dispute in Beijing

Almost all the top leaders of the CCP accepted Mao's decision to
split with the Soviet Union. The failure of the Great Leap Forward,
however, raised serious questions about Mao's leadership. He did
not have sole responsibility for the Great Leap – most of his colleagues had been just as unrealistic as Mao during the euphoria of
late 1958 – but as the supreme leader of the CCP he bore primary
responsibility for having led it on a disastrous course. Unfortunately, the first open challenge to his policies came at the
worst possible time, and caused Mao to reaffirm his support for the
policies of the Great Leap instead of persuading him to abandon
them.

By the spring of 1959 it was already becoming apparent that
some of the policies of the Great Leap were having a very bad effect
on the economy, and that many claims of fantastic increases in
production were gross exaggerations. At this point, the CCP began
abandoning the extreme policies of the Great Leap. The policy shift
was handled quietly, and Party leaders carefully avoided discussing
the question of who might be responsible for the policies that were
being reversed. Mao took much of the initiative in this effort to bring
the Great Leap under control, just as he had taken the initiative in
starting it during the previous year. However, when the top leaders
of the Party met at Lushan, in July 1959, Minister of Defence Peng
Dehuai presented Mao Zedong with a written statement saying, in
effect, that the Great Leap had been a disaster and that Mao had
caused it. This suddenly made the issue a matter of personal pride
and personal power for Mao.

Peng Dehuai does not seem to have wanted or expected an open conflict at this time. He gave Mao his denunciation of the Great Leap privately, in writing, rather than standing up and speaking his mind before all the Party leaders gathered for the meeting. However, Mao immediately launched an all-out attack; he was not willing to wait for Peng perhaps to start an open conflict at some later date of his own choosing. Peng was defeated before he could even organize an effective presentation of his case. He was replaced as Minister of Defence by Lin Biao. For practical purposes he ceased to be a member of the Party leadership, though he nominally retained a high Party post.

To justify the purge of Peng Dehuai, Mao had to deny Peng's charges that the Great Leap was a failure. Mao vigorously reaffirmed the policies that just before the Lushan meeting he had been discarding as failures. He had built up so much credit from the spectacular successes that had marked his first twenty years as head of the CCP that even in 1959, when the true results of the Great Leap were becoming fairly clear, he was able to persuade the rest of the Party leadership to go along with him. The Great Leap continued for more than a year after the Lushan meeting, with appalling results.

The Great Leap was the first great example of the lack of realism for which Mao has been much criticized since his death. At its beginning, trying to interpret China's problems as advantages, he said:

> Apart from their other characteristics, China's six hundred
> million people are, first of all, poor, and secondly, 'blank'. That
> may seem like a bad thing, but it is really a good thing. Poor
> people want change, want to do things, want revolution. A
> clean sheet of paper has no blotches and so the newest and
> most beautiful words can be written on it, the newest and most
> beautiful pictures can be painted on it.

There are two striking anomalies in this metaphor. One is that extreme poverty is not conducive to blankness; it tends to scar people. Whatever the characteristics of the Chinese people, nothing remotely resembling 'blankness' was among them. The other is that, even had they been blank, this would have been of dubious desirability. The transformation of Chinese society was not something that could be done *to* the Chinese people, it would have to be done *by* them. Blank paper may be desirable for writing; a blank-minded author is not. On both of these counts, Mao was deviating from his own usual attitudes. Most of the time he maintained a vivid awareness of the living strength of China's cultural tradition, both negative (as when he discussed the tremendous difficulty of overcoming 'feudal' attitudes) and positive (as when he drew on ancient sources for some of his military strategies, and for that matter when he wrote poetry which drew far more on classical Chinese models than on 'socialist realism'). Also, he usually emphasized the active and creative role of the masses rather than talking about them as objects to be manipulated by a revolutionary leadership. However, the boundless optimism of this statement, its emphasis on will and the desire to make revolution as the most important determinants of success, and its claim that the impoverished masses of China have the will and the ability to transform their society, were all typical of Mao's thinking.

Traditional Marxists, and probably most leaders of the CCP, believed in an interpretation almost exactly opposite to Mao's. Socialism and communism were supposed to emerge from a highly developed economy. To the extent that the Chinese people were poor and blank, this would make it difficult for them either to formulate plans for a communist society, or to find the material means to carry out such plans once formulated.

The Great Leap was finally abandoned late in 1960. In place of massive increases in production and efforts to achieve a radically egalitarian society, the CCP concentrated on getting China out of the crisis it was in and restoring order to the economy.

Most of the peasants who had gone into industrial production were sent back to the fields, in a desperate effort to revive agricultural production and resolve the problem of food shortages. On the average, each of the communes created in the Great Leap was split into three smaller ones. Within each commune, the income of individual families, or of production teams (work units that might comprise twenty families) was related much more closely to the actual performance of the family or team. It became less common for members of a commune or of a subdivision within a commune to share their income equally, without regard to the relative contributions of different families ('eating out of a big pot').

Individual freedom in economic matters was increased to some extent. The peasants' private plots, which had been almost eliminated during the Great Leap, were restored. Rural markets at which individuals could sell part of their produce on a private basis were revived. However, it should not be supposed that all restrictions on individual freedom were relaxed, or even all restrictions in economic freedom. Urban workers did not have the right to choose jobs that suited them; state labour bureaux decided who would work for which enterprise. The assignments were often made without much regard for the wishes or even the exact skills of the people involved. The assignment was usually for life. (While this system had disadvantages, it did provide great job security. A reasonably well-paid job that one could depend on retaining for one's entire working career was referred to as an 'iron rice bowl'.)

A system of residence permits prevented people from moving from one city to another, or especially from the countryside into the cities, without permission. It was possible for some peasants to work on contracts in the cities, as short-term labour, without job security or the medical and retirement benefits received by regular city workers. However, it was extremely difficult for peasants actually to obtain residence permits for the cities, which would allow them to remain permanently. The CCP had partially re-created a phenomenon usually considered a relic of feudalism: a peasantry bound to the soil.

Economic plans based on very modest goals, a revival of free markets, and the desire of each peasant household to worry first about its own welfare, did not suit Mao's inclinations. However, in the years immediately after the Great Leap, economic policy was made mainly by a group of more moderate leaders centring on Chief of State Liu Shaoqi, Premier Zhou Enlai, and CCP Secretary-General Deng Xiaoping.

There had long been agreement among top leaders, including Mao, that he should to some extent withdraw into the background and allow others to do more of the routine work of running China. Shortly after the Great Leap began, Mao had handed over the position of Chief of State to Liu Shaoqi. At the time Mao did this on a voluntary basis. He was not being stripped of his power as a result of the failure of the Great Leap (which had not yet become obvious), he was simply shedding a job he no longer needed. Two years later, however, when CCP leaders were formulating the policies designed to pull China out of the crisis of the 'three bitter years', the group often called the 'pragmatists' pushed Mao considerably further into the background than he had expected. Mao was still Party Chairman; the Chinese public continued to regard him as the incarnation of the revolution. He still had much influence in policy formation. However, when a substantial number of other leaders were united on an issue, they could and sometimes did overrule him. He later said, with some exaggeration, that he had been treated in this period like a dead ancestor – someone who is worshipped but not consulted. Mao was especially bitter about the attitude of Liu Shaoqi and Deng Xiaoping.

8

The Cultural Revolution

By the mid 1960s, the Chinese Revolution seemed to have settled down to the job of ruling China. Its main goals were essentially nationalist: a prosperous modern economy, and a government capable of maintaining national unity and upholding China's place in the world. It was a meritocracy: positions of power and prestige had to be earned. While there continued to exist substantial economic inequalities, the distribution of wealth was probably a bit more equal than in most Western countries, and significantly more equal than in pre-revolutionary China. One could say that the Chinese were trying to carry out an improved version of the Russian Revolution – improved by the fact that China had not gone as far as the Soviet Union had gone under Stalin in regard either to extremes of internal terrorism or to Stalin's tremendously wasteful methods of forced-draft economic development. Almost all CCP leaders were happy with this picture. Mao Zedong was not; he felt that some fundamental goals of the revolution were being abandoned.

Education was functioning as the basis of a caste system, which to Mao seemed unpleasantly reminiscent of the system by which the Confucian scholars had dominated traditional China. He could observe that the Soviet Union was, quite literally, ruled by the graduates of advanced technical schools. This group not only managed the factories, it held an overwhelming majority of the positions on the Central Committee of the Soviet Communist Party. China seemed to be headed in the same direction. Educated people not only got the best jobs and the highest pay, they had high prestige. They felt (and many of the non-educated agreed with them) that an educated person was fundamentally superior to an uneducated one, entitled to look down on the masses, give them orders, and avoid, *as a matter of right*, having to do any form of manual labour. China's poverty and the lack of qualified teachers restricted access to education. Even primary schooling was far from universal; graduation from secondary school, especially from one of the best schools in the major cities, marked a person destined for a position well above the average in Chinese society.

While there were great variations in income between different villages, and between different jobs in the urban sector, the overall averages showed a clear pattern: the cities were much richer than the countryside. Most capital investment was going into urban industries. The urban workers, using a considerable amount of expensive machinery, had a much higher average level of productivity per hour than the rural workers, who lived mainly by farming but did not have enough land, machinery, or fertilizer. The natural consequence was for the city people, with their greater economic power, not only to arrange for themselves an average income level about twice as high as that in the countryside but also to dominate Chinese society in other ways.

Finally, the bureaucrats of the Communist Party and the government, who dominated Chinese society more thoroughly than the Confucian scholars or the Guomindang had ever managed to do, made Mao uneasy. They formed a ruling caste, which felt entitled to make all real decisions and demand instant obedience from the people.

All three of the marks of privilege – education, urban residence, and Party or bureaucratic status – were to a considerable extent hereditary. This was not just a matter of fathers using their influence to arrange favoured status for their children on an individual basis, or even of institutional arrangements like the strong special preference given to the children of veteran Communist cadres in the competition for admission to secondary schools and colleges. It was fundamental to the system. The children of city people tended naturally to live in the cities where they had grown up, while the children of peasants had great difficulty if they wanted to move into the city. Even if educational opportunities had been equal for all, the children of educated parents would have performed on the average much better in school than the children of the uneducated. Opportunities, however, were not equal; urban areas where many of the parents were educated had better schools than were found in the countryside. As long as good positions in life, including positions in the Party and government bureaucracies, were allocated largely on the basis of educational attainment, membership in the élite would tend to be hereditary even in the unlikely event that actual nepotism could be totally eliminated.

Family background played, in one way or another, a tremendous role in the educational careers of Chinese students. All students had an official class label, based on the status of their parents. The level of academic competence one had to show in order to win admission to a selective school depended on one's class label.

- The children of revolutionary cadres were given a strong preference in admission to good schools, and also the average educational level of their parents was somewhat higher than the average for the population as a whole. They therefore formed a large proportion of the student body at the better secondary schools and colleges.
- The children of ordinary workers and poor peasants had to meet somewhat higher academic standards to win admission, and since their parents were generally uneducated, few of them were able to do so. Partial figures are available for thirty upper middle (senior high) schools in Guangzhou; the children of ordinary workers and peasants made up, on the average, less than one-sixth of the students of these schools.
- The children of the middle class had to meet still higher standards, but thanks to the educational background of their parents, many were able to do so; they made up about half of the student body of the Guangzhou schools mentioned above.
- The children of the 'bad classes' (landlords, counter-revolutionaries, rich peasants, capitalists, and 'rightists' who had spoken out against the Communist system during the Hundred Flowers episode of 1957) had to meet the highest standard of all to win admission, but a significant number were able to do so.

The differential admissions policy led directly to differentials in the average academic competence of the students in each category. Middle-class students tended to be academically above the average in any given school, and students from the 'bad classes' very far above the average, simply because if they were not above average they would not have been allowed in the school. Students of below-average competence were generally the children of revolutionary cadres or of ordinary workers and peasants. This led to serious conflicts over the criteria to be used in choosing students for the next higher level of education, since a selection process emphasizing academic competence would clearly favour the middle class and the 'bad classes'.

The peasants of China were better off than before the revolution. They had a higher average standard of living, and more security against unexpected disasters. The élite was more solicitous of peasant interests than had been true in the old society. However, while a good many individual peasants had managed to work their way up into the élite, the peasantry as a whole was still, quite clearly, a lower class with a subordinate position in society. This was not what the revolution had been intended to accomplish.

China was having far more difficulty escaping from its past than Mao had expected. Marxist theory predicted that after the initial establishment of a socialist society, there would be a continued upward movement towards forms of society having less and less in common with pre-revolutionary patterns. Chinese tradition, however, said that the high point of each dynasty had always come shortly after it was founded; dynasties tended to decline from that point onward. Inequalities of wealth were smallest at the beginning of a dynasty, and increased later on. Mao looked at the younger generation, the people who would someday inherit power in China, and he was not reassured. Conditioned to accept substantial inequality in society, conditioned to obey authority without question, lacking experience of revolutionary turmoil or personal knowledge of what China had been like before 1949, how could they have any real understanding of the revolution? How could they be expected to preserve its ideals once the older generation was gone?

Aside from being distressed by the direction the revolution had taken, Mao felt increasingly outraged by the difficulty he sometimes had in making his beliefs felt. In some respects he seemed as powerful as ever. His picture was displayed everywhere, and the general public continued to regard him as the incarnation of the revolution. The army came increasingly under his influence after his enemy Peng Dehuai was replaced as Minister of Defence by his ally Lin Biao in 1959. Mao took advantage of this by initiating a campaign to 'learn from the People's Liberation Army', which increased the army's influence in the Party and the civil government. Much of the Party bureaucracy, however, did not share his fundamental attitudes and in any case did not like the way some of his mass campaigns had disrupted orderly government. On many issues, especially those involving economics, the bureaucrats had shunted him out of the main line of policy formation after the failures of the Great Leap Forward.

Mao's struggle both to re-establish his personal power and to shift the overall course China was following led to the 'Great Proletarian Cultural Revolution': three years of intense struggle from 1966 to 1968, and a lingering aftermath lasting until Mao's death in 1976.

Most observers, both Chinese and Western, feel today that Mao had simply lost touch with reality; that in his old age he had become willing to throw away everything he had built, in his blind pursuit of Utopian dreams and personal power. Certainly Mao's optimism about the social transformation he was trying to bring about has turned out to be unjustified. Still, if he had cared to respond to the charges he knew were being made, that he was being unrealistic, he might have said: Marxist doctrine taught that in a socialist society, there would be a natural tendency for social inequalities to shrink, for greed to give way before the habit of unselfish cooperation, for the gaps separating mental from manual labour, peasants from industrial workers, cities from countryside, to fade away. More than a decade of socialism in China, and more than four decades in the Soviet Union, had provided little evidence that any such natural tendency was going to emerge. What would it be most 'realistic' for him to do? To abandon his most cherished goals without a struggle? To sit back and continue to hope that all would somehow work out for the best, despite the evidence he could see all around him? Or to fight to *make* the promises of Marxism come true, as ruthlessly as he had once fought, against odds that looked even more impossible, in the hills of South China?

Whether or not one thinks Mao's decision was so irrational as to reflect a loss of contact with reality, there can be little dispute that the results of the decision were disastrous. He failed to reach his goal, to get China off the path he called the 'capitalist road'. The country was more firmly set on that path by the 1980s than it had been in 1965. Furthermore, the cost of the unsuccessful attempt to change course was ghastly, no matter how one measures it – lives lost, students not educated, economic growth set back for years. The Chinese leadership later referred to the period from 1966 to 1976 as the 'Ten-Year Catastrophe'.

At the time the Cultural Revolution was going on, some people were puzzled that it seemed to be so much the personal creation of Mao Zedong. His name was repeated endlessly in the documents of the Cultural Revolution; it will be repeated endlessly in the account of the Cultural Revolution in this book. Great historic movements do not normally spring from the head of an individual, they arise from the logic of a situation. It seemed incredible that the social, economic, and political structure of the largest nation on earth was being drastically revised because one man willed it.

Today, after the failure of the movement, the pattern of events makes more sense. While Mao was able to find a certain natural base of support for the Cultural Revolution in Chinese society, this natural base was weak enough so that nothing remotely resembling the Cultural Revolution would have been likely to occur if Mao had not decided to make it occur. That is why it ended in failure.

1966: 'To rebel is justified!'

The conflict between Mao and his opponents came to a head in 1966. The Deputy Mayor of Beijing, Wu Han, was an academic who had not been a member of the Communist movement during the Civil War, but who had been recruited along with many other intellectuals during the 1950s. In 1961, Wu Han wrote a play called *Hai Rui Dismissed from Office*, about a wise and virtuous official of the Ming Dynasty, devoted to the welfare of the people, who was dismissed from office by an egotistical emperor (see Ch. 1). It may well have been written innocently, but it looked suspiciously like a disguised criticism of Mao for the way he had purged Peng Dehuai in 1959. When Mao became disturbed by the parallel, he found that he could not even arrange for publication of an attack on the play in the major Party organs in Beijing. He had to go to Shanghai, where his own influence was greater and Wu Han's was less, to get his view into print.

Wanting to cut down the power and privileges of the ruling élite of China, Mao obviously had to find allies outside that élite. His supporters in the army would eventually play a major role, but it was students who led during the opening stages of the movement.

The Great Proletarian Cultural Revolution began as a campaign to root out 'bourgeois' influences in art and literature. By the spring of 1966 it had been broadened to deal with bourgeois influences among the intellectuals in general. Party authorities in Beijing sent out teams of cadres to conduct the movement in various schools, factories, and other organizations. Nothing suggested that this was going to become a matter of great importance; the movement seemed directed mainly against intellectuals from middle-class backgrounds, the type of people who had been attacked in the Anti-Rightist campaign of 1957. The Party bureaucracy, not Mao Zedong, controlled the teams of cadres supervising the movement.

Then, in May 1966, a young woman named Nie Yuanzi (Nieh Yuan-tzu) put up a wall poster at Beijing University. She argued that the Cultural Revolution should be a vigorous mass movement, and she denounced the administration of Beijing University for restricting it and keeping it from developing properly. Mao had her poster reprinted in the *People's Daily*. In the summer of 1966 students in Beijing began, with Mao's support, to organize themselves as 'Red Guards'. They took an increasing role in the effort to root out bourgeois influences from the faculties and administrations of their universities. Wall posters attacking various professors and administrators proliferated fantastically. Before long there were far more posters than space available on the walls; rooms and courtyards had ropes strung across them like clothes-lines, from which posters could be hung. People walked along the narrow alleys between the rows of posters, reading them or putting up posters of their own.

Mao had the work teams pulled out of educational institutions in late July. With their restraining influence removed, the Red Guard movement was able to spread to institutions throughout China. The Red Guards attacked the 'Four Olds': old ideas, old culture, old customs, and old habits. They also attacked anything that they felt represented the influence either of the Soviet Union or of the Western capitalist countries. They smashed images in Buddhist temples. They raided the homes of professors and other intellectuals, confiscating or destroying Western-style clothing, books and paintings representing the Four Olds, and anything else that offended them. The owners of such materials were abused both verbally and physically. Within weeks, the first incidents in which Red Guards beat people to death began to occur. The police and the military were under orders not to interfere.

The students involved, in the first months, were mostly from backgrounds considered 'pure'. Many, in fact, were the children of important Communists. They were stepping outside the bounds of behaviour normally permitted by the Communist system, and they were putting a severe strain on the system when they attacked academic administrators many of whom belonged to the Communist Party, but they regarded themselves basically as defenders of the system. They had a variety of motives for joining the Red Guards. Most were convinced that anything Chairman Mao urged them to do must be correct. Many genuinely resented the authoritarian behaviour that characterized many teachers and administrators. Many had a longstanding dislike of 'bourgeois'

intellectuals, a dislike that had grown out of the competition that pitted cadres' children against students of greater academic talent who came from bourgeois backgrounds. Almost all the Red Guards were desperately eager to meet whatever criteria were currently being used to measure correct political attitude, since if their political attitude were not considered correct, their chances of further education and thus a better life would become miniscule.

On 5 August 1966, the direction of the movement began to change. Mao Zedong himself issued a statement titled 'Bombard the Headquarters', in which he charged that there were people in the CCP at all levels up to the very top who were following reactionary, essentially bourgeois policies. He did not name those he was attacking, but it soon became clear that they included both Liu Shaoqi (Chief of State of the PRC) and Deng Xiaoping (General Secretary of the CCP). On 15 September, Lin Biao told a mass rally in Beijing, attended by Red Guards from all over the country, that the main target for their movement should be the individuals in power who were following the capitalist road. Soon, more and more senior officials were being attacked and humiliated. Many of them, including Liu Shaoqi, eventually died as a result of the mistreatment they suffered.

At schools where the movement had at first been dominated by the children of revolutionary veterans, competing groups appeared, containing more students from middle-class backgrounds, who had long resented the special preference given to the children of cadres. They attacked the Communist Party bureaucracy, and indeed most of the authority structure that had ruled China. Before the end of 1966, many of the original Red Guards, children of the Party bureaucracy, were rallying to the defence of that bureaucracy and struggling against the newer Red Guard units.

In September 1966, student Red Guards from colleges and even some from secondary schools were invited to go travelling through China to share information and experiences, and to learn more about revolution. They were given the right to travel free on the railroads, but tens of thousands marched on foot across the countryside, visiting Chairman Mao's birthplace, the CCP strongholds of the 1930s in Jiangxi, and other famous revolutionary sites. They hoped both to find inspiration there and to toughen

8.1   Teachers and students at Beijing University read big-character posters repudiating Deng Xiaoping.

themselves by enduring physical hardships along the way. About 11 million went to Beijing to attend mass rallies where they could actually glimpse Chairman Mao in person. The general right of Red Guards to travel everywhere was rescinded in December, but they continued to move about to a significant extent. They were ordered to return home in February 1967.

Organizations analogous to the Red Guards began to be formed among industrial workers. By the end of 1966, workers' organizations in Shanghai were already showing the same pattern of factional division that had appeared among the student Red Guards in many cities: there were radical organizations attacking the Party apparatus, and more conservative ones defending it.

The 'mass organizations' – student Red Guards and workers' groups – were not simply operating on their own. Shortly after Mao had pulled the Party organization's work teams out of the universities in the summer, he had begun sending in work teams of his own. However, the situation in which competing authorities issued conflicting orders to conflicting organizations of workers and students amounted to a breakdown of central control. In the confusion, many students and workers broke free of almost all organized restrictions; one or another group attacked almost every sector of the authority system that had formerly governed China. Professors probably suffered the most, but factory managers, government officials, and Party leaders also found their authority vanishing and themselves being held up to public scorn as followers of the 'capitalist road'. Many were subjected to savage physical abuse; some died.

Mao's objections to the way society had been developing probably had not involved strong objections to the lack of individual freedom in China. He seems to have felt, most of the time, that it was reasonable for individuals to be subordinated to the group, and to be forced to adapt not only their actions but even their innermost thoughts to suit the demands of the group. However, he had enough affection for the idea of individual freedom to be willing to endorse it under certain conditions. In 1966, as in 1956–57, he decided that a substantial relaxation of the controls on individual expression would be likely to promote his goals. The range of conflicting opinions that could be and were expressed on wall posters became remarkably broad, by the standards of a Communist society.

Mao had once said, 'In the last analysis, all the truths of

Marxism can be summed up in one sentence: "To rebel is justified." ' He did not feel that there was anything sacred about the Communist Party. He had been a rebel against the warlord regimes of his youth; he had spent the best years of his life rebelling against the Guomindang; he saw nothing wrong with rebelling, and inciting the students to rebel, against the Communist Party structure once he had decided that the Party was leading China in the wrong direction. Loyal opposition would not do. The authoritarian traditions of Chinese society had combined with the authoritarianism of Communism to produce a structure so intimidating that there was no possibility Mao could persuade great masses of people to act as a loyal opposition, to put pressure on that structure while continuing to respect it. They would follow him against the structure only if he could persuade them to reject its authority totally, and set out to overthrow it.

Most Communists, once in power, become in a sense rather conservative. A few actually develop a respect for formal law, under the slogan of 'socialist legality'; they argue that the laws of a Communist state have been designed to protect the interests of the state and the people, and therefore everyone, including the Communist Party, must obey those laws. Most place Party policy above the law, and are willing to flout the law when the interests of the Party require it, but they have a great respect for the structure of Party authority. In the Cultural Revolution Mao showed utter contempt not only for formal law but for the authority of the Party, and for the normal rules governing politics within the Party. The only rule he respected in the game of politics was that the true revolutionaries must win.

With hindsight it is possible to discern approximately what Mao was after, but he did not explain his goals clearly at the time. Indeed, despite the way the Cultural Revolution lifted him almost to the status of a god, he was hardly presenting his ideas in public at all. The official edition of his *Selected Works* only covered the period up to 1949. *Quotations from Chairman Mao*, a collection of short excerpts from his writings which in a pocket edition known as the 'Little Red Book' became almost a bible for the Red Guards, contained very little written after 1959; most of it dated from before 1949. The man who during the 1930s and 1940s had been writing long and informative analyses of major problems was by the 1960s allowing his views to be represented, for the most part, either by things he had written many years before or by the frenzied and often absurd statements of his followers.

His actions make it unmistakable that he was vitally interested in a wide range of policy questions. He cannot have believed that the Chinese people already understood his beliefs well enough so that he had no need to write about them further; there were too many conflicting interpretations of his ideas in circulation. Despite the effects of age and illness, he retained enough vigour and alertness to fight and win major political power struggles; surely he was still capable of the much easier task of writing out his views, or at least of allowing some assistant to edit into publishable form the texts of the speeches he was giving. It is difficult to escape the conclusion that, for a whole range of reasons, he had made a conscious and deliberate decision not to explain his thinking in print. Probably he wanted to let his followers experiment, and find their own way without the inhibition of too much guidance from him. Probably he was to some extent being Machiavellian, and was hoping to win the support of

8.2   In late-1966 and early-1967, senior CCP and government members were publicly humiliated. Here, a government official is paraded through a Beijing street before Red Guards, wearing a cone-shaped hat as a sign of shame for involvement in an anti-revolutionary group.

some people who would have opposed him if they had understood his real goals. Probably, feeling his way by trial and error through very difficult questions, and knowing his enemies would seize upon any error, he was reluctant to commit himself too publicly to answers which were still tentative. In earlier years he had been more confident; the tide of history had been running his way. He had been prepared to explain his views and the logic behind them; to be reasonable, even generous, with opponents whom he had defeated by proving that his own policies were superior. The conditions of the late 1960s, when he was being driven to increasingly desperate expedients in his efforts to regain control of a revolution that had slipped from his grasp, were less conducive either to civility or to candour.

The Maoists presented the Cultural Revolution not as a conflict between two conceptions of the revolution, one more egalitarian than the other, but as a conflict between revolutionaries and enemies of the revolution. This was necessary in a propagandistic sense; they needed to present an almost apocalyptic vision if they wished to persuade loyal Communists to attack the Party apparatus, and educated young people whose own self-interest lay in the existing system to attack that system. But Mao was spreading fear that the revolution was endangered, and unleashing a mass struggle to defend the purity of the revolution, without having either a coherent organization he could trust to guide it, or a clear and concrete definition of the enemy against which the struggle was to be conducted.

A number of passages in this book attempt to describe, as clearly and rationally as possible, what Mao was promoting and what he opposed. It is important to remember, when reading these passages, that they have had to be based to a considerable extent on reconstruction of Mao's goals from his actions. Neither Mao nor his followers were publishing any such clear, rational explanations of their goals during the Cultural Revolution. Statements by the radicals in this period often referred to the enemy as 'ghosts and monsters', 'freaks,' or 'demons'. The intent of these phrases was to indicate that anyone so vile as to oppose the true revolutionary doctrines of Chairman Mao could hardly be considered human. With hindsight, however, such language looks like a symptom of the fact that some of Mao's followers, not having been told exactly who or what they were struggling against, were having to conjure pictures of the enemy out of their imaginations. The result was chaos.

The radicals tried to connect their enemies as much as possible to the old enemies of the revolution, the landlords and capitalists. There were certain elements of reality in this. Policies that offered advancement to young people with academic talent had given an advantage to the children of educated parents, many of whom were the children of the pre-revolutionary élites. The manager of a state-owned factory in China could be sufficiently similar to the manager of a factory in a capitalist country, in the nature of the problems he faced, the nature of his relations with his workers, and his conception of his role, that it was by no means nonsense to refer to the Chinese manager as following the 'capitalist road', although the way this phrase brushes aside the question of ownership is perhaps odd. The radicals, however, carried their fears of landlord, rich peasant, and bourgeois influence to remarkable extremes. Two radicals who had seized power in one production brigade in the countryside decided it was necessary to carry out a complete extermination of the 'bad classes' – landlords, rich peasants, counter-revolutionaries, bad elements, and rightists. They called a meeting of leaders of neighbouring brigades (one brigade usually meant one village), and the slaughter was carried out in ten brigades. The victims included children who had not even been born at the time their parents committed the actions that had caused their families to be labelled 'bad classes'.

To the Maoists, the essential characteristic defining the capitalist road was selfishness. All policies that either rewarded or encouraged individual selfishness were deemed capitalist. This definition, which does not seem very Marxist, combined what were in fact two very different types of people under the general heading of 'capitalist roaders'.

1.   The typical Communist bureaucrat believed in an authoritarian meritocracy. People should compete with one another, in school and elsewhere, and the winners should be rewarded with top positions in a steeply hierarchical structure of privilege and power.

2.   Many intellectuals and some economic planners, on the other hand, believed that individual freedom should be substantially expanded. Writers should be allowed to write as they pleased; farmers should be permitted to grow whatever crops they thought most profitable; more people should be free to search for jobs that suited them, rather than being assigned jobs by the state. Many of the common people, while not involved in

theoretical debates, wished that they as individuals could have more freedom to choose how they would make a living.

Lumping the proponents of centralized bureaucracy and of individual freedom together under a single label was not conducive to clear discussion of the issues. There were only a few policy positions, such as a desire to stress academic competence in the educational system, on which the two types of 'rightist' were really in accord.

The three supreme elements of Maoist revolutionary purity became: personal selflessness, belief in 'the masses', and belief in Chairman Mao.

Everyone was supposed to be preoccupied with service to society, and care nothing for their own welfare. 'Craving for a comfortable life and continuing the revolution are as incompatible as fire and water.' In fact, selflessness was supposed to be carried to a point where people would sacrifice their own interests out of loyalty to the revolution without even thinking very much about whether their sacrifice would bring any concrete benefit to the revolution. The press gave considerable publicity to a story about a man who was carrying a message about Cultural Revolution policy to a remote village, and found his path blocked by a flooded river. He hurled himself into the waters, and (rather implausibly) died just as he delivered the message on the far side. There was nothing genuinely urgent about the message. One might think that he could have served Chairman Mao better by waiting for the waters to subside, delivering the message, and then making himself available for another assignment. This logic, however, was ignored; his readiness to die for the revolution made him a hero.

Everyone was supposed to believe that the common people had both the right and the ability to run society; the right to avoid being dominated by a few bureaucrats, and the ability to carry out any task of great importance without having to depend on highly trained experts.

On the other hand, everyone was supposed to have faith in the infallible guidance of Chairman Mao. Intensive study of the 'Little Red Book' became the official source of inspiration for almost any activity; it taught people how to grow more wheat, make better light bulbs, and heal the sick. Great crowds chanted it in unison.

The years of chaos: 1967–1968

In January and February of 1967, Mao began to encourage an actual seizure of government by radicals organized in a three-way alliance: (1) 'mass organizations' (Red Guards among the students, and equivalent groups among the industrial workers); (2) the military; (3) officials of the government organs being seized who were willing to change sides and join in the overthrow of their own organizations. Such seizures began to occur in city governments, province governments, and ministries of the national government. Once in power, unfortunately, the new power-holders fought savagely among themselves. Different groups had different private interests to promote, and different conceptions of revolutionary purity.

In Beijing, the central leadership under Mao was also divided into three parts. (1) Most radical was the committee called the Cultural Revolution Group, of which Mao's wife Jiang Qing was a conspicuous member. The Cultural Revolution Group supported many of the most radical Red Guard factions. (2) Somewhat less radical was the military high command under Lin Biao. (3) Most moderate were the surviving sections of the civil government, under Premier Zhou Enlai. Mao stood above these three groups, balancing them against one another.

There was no simple relationship between the three leadership groups in Beijing and the different groups struggling for power in various parts of China. Many Red Guards accepted policy guidance from the Cultural Revolution Group, but some supported Lin Biao and some backed relatively moderate officials. The same divisions existed within the military, and among civil officials. If a provincial town were split by a fight between radical and conservative factions, there might well be some soldiers, some civil officials, and some Red Guards supporting each side. Participation of the army in actual street fighting was restrained by a policy (enforced to some extent, though not universally obeyed) which forbade the army to use armed force against Red Guards. However, if a military unit wished to weaken a certain Red Guard organization, it would often do so by issuing weapons to some competing Red Guard organization.

Chinese Communism had for years accepted three assumptions: (1) In any situation there exists a correct political line; (2) it is absolutely vital that everyone be made to conform to this political line; (3) therefore, anyone who defies the correct line must be forced into submission by whatever means are necessary. In the

8.3 During the Cultural Revolution, Mao's wife, Jiang Qing, dominated theatre, ballet and the cinema in China. All the works produced under her supervision were characterized by very heavy-handed propaganda themes. This scene is taken from *The Red Detachment of Women*.

early 1950s, the CCP had been willing to be gradualistic in its approach to the goal of ideological conformity; it had been so confident of the eventual acceptance of its political line that it could remain fairly calm when confronted with momentary nonconformity. By the beginning of 1967, however, the future had become very uncertain. When two groups with different versions of the truth confronted one another, each dedicated to ruthless enforcement of what it regarded as correct revolutionary doctrine, then even minor differences in actual beliefs could provoke incredible explosions of violence, especially among the Red Guards. The situation would have been bad enough if the competing factions had been armed with knives and clubs, but soon they were using military weapons.

Changsha, for instance, the capital of Hunan province, was split for several months early in 1967 in a civil war between a 'conservative' Red Guard faction wanting the Cultural Revolution to be directed mainly against bourgeois intellectuals, and a more radical 'Rebel' faction wanting the movement to be directed more against Communist Party bureaucrats. Both sides conducted the fight with great brutality, sometimes torturing or beating to death prisoners taken from the opposing group. The 'Rebel' faction won a decisive victory, but by the summer it in turn had split into moderate and radical subgroups. Each group was very heavily armed. A young man named Liang Heng, who was in Changsha at the time, later recalled:

> The guns distributed to the Rebels' small official militia by the . . . Army scarcely satisfied them. They added what they had seized from the Conservatives, stole from the local militias, stopped trains for weapons shipments, broke into arsenals, and attacked military bases. Then they started shooting at each other in order to decide arguments about who was going to be in charge. The 'moderate' Workers' Alliance was the huge faction cooperating with the army; their opponents were the Xiang River Wind and Thunder group, which wanted to seize power from the military.

The doctrinal differences between the two types of 'Rebels' were not nearly so large as those that had separated 'Rebels' from 'Conservatives' in the spring of 1967. In hindsight, their quarrel seems to have been primarily a struggle for simple political power. At the time, however, each group was sure that it was involved in a fundamental struggle of good against evil. Most members were convinced that their cause was worth dying for, and many were as careless with their own lives as they were with the lives of their enemies or of innocent bystanders. Liang Heng was near the office of the newspaper *Hunan Daily* when a battle between the two factions of 'Rebels' broke out there in the summer of 1967; his account illustrates the extraordinary fanaticism of these young people.

> Suddenly, fifty or sixty men carrying machine guns ran past the gate of the *Hunan Daily* toward me. A short man in black carried the flag with the words *'Young People's Bodyguard Squad'* on it, the name of one of the groups in the Xiang River Wind and Thunder faction. I instinctively flattened myself against the wall and a number of people leaped for their bicycles in fear; when the men were almost abreast of me they opened fire, aiming off down the road into the distance, shaking with the vibrations of their guns.

The enemy was out of sight, but it responded with force. The bullets whizzed through the air and, as if everything were in slow motion, the flagman fell in front of me and rolled over and over like a lead ball. The flag never touched the ground. Someone caught it and raised it, hardly breaking stride. Then he crumpled and rolled and someone else seized it and carried it forward. They never hesitated to take their places in the front line, always running erect and proud, then falling and rolling. The pool of blood widened to within a few feet of my bare toes. I thought I would vomit.

At last there was too much blood for the Young People's Bodyguard Squad, too, and they retreated to the nearest shelter. This happened to be the *Hunan Daily* . . .

Other Bodyguard Squad members were waiting inside the *Hunan Daily*'s gate with trucks and stretchers. As wounds were staunched and bandaged, those still unharmed reloaded madly, breaking open huge wooden crates and spilling the long pointed bullets in random hillocks on the ground. There were a number of army men in the gateway, but since official policy was neutrality, they neither helped nor interfered. Still, when they saw the foolish way the young Rebels were planning to march out into the street to retrieve their fallen, they couldn't restrain themselves. 'Crawl, you fools,' they cried. 'Do you want them to be able to pick you off with their eyes closed? . . .'

In the meantime, three shining black cannon had been taken off the trucks and the Rebels were trying to get the soldiers to show them how to use them. The soldiers were refusing, and voices were loud and angry. The cannon looked splendid and terrible, of the sort intended for use in Vietnam against the American Imperialists. Finally the Rebels despaired of enlisting the aid of the military and decided to go ahead without instruction.

They shot three times, but each time the shell went wildly astray, one exploding through the roof of the black tiled roofs across the way, another landing in the road, another smashing directly into a car parts factory.

Violence on a greater or lesser scale broke out in every province of China; it reached a peak in August 1967. It did not involve only the 'mass organizations'; the army was directly involved in some areas. In September Chairman Mao called for students to return to their schools, and ordered that military weapons be handed back to the military. The army was given the right to use armed force against the Red Guards in the suppression of factional fighting. Mao began pressing the various factions among his followers to compromise their differences and join in unified organizations. Soon, some of the most radical members of the Cultural Revolution Group were arrested on charges that they had been plotting against Zhou Enlai and the military.

These measures did not cure the problem, however. The level of armed conflict died down for a while, but then flared up again. Street fighting in the spring of 1968 sometimes involved tanks and artillery. As late as July 1968, a dispute among Red Guards in Beijing itself left fifteen students dead.

At the end of that month, Mao finally agreed with the more moderate of his supporters that the chaos had to end. 'Worker–peasant Mao Zedong thought propaganda teams' including a large number of military personnel began moving into educational institutions all over the country, and breaking the independent power of the Red Guards. Revolutionary committees, on which the military was heavily represented, became the principal administrative units everywhere. Millions of Red Guards, from all factions, were soon shipped out to the countryside and put to work on the land. Open violence ended in the streets of most cities, though it continued in a few places.

The struggle Mao had launched involved the fundamental nature of the revolution. However, basic issues had often become blurred as China disintegrated into a mass of warring factions, spewing forth their views and denouncing their opponents in uncountable millions of handwritten wall posters.

The extent to which political issues were reduced to personalities was quite striking, and today it inspires vigorous denunciations of the 'cults of personality' practised during the Cultural Revolution. Chairman Mao, as an individual, became the incarnation of the revolution to an even greater extent than he had been before 1966. People bowed before his image after getting up and before going to bed. When a PLA soldier saw a school building on fire, his first thought was to save the portraits of Mao that hung in the classrooms. Only after he had done this did he turn his attention to saving human beings trapped in the building; he got the last of them out only seconds before the building collapsed. When the story was published, his priorities were not criticized; he was treated as a hero.

When the CCP issued a new constitution in 1969, Mao's name appeared in it eleven times; it repeated endlessly that 'Marxism–Leninism–Mao Zedong Thought' formed the guiding line of the Party. Lin Biao, who as head of the Army had been Mao's greatest supporter in the Cultural Revolution, was designated by name in this constitution as Mao's heir. The most bizarre thing, however, is that the Party constitution phrased the reasons for Lin Biao's elevation purely in terms of his relationship with Mao; this had become more important than Lin's concrete accomplishments. It said: 'Comrade Lin Biao has consistently held high the great red banner of Mao Zedong Thought and has most loyally and resolutely carried out and defended Comrade Mao Zedong's proletarian revolutionary line. Comrade Lin Biao is Comrade Mao Zedong's close comrade-in-arms and successor.'

Mao later charged that the cult under which he had become such an object of worship had gone too far, had in fact been something that Lin Biao had whipped up in order to manipulate it for his own benefit. However, when he reached this conclusion he only moderated some of the extremes of the cult; he did not try to renounce it. When a new version of the Party constitution appeared in 1973, Mao's name appeared in it three times.

The cost of the Cultural Revolution had been monumental. There was a general attack on intellectuals, the 'stinking ninth category'. All institutions of higher learning were closed for several years, due both to the struggles being conducted against their administrations and faculties, and to the fact that the students were busy being Red Guards. A significant number of colleges were reopening by 1970, but others did not do so until 1972, and the academic quality was far below the levels that had prevailed in 1965. For a relatively backward country trying to modernize itself, this was a hideous disaster. The disruption was less severe in primary and secondary education, and in industry, but still significant. The take-over by Red Guards of considerable portions of the railroad network had affected almost all sectors of the economy.

In more general terms, China suffered from a general breakdown of law and order, the effects of which endured long after the Red Guards had been shipped out to the countryside. Crime rates increased drastically, and street gangs appeared in many of China's cities. The enforcement of birth-control policies slackened, and took several years to restore. Corruption within governmental and economic units flourished. Most fundamental, the relationship between political discourse and reality was severely damaged. Most governments tell a certain number of lies, but the level of lying in Chinese public life reached incredible levels during and after the Cultural Revolution.

The process by which China had been breaking out of its international isolation was also set back by several years. As all aspects of revolutionary purity became crucial, foreign influences especially came under attack. The PRC, which despite its conflicts with the Soviet Union and India had won steadily greater international acceptance, and by 1965 had been approaching its longstanding goal of replacing the Guomindang as the representative of 'China' in the United Nations, withdrew into virtual isolation. Ambassadors to foreign countries were called home. After the radicals had taken over the Foreign Ministry, China's remaining foreign contacts came to be conducted in a rather strident fashion. When Chinese in various countries came into conflict with the governments of those countries, Beijing mobs sometimes invaded the embassies of the offending governments.

Probably the worst such incident was the attack on the British Embassy. There existed a substantial Communist organization among the Chinese population of the British colony of Hong Kong. In 1967, the PRC began encouraging the Communists in Hong Kong to seize control of the colony. The British administration in Hong Kong resisted successfully, and with remarkably little use of physical violence. In August 1967, a mob of Red Guards protested British actions in Hong Kong by sacking the British Embassy in Beijing. They gave the chargé d'affaires a severe beating, tore the clothing from female members of his staff, etc. This incident was so clearly harmful to China's interests that in its aftermath Zhou Enlai was able to reduce the radical influence on the conduct of China's foreign relations, and rein in the Red Guards somewhat. This did not undo the damage already done.

In some vital areas, however, no such chaos was permitted. In the rocketry and nuclear weapons programmes, Western-trained experts went about their work with relatively little interference. China detonated its first hydrogen bomb in 1967, and orbited its first satellite in 1970.

Perhaps the most striking thing is the way, while the revolutionary frenzy was permitted to disrupt China's relations with much of the world, the crisis in Vietnam, which posed serious dangers to China during the American escalation of 1965–68, was handled calmly and rationally. The PRC put tens of thousands of military personnel in the northern section of North Vietnam, mostly construction units working to keep the railroads open, but also anti-aircraft gunners and so on. This constituted an unmistakable warning to the United States that China would if necessary fight to defend the Democratic Republic of Vietnam. However, none of this was given much publicity. The Chinese personnel were clearly visible to US reconnaisance – indeed in some cases they did not dig in against air attack as much as they might have wished, because to do so would have rendered them less visible – but the attention of the American public was never drawn to this fact, so when the United States government limited its actions against North Vietnam it did not appear to be giving in to Chinese pressure. The careful way the PRC avoided inflammatory rhetoric on this one issue is remarkable in the context of the times.

The organizational structure of the Communist Party was destroyed in most areas. However, while many individual military officers were purged, order and discipline were at least partially preserved in the armed forces. Even the administrative structure of the government got some protection. Zhou Enlai, who as Premier headed the government hierarchy, served as a sort of moderator in the Cultural Revolution, trying to limit the spread of chaos. He did not try to oppose the Cultural Revolution; either he saw significant value in it or he decided he was not strong enough to fight Mao. However, Zhou did what he could both to preserve the government as an organization and to protect many of the individuals who were attacked as followers of the capitalist road. The most extreme radicals naturally hated him, and he later became almost a patron saint to those who wanted to repudiate the Cultural Revolution. Mao, who was well aware that China needed some of the trained people whom Zhou was trying to protect, tolerated Zhou's activities and quashed all attacks on him; indeed, Zhou remained Premier until his death in 1976.

Even on less vital matters the frenzy could be moderated in practice. When the Cultural Revolution began to attack the 'Four Olds', the treasures of China's traditional art came under suspicion as 'relics of feudalism'. Any museum or private home where they were displayed was in danger of attacks by Red Guards. However, the destruction of art was not by any means all-encompassing; large quantities were trucked off to safe warehouses. Today some of this material is once again on display in Chinese museums, and other pieces have recently been sold to the Westerners, at premium prices, to raise money to help pay for China's modernization.

The initial results

As comparative order was restored in 1969 and 1970, and 'Revolutionary Committees', many of whose members came from the PLA, were established to replace the administrative structures that had collapsed in the preceding years, some of the concrete goals of the Cultural Revolution became more clearly visible. The May Seventh Cadre Schools, the 'barefoot doctors', and a massive reorientation of the educational system exemplify these.

Many administrators and intellectuals were sent to May Seventh Cadre Schools, which combined prolonged and sometimes very unpleasant manual labour with intensive indoctrination. They might be less likely to look down on people who worked with their hands after having done so for several months or years themselves, probably without much skill due to their lack of practice. Late in 1969 a rotation scheme was proposed under which, at any given time, one-third of the personnel of leading organizations would be released from their administrative duties to engage in manual labour in farming or industry.

The 'barefoot doctors' were peasants who were given a few months of medical training and were then set to providing rudimentary health care at the village level, referring only the more difficult cases to clinics having real doctors. These people really did make a contribution to Chinese health care. Real doctors had several major disadvantages. They were very expensive to train, and a poor country like China could not possibly afford enough of them to provide for all the patients needing care. They tended to congregate in the cities, where the living conditions were best and where most of the people with sufficient influence to demand good medical care were found. Finally, highly trained doctors often developed a liking for cases which challenged their skills, which generally meant cases on which one had to devote a great deal of time and effort to a single patient, and even then possibly fail to effect a cure. For the cost of training one real doctor specializing in heart surgery the government could train a great many 'barefoot doctors', and even a single 'barefoot doctor', by doing relatively routine work on tasks like the eradication of snail fever, might succeed in doing more good for more patients than the heart surgeon.

The whole spirit of the educational system was altered to reduce gaps between the educated and the uneducated, between mental labour and manual labour. A system that had been geared to giving a fairly good education to a few people was redesigned to give a lower level of education to a great many people. Enrolment in secondary schools expanded dramatically, while enrolments in colleges and universities, when these finally reopened, remained below 1965 levels. The duration of schooling was reduced (at the college level, five-year courses of study were typically cut to three years). Even during those years the number of hours of academic learning was reduced, so the students could devote a considerable portion of their time to manual labour, enough so their labour actually had economic value. Some grew vegetables in school gardens. Others worked in school workshops, which might turn out consumer goods and other simple products, or even have a contract with some nearby factory to produce components for large machinery.

There was a great expansion in the programme, originally begun in the 1950s, for sending young people out to the countryside as soon as they finished secondary school. About 17 million were 'sent down' between 1968 and 1978, of whom about 10 million were still in the countryside in 1978. The effect of this was to spread the educated people more evenly in society, and to reduce the extent to which education would be seen as an avenue to the good life. Knowledge was supposed to be intensely practical, sought so that one could serve the people; it was not to be valued for its own sake or for the prestige it could confer.

The ability to demonstrate academic competence, through written examinations, was de-emphasized; this had been one of the first major slogans under which the Cultural Revolution began, in 1966. In any given school, almost all students from middle-class and 'bad-class' backgrounds were academically above average; given the class-oriented admissions policies in effect, they would have been unlikely to win admission to the school if they had not been superior to the average level of students from worker, peasant, and cadre households. Anyone who looked at the schools could see that a policy which stressed the importance of examination results, and used them as the main criterion for deciding who could go on to the next higher level of education, would be a policy benefiting the students from middle-class and especially from 'bad-class' backgrounds. Examinations were, therefore, denounced as a device which had been used by bourgeois intellectuals in positions of academic authority to promote the interests of people similar to themselves, and frustrate the ambitions of the ordinary workers and peasants. In the early 1970s, when an attempt was made to revive written examinations as part of the selection process for college admissions, one student handed in a paper that consisted simply of a denunciation of examinations and those who did well in examinations.

> To tell the truth, I have no respect for the bookworms who for many years have been taking it easy and have done nothing useful. I dislike them intensely. During the busy summer hoeing time, I just could not abandon my production task and hide myself in a small room to study. That would have been very selfish. If I had done that, I would have been guilty of being unworthy of the revolutionary cause which concerns both the poor and lower-middle peasants and myself, and I would have been condemned by my own revolutionary conscience.

His statement was given national publicity, and he became a hero for having expressed such a correct revolutionary attitude.

College students were no longer recruited straight from the secondary schools, and were no longer selected by primarily academic criteria. Graduates of secondary schools had to complete at least two years of manual labour in agriculture or industry before becoming eligible to be nominated by their co-workers to go to college. Proper political attitudes, and a willingness to respect manual labour and those engaged in it, were supposed to be key criteria in this selection. Beyond this, when the colleges and universities began to reopen in 1970, many of the students selected for admission were not secondary graduates at all. Some had never even graduated from *lower* middle (junior high) school.

Such policies may have had some success in producing a crop of college graduates less isolated from the masses than those of former years. Unfortunately, they also produced college graduates whose level of academic knowledge was quite low, sometimes below the level of the best secondary graduates of the days before 1966. The fact that political criteria were more important than academic ones also helped to ensure that politically powerful individuals would be able to ensure admission for their children, or the friends of their children, or just someone who had offered them a bribe. This was known as entry through the 'back door'. Personal influence became, in fact, a far greater factor than before the Cultural Revolution; it would have been the height of folly for anyone evaluating the political attitudes of college applicants to find fault with someone favoured by a powerful official.

Aftermath: 1969–1976

In 1969 the formal apparatus of the Communist Party, which had fallen apart during the Cultural Revolution and had been replaced by the Revolutionary Committees, began to be restored. By late summer of 1971 there was, once again, a CCP provincial committee in every province. Military men still had a major role, and Lin Biao, Minister of Defence, was openly acknowledged as Mao Zedong's chosen successor. However, as public order was restored and the Party apparatus was revived, Mao felt less need for the army and its commander, and he began to cut down on Lin Biao's authority. Lin, perhaps uncertain as to how far this would go, and not willing to give up the supreme power that had seemed within his grasp, apparently began plotting against Mao.

The details are difficult to discern; most of what we know comes from statements made, after Lin Biao was dead, by the people who had sided with Mao. They include some truly preposterous slanders against Lin, ranging up to the claim that Lin had been planning to make China a colony of the Soviet Union, and also that he had been planning to abolish socialism, handing the factories over to the capitalist class and the land to the old landlords, as private property. The propaganda of Chinese power struggles had abandoned all concern for truth or even plausibility. What seems fairly clear, however, is that a power struggle occurred, and by September 1971 Lin had lost. He and some of his followers apparently tried to flee to the Soviet Union by air, but were killed when their plane crashed in Outer Mongolia. The cause of the crash is still uncertain.

The fall of Lin Biao was not revealed at once to the Chinese people. For a while Party leaders said nothing in public. Then there was a long period during which they denounced Lin Biao in the most extravagant terms, but without mentioning his identity; their denunciations simply used the euphemism 'political swindlers like Liu Shaoqi'. By the time they were willing to attack Lin Biao by name in the press, he had been dead for almost two years.

Mao had removed a great many people from important positions on a purely temporary basis during the Cultural Revolution. It had always been assumed that most of those sent to May Seventh Cadre Schools would eventually return to their former work, once they had been subjected to intensive reindoctrination, and once radicals satisfactory to Mao were ensconced in some key positions. The defection of Lin Biao increased Mao's need to broaden his base of support by bringing non-Maoists back into the

Party and the government. During the early 1970s, even people who had been charged with the most serious crimes during the Cultural Revolution, and who seemed to have been placed permanently beyond the pale, were in many cases rehabilitated and restored to positions in the Party and government. The most important of them was Deng Xiaoping, rehabilitated in 1973. By 1975, as both Mao Zedong and Premier Zhou Enlai became too ill to handle any great amount of business, Deng was given control of the day-to-day operations of the Communist Party's Central Committee. Some of the most extreme leftists, such as those responsible for attacks on foreign diplomats in Beijing in 1967, were repudiated and even put on trial. Not all leaders purged during the Cultural Revolution were rehabilitated, but even so the range of those being asked to work together was very wide.

Extreme Left-wing leaders who had risen to power in the Cultural Revolution felt that the past was returning to haunt them. They had long been worried about the danger posed by old attitudes and traditions, hence the enthusiasm of their attack on the Four Olds starting in 1966. When they saw the enemies they thought they had defeated returning to power, however, their worry about the strength of the past increased still further.

When attacks on Lin Biao finally began to mention him by name, they did so in the context of a 'Campaign to Criticize Lin Biao and Confucius'. The CCP propaganda apparatus charged that Lin Biao had been a Confucian, that he had used the ideas of Confucius to try to turn back the clock and undo the work of the Communist Revolution. Party propagandists tried to portray Confucius, in turn, as a reactionary who in his own lifetime had been trying to defend an old, declining ruling class – the slave-owners – against the encroachment of feudalism. The CCP praised Shi Huangdi and the Legalists (previously the villains of Chinese historiography) as valiant advocates of reform and progress, who had set out to destroy Confucianism as part of their struggle to destroy the slave-holding system the Confucians defended. The curious thing is that the people who conducted the Campaign to Criticize Lin Biao and Confucius were saying both (a) that Confucianism had already been the ideology of an outmoded and declining class of exploiters even in the third century BC, and (b) that the power of Confucian ideology was still dangerously great in the 1970s.

The ideological journal *Red Flag* said that Shi Huangdi had been correct in burying alive 460 Confucian scholars to stop them from 'recounting the past to the detriment of the present'. Apparently, as the radicals watched conservative CCP leaders purged in the 1960s returning to power, they were beginning to feel that the oppressive influence of the past was almost immortal. No measures were too drastic to use in the effort to destroy this influence, and no measures could give one any confidence that one would succeed in destroying it.

Left and Right

The Chinese political structure of the mid 1970s was an uneasy amalgam of incompatible elements. Government and Party policies were set mostly by the leftists – very radical followers of Chairman Mao. Many of those who were supposed to implement policy, however, were rightists who had been purged between 1966 and 1968 but later rehabilitated. (They themselves would have rejected indignantly the label of 'rightists', but to the outside observer it appears justified.) The conflicts between these groups were greatest in regard to economics.

The leftists emphasized the importance of egalitarian attitudes. They did not like too much use of bonuses or salary differentials to reward those who did the most, or the most useful, work. Not only would this, by definition, imply considerable differences in income, but it would undermine the socialist ethic the leftists were trying to instil. A system of economic incentives would reinforce the old habits of trying to obtain as much as possible for oneself, instead of inculcating the socialist idea of doing what was best for society regardless of personal profit.

The leftists objected very strongly to the idea that a person or an enterprise could acquire great power by exercising the functions of middleman, shuffling goods around between producers and users, and skimming a profit off the transactions. Although they would have been outraged if anyone had tried to tell them so, their attitude had some of its roots in Confucianism. Traditional Chinese social theory had held that a merchant, a man who makes a living by buying things in one place and then selling them elsewhere at a higher price, is fundamentally a parasite; he has made a profit without actually having produced anything.

They even disliked the idea of a productive enterprise making a large profit, out of proportion to the amount of work done in the production of goods, by concentrating on some product which was in great demand and for which a high price could therefore be charged. Skill in production was respectable; skill in distribution and exchange was not. In one extreme case, a foreign visitor saw a small tractor factory with finished tractors sitting beside it, rusting, for lack of procedures for getting them to the potential users. In a capitalist system, if some financial crisis had rendered the farmers unable to pay for new tractors, such a situation might not have been unnatural. Tractors are manufactured for the purpose of being sold, and go only to those who can pay for them. In a socialist system, desperately short of farm machinery, it must be considered bizarre.

In more general terms, the leftists did not like or trust specialized economic managers. This was partly expressed in a direct way, as they tried to cut down the power and prestige of such people, but it was also expressed in policies that reduced the need for skilled managers. The leftists preferred small factories to large ones. They preferred to make as many enterprises as possible self-sufficient, thus eliminating the need for skilled management of the exchange relationships between enterprises. They praised their model industrial enterprise, the Daqing oil complex, not only for the hard work and self-sacrifice shown by its staff, but for the fact that it intermingled oil facilities with farmland in such a fashion that a considerable portion of the workers' food was grown within the facility.

The leftists were crude and inflexible in their management of the economy. They did not even bother to collect the kind of information on which sophisticated national planning might have been based; in 1976 there were only about one-tenth as many statisticians in the State Statistical Bureau in Beijing as there had been in 1966. The push towards self-sufficiency meant that each area was supposed to devote much of its efforts to the production of basic necessities, especially grain, and it might not have many resources left to produce things to which local conditions were particularly suitable. Every commune was supposed to try to become self-sufficient in grain; in areas where far more value could have been obtained from the land by concentrating on tea, vegetables, or industrial crops, this was economically inefficient. The leftists were at least half sincere in stressing the need for imagination and local initiative in economic management, but what they primarily meant was that local people should think of ways to make production more efficient, and to put to work resources, such as industrial waste products and underemployed individuals, which had not previously been used. They were much less happy about people deciding, on a local level, to shift resources that were already in use

8.4 The peasants of Dazhai, in Shanxi Province, won tremendous praise for the way they had converted barren and unusable hillsides into terraced fields.

to the production of a different product, which would be more profitable.

The practical effect of leftist policies was not always beneficial even to the type of small local industries that in theory the leftists favoured the most. They wanted to build a decentralized, self-sufficient local economy through the application of correct socialist attitudes, but their definition of correct socialist attitudes often inhibited the development of the local economy. They wanted all of China to advance to prosperity together, without allowing one person or group selfishly to get ahead of the rest and start enjoying the good life while others were still poor. Some regions remained almost exclusively agricultural, and efforts to set up local industries and 'sideline production' were inhibited by the fear that one would be accused of 'following the capitalist road'. There was a short list of standard products for which production was encouraged in every part of China. These included iron and steel, chemical fertilizer, coal, cement, agricultural machinery, and agricultural implements. But if anyone in a backward commune wished to go beyond this list, and produce something for which local conditions were particularly suited or for which there was a special local need, it would be necessary to pick some product which could be produced profitably, divert funds and manpower from agriculture to get the operation started, buy equipment, make deals outside the normal structure of distribution to obtain raw materials, and so on. In short, the project would need an aggressive and flexible entrepreneur. The leftists were not friendly to such people. The Deputy Governor of Shandong province, in much of which attempts to diversify the rural economy had been almost totally blocked by fears of following the 'capitalist road', remarked a few years later:

> One major problem we have in developing the diversified economy is caused by the ultraleft pernicious influence, which considers socialists as people who plant grain crops, engage in collective production and develop a self-sufficient, small-scale peasant economy, and considers capitalists as people who strive to make money, engage in sideline household occupations and develop consumer goods production. Some comrades still think it improper to let certain commune members become wealthier than others.

The leftists tried in some ways to reduce the gap between the cities and the villages. They shipped a very large proportion of the new graduates of medical schools out to the countryside. They also sent out urban secondary-school graduates in enormous numbers. These people were much less useful than the medical personnel; their skills were seldom directly relevant to the tasks of farming, and their morale was often low. The villages actually had to be paid to accept them, since at least in the period immediately after they went out, they were not sufficiently useful as workers to pay for the cost of their subsistence. However, in the long run it could be hoped that the presence of a substantial leavening of educated people in the villages would not only make the introduction of modern knowledge (including scientific farming techniques) easier, but also reduce the intellectual isolation of the rural population. Some of the young people 'sent down' were actually persuaded to look on this as an opportunity to 'serve the people', but for most it was agony. If they managed to grit their teeth and smile it was from fear that if they opposed the programme they might be punished by being kept in the wilderness for life. They were reluctant to marry; a settled family life would reduce their chances of getting permission to return to the city. However, the very reasons they found life in the villages so hateful – the much lower level of material and cultural life, the paucity of educational facilities, and the intellectuals' traditional lack of respect for manual labour and the people who engaged in it – were the reasons Mao and his associates felt it was so vital to break down the barriers between city and countryside, at whatever the cost. Mao felt that people who despised village life so totally were, *ipso facto*, unqualified for the leading positions in society that the young graduates were hoping to fill.

For the most part the leftists realized that they would have to temper their actions at least in the short run, and tolerate some persons, activities, and institutions distasteful to them. This applied especially to their dislike of economic incentives. The Chinese people's mode of thinking could not be changed overnight, and institutional changes could not get too far ahead of changes in thought patterns. Leftist officials in some areas decided to abolish the peasants' private plots, collectivize pigs and other livestock which had been privately raised, and end the work-point system under which the income a peasant family drew from the production brigade had been dependent on the amount of work done by the family, but such drastic steps towards egalitarianism were not national policy.

The leftists advocated putting 'politics in command'. If someone argued that a coal-mine which operated at a loss should be closed down, they said that this was putting 'profits in command', and that the national need for more coal should take precedence over the selfish desire for profit. They did not consider that if a mine operated at a loss – in other words, if the value of the coal it produced was less than the cost of operating it – this might be a sign that its continued operation was not really in the national interest. 'Politics in command' also meant that people should do their work out of a desire to build socialism, not in order to win higher incomes for themselves. Selfishness was very nearly the ultimate sin. (Note the extreme contrast with traditional Chinese values, in which accumulating wealth for oneself, in order to be able to provide security for one's family, was a virtue.)

Everything would work out well if the mass line were followed. Managerial personnel should make decisions in cooperation with the workers, and not simply try to impose their views by fiat. Production workers should be encouraged to make technical innovations, rather than leaving such things to technical experts, and using uncritically the machines and procedures given to them.

The rightists felt that the most important task of the revolution was to build up a strong and wealthy China, and that this task required stability and hierarchy. China was an underdeveloped country; everywhere one turned there were problems that were not being solved fast enough because of the shortage of technically trained personnel. To strip a qualified engineer of the authority he needed to manage a construction project simply because he did not have the correct political attitude, or to choose for engineering training, on political grounds, someone other than the candidate who showed the greatest technical aptitude, were luxuries China could not afford. Deng Xiaoping, by the 1970s the leading spokesman for the Right, used to say that he did not care whether a cat was black or white as long as it could catch the mice. The rightists felt that a modernized, technologically advanced economy had to contain elements almost incomprehensible to the uneducated masses. It had to include the sort of industrial plants that could be designed only by highly trained experts (in many cases only by foreign experts), which to run properly would have to have powerful and technologically oriented managements, and in which the common workers, if they tried to make innovations before they had spent a considerable time getting used to the system and getting to understand how things fit together, would only make a mess.

Aside from disliking the idea of giving too much emphasis to any political criteria in running the educational system and the economy, the rightists disliked the particular political ideas the leftists were pushing. The rightists were, fundamentally, the urban élite of China – technicians, managers, administrators, and intellectuals. They were convinced that the work they did required far more skill than farming, and was of vastly greater benefit to society. If they enjoyed much greater status and respect than the peasants, and used their status to acquire better food, clothing, housing, and medical care, and to arrange better education and career prospects for their children, they felt that they had earned these things. Even after the improvements brought about by the revolution the life of the typical peasant was not a pleasant one. Both pride and self-interest made many people cling, despite prolonged Maoist indoctrination, to the idea that they were entitled to something better.

Rarely could members of the Left and Right really talk to one another. The savagery with which the Left suppressed unacceptable ideas, even in the aftermath of the Cultural Revolution, made open debate impossible. Indeed the leftists may have executed more people in 1970 and 1971, quietly in various prisons and cellars, than during the publicly visible mass struggles of 1966–68. When major leftist leaders were brought to trial in 1980, it was charged that between 1966 and 1976 their persecution of their opponents had caused the deaths of about 34,000 people. Besides outright executions, this figure apparently included people driven to suicide, and those such as Liu Shaoqi who simply died of abuse and neglect while imprisoned, but it probably did not include the casualties of the street fights of 1967 and 1968.

The leftists had written principles of free expression into the Constitution, but they were not above surgically severing the vocal cords of a woman who expressed herself in a manner they found too objectionable. Dominating the media of public propaganda, they presented their one-sided argument with all the carelessness of people who know that if they confound logic, falsify the facts, or misrepresent the views of their opponents, nobody will dare to point out the errors.

Argument in terms of allegory, and indirect language which avoided saying outright what the author meant, had proliferated. There had been a long period during the Cultural Revolution when the press had been filled with denunciations of 'the chief person in power following the capitalist road', also known as 'China's Khrushchev'. At least in that period everyone knew that the un-named culprit was actually Liu Shaoqi. In 1973, people similarly understood that denunciations of 'swindlers like Liu Shaoqi' actual-ly referred to Lin Biao. But in 1974, when a campaign to criticize Lin Biao and Confucius became so important that it was clearly intended to be relevant to current political struggles, it was not obvious which living persons were the real objects of this criticism nominally directed against dead ones.

Complex political ideas were summed up in slogans so short that nobody who did not already know would have been able to deduce the real meaning. This practice had many disadvantages. It encouraged fuzzy thinking. It was élitist, since the ordinary person was not able to understand policy statements without the help of some knowledgeable interpreter. It was ideally suited to the con-venience of those who wished to misrepresent the content of impor-tant policy statements, and it helped Mao's enemies to misrepresent his ideas quite seriously after his death. But Chinese culture had for many centuries respected indirect, allusive language, while clear language would have made more difficult the vital task of misrepre-senting the views of one's own enemies.

The difficulties of dialogue and compromise were increased by the way the policies of each faction formed an interrelated whole. In military strategy, for example, the Left favoured a defence in depth. A foreign invader would be able to penetrate a considerable distance into China, but would then be chopped up by guerrilla warfare and eventually forced to withdraw. This form of warfare would not be crucially dependent on sophisticated modern weapons of a type that could only be produced in very large modern factories. Indeed it could not afford to be, since most such factories would probably be captured or destroyed by the enemy in the first weeks of war. Instead what China would need would be a great many smaller and less sophisticated factories scattered across the country. The military, lacking sophisticated weapons, would not need highly skilled technicians to run them, and therefore would not need an educational system geared to rewarding technical excellence. Since combat would not involve a great deal of complex knowledge, the army in peacetime would not be forced to spend all its time practising military tasks in order to maintain the necessary level of proficiency. It would have time to spare for political training (vital if it were to have the cooperation of the civil population in a future guerilla war), and to do productive labour.

The rightists, on the contrary, wanted armed forces capable of preventing China from being invaded, which meant they wanted modern weapons capable of standing up to those of the invader in open battle. Such an army required modern heavy industry to supply it. Such industry, in turn, would be concentrated in large and vulnerable plants which could only be defended by regular armed forces; guerrillas would not do. The army would not require tactical cooperation from the civil population in a war, so political training would be of little military value. On the other hand high professional standards, and continuous training leaving little time for non-military activities, would be necessary if complex arms were to be used effectively.

It would be difficult to justify a military policy halfway between the two extremes, and almost impossible to devise a rational policy which took the leftist attitude on some questions and the rightist attitude on others. The rightists' military strategy *required* a rightist pattern of industrial development, and so on.

The same was true of many other key issues. Attempts to compromise between Left and Right on the question of free-market activity by the peasants led to continual troubles. The norm for China, since the collectivization of agriculture in 1955–56, had been to allow the peasants to have small private plots on which they could grow what crops they wished, and raise their own livestock. At some periods, especially during the relaxation of controls in the aftermath of the Great Leap Forward, the peasants had been allowed considerable freedom to sell their produce at local markets, for whatever they could get for it. Where there were acute shortages of many products, such free-market activities could be extremely profitable. The head of one commune discovered in the early 1960s that the peasants were selling privately raised chickens at the local market for five times the price of chickens marketed through government channels. He decided that this was a very dangerous phenomenon; it would lead the peasants to use the desire for profits as the guide to their actions, and to neglect collective production in favour of private production, where they could obtain higher incomes without having to work any harder. He applied pressure to prevent the peasants from using the local market. In the mid 1970s, some peasants on another commune decided to take some of the land on which they had been growing grain, and use it instead to grow melons, which were in great demand and were commanding high prices. This was collective production, not private, but it was following the 'capitalist' principle of 'putting profits in command', and it clearly had the potential to make these peasants much richer than those of their neighbours who were adhering to the ideologically correct course of growing grain. Local authorities responded by destroying the melon crop shortly before it would have been ready for harvest.

A policy permitting only collective, ideologically correct forms of production was internally consistent, although it tended to lead to shortages of meat, vegetables, and other products which required more flexibility than the collective production system usually showed. A policy permitting really extensive free-market activity, adequate for competition to push the prices of free-market goods down to reasonable levels, might work reasonably well. Logically, it should ensure greater supplies of goods to consumers without creating tremendous inequalities in wealth. Participation would be open to all peasants in a given area, and competition would keep any of them from obtaining preposterous prices for their produce. The compromise policy of tightly restricted free markets, however, combined many of the disadvantages of both worlds. Tightly limited markets were unable to satisfy consumer needs adequately, and at the same time the gap between supply and demand ensured that the small amount of free-market activity permitted was so profitable as to undermine people's respect for collective production.

One of the great weaknesses of the radicals – one reason why their policies produced such disastrous results and were so totally repudiated after 1976 – was that they attacked people more than they attacked problems. When they had important goals, and saw that there were people who opposed these goals, they sometimes seemed to be concentrating more on tearing down the opposition than on achieving the goals. They were very good at vilifying and attacking the followers of the capitalist road. Cases such as the 'barefoot doctors', in which the leftists showed real talent in following the socialist road, occurred but were far less common.

They had a general tendency to emphasize spirit over concrete reality; to choose a policy that would reflect their own correct revolutionary attitudes, and inculcate correct revolutionary attitudes in others, rather than basing their actions on the concrete results of this or that policy. This could go to preposterous extremes. Thus we have the story, supposedly true, of a man who was fighting a large forest fire. Lacking effective tools for the job, he finally gave a loud cry of 'Long live Chairman Mao', lay down, and tried to put out the flames in his immediate vicinity by rolling on them. This had no significant effect on the fire, and he was quickly burned to death. His sacrifice accomplished nothing, and it rendered him unavailable for constructive action, but it demonstrated tremendous revolutionary dedication and lack of concern for self-interest. He was praised as a great hero.

The emphasis on spirit over results had some of its most important expressions in policies dealing with salaries and incomes. When the leftists looked at a capitalist roader who was doing something important in the economy, and collecting a very high income as a result, they did not object merely because his income might better have been diverted to the poor. They were also offended – some of them seemed most offended – by the fact that he was a piece of living propaganda for the *attitudes* characterizing the capitalist road. All who saw him would be influenced to think: (1) that the work he was doing really was more important than that done by other people; (2) that he was earning his high income, and deserved to go on getting it; (3) that the reason for doing important work is that it will get one a high income. If attitudes constituted one's major worry, one could conclude that the most dangerous situations were precisely those in which a person was getting a high income as a direct and visible result of doing something valuable. A capitalist roader who was getting a high income that he was *not* earning was less worrisome, since such a person would not appear to illustrate the virtues of the capitalist road. In the early 1970s, few of the senior professors who had once dominated Chinese universities were doing much of importance; both their morale and their prestige had been virtually destroyed. However, they continued collecting very high salaries, much higher than those of the people who were now doing most of the real work on their campuses. Intellectuals sent out to the countryside to reform themselves through manual labour sometimes continued to collect the full salaries appropriate to the jobs they had held in the cities, giving them a much higher income than the peasants among whom they had been sent to work.

In industry, the leftists virtually abolished the practice of giving bonuses to people who worked especially hard. However, they made little effort to abolish the large differentials in basic salary levels between different workers. In other words, it was permissible for a factory to pay Mr Wang half as much again as Mr Chen during a particular month on the grounds that Mr Wang had seniority, or that he was classified as a regular rather than a temporary employee, or that he simply held a position for which a high salary was traditional. It was not permissible to pay Mr Wang more if the reason was that Mr Wang had worked harder during that month. There may have been other reasons for such impractical choices in policy, such as a desire to take discretionary decisions on the awarding of bonuses out of the hands of factory managers, but the Left's feeling that the attitude of selfishness was a worse evil than the fact of inequality clearly influenced matters. It is not surprising that labour discipline suffered. Many factories suffered from absenteeism, laziness, or simple indifference on the part of their workers. Industrial growth slowed.

Many Communists had shown a similar preoccupation with attitudes in the earliest years of the revolution, for some of the same reasons. Most people have a certain view of the way the world works. If they are presented with a single new idea or a new situation, they can usually fit it into their existing mental structure without having to discard old assumptions wholesale. However, if they try to assimilate too many new ideas in a short time, the old world view may collapse through inability to integrate the new material. The problem is that the new material will not automatically organize itself into a reasonably complete and coherent world view, capable of replacing the old. People in such a situation often find themselves unable to answer fundamental questions. In their struggle to organize a new world view they will probably have to oversimplify matters somewhat, and they may become rather inflexible. Only gradually will they acquire enough confidence in the new structure of ideas to be able to apply it flexibly and effectively in a variety of situations.

Communism in the 1920s had represented such a departure from the traditional world view that few Party members could really predict the results of a given policy. They had no mental landmarks to tell them which way to go, to tell them that one policy would work while another would not. For lack of a better option, they often chose to do whatever would show a correct revolutionary attitude. Experience gradually filled in the gaps in what had at first been a sketchy and incomplete as well as inflexible Communist world view; it taught them how to work within the new system and how to judge what the actual results of a given policy might be. The making of Party policy had begun to be based on concrete realism by 1935, and was so based to a very large extent by 1949. Mao, however, had cast his followers adrift again in 1966. He demanded that they abandon the patterns of thought and behaviour that had become standard since the Revolution of 1949, and once again they were left frantically trying to learn how to apply a totally new world view to the complexities of the world. The results were the same as they had been a generation before: confusion, bad decisions, and a tendency to mask one's own inner uncertainties by acting self-righteously and attacking one's opponents with exceptional fanaticism and ferocity.

The full extent of the leftists' failure can be seen in the fact that some of the phenomena they detested most actually became more widespread during the period of their domination. Before 1966, moderate CCP leaders had established mechanisms by which the market, and the forces of selfishness in general, were harnessed to serve CCP goals. The leftists, their sense of revolutionary purity outraged, abolished many of these mechanisms during the Cultural Revolution. Selfishness and the market did not disappear, however. What happened was that selfishness and the market were unharnessed; they no longer operated in such a way as to serve CCP goals.

In the early 1960s the market had played a significant role in the economy. It had for the most part been a rationalizing force, which rewarded those who produced needed goods, and directed goods to those who wanted them. In the early 1970s the market played an even greater role, but it was primarily a market in favours, influence, and bribes. Under the old market system one might have obtained scarce raw materials by paying for them, at so much per ton. In the new market one gave the relevant official a banquet, a hundred cartons of cigarettes, a dozen melons, or permission for his nephew to enter college. If one had *guanxi* (personal ties) with the relevant people, a tremendous range of goods and services were available through the 'back door'. Cadres and officials unselfishly dedicated to duty and the public interest were probably less common in 1972 than in 1965.

One can only speculate as to whether the Maoist ideology of the 1960s could have matured into a flexible and effective world view if given enough time, repeating the process that had transformed the dogmatic radicalism of 1930 into the mature Communism of 1949. What is plain is that the Maoism of the Cultural Revolution was not capable of making this transition in ten years, and ten years was all the time it was allowed.

International relations

During the Cultural Revolution the Left had been highly xenophobic, but this was more a matter of the Red Guards' determination to demonstrate their revolutionary purity than a reflection of Mao's fundamental goals. Once the frenzy had died down, the Left and the Right agreed on the desirability of resuming the movement, broken off in 1966, towards broader diplomatic and trade ties with non-Communist nations including the United States. The US government, on the other hand, had realized that good relations with China would improve its position both in the Vietnam War and in its world-wide competition against the Soviet Union. Henry Kissinger, President Nixon's National Security Adviser, made his first visit to Beijing secretly in 1971; President Nixon went with great publicity in 1972. The problem of Taiwan still remained a stumbling-block, but the United States was clearly on the road to full diplomatic recognition of the PRC.

The USA had long applied pressure on the international community to keep China in isolation and continue recognizing the Guomindang leaders in Taibei as the government of China, but this pressure was weakening. Canada shifted diplomatic recognition from Taibei to Beijing in October 1970; other nations followed in rapid succession.

The shift was most visibly measured in the UN, where for many years a motion had come annually before the General Assembly to replace Taibei with Beijing as the representative of 'China'. The resolution had gradually gained support, and in 1965 had come fairly close to success. The Cultural Revolution interrupted the trend for four years, but in 1970 this motion actually won a majority, 51 to 49, in the General Assembly. The USA managed only to postpone the inevitable by pushing through a procedural resolution stating that this was an 'important question' which would require a

8.5   In 1971, Dr Henry Kissinger (National Security adviser to the US President, Richard Nixon) made a secret visit to Beijing, met with Zhou Enlai, and began the re-establishment of friendly relations between China and the United States.

two-thirds margin to pass. In 1971, realizing that the PRC might be about to win, the USA belatedly introduced a resolution that both Beijing and Taibei should be represented in the UN, as separate governments. This 'Two China' policy might have had some success if it had been tried when the United States still had the power to say that the PRC could enter the UN only at the cost of coexisting with the Taibei representatives there, but by the time the United States made the offer it had no such power; the PRC had the votes to enter the UN without having to make any concessions. Besides, Chiang Kai-shek's government vigorously denied that it was in the UN as a representative of the area it actually ruled – the island of Taiwan. It still claimed to be in the UN in its capacity as the sole government of China as a whole, and denounced the American 'Two China' proposal as a 'gross insult'. In October 1971 the General Assembly voted 76 to 35 to expel the representatives from Taibei and seat those from Beijing.

Trade with the capitalist countries grew along with diplomatic contacts, so much so that China had to expand its port facilities quite substantially by the mid 1970s. In July 1971 Britain once again abandoned the discriminatory treatment of China in regard to export restrictions; from this point onward British businessmen could sell to China as freely as to the USSR. The following month, Britain signed a £20m. contract for commercial jet aircraft. In February 1972 the United States followed the British lead in allowing China to purchase as wide a range of non-military goods as the Soviet Union. Before the end of 1972 the Chinese were negotiating to buy jet airliners from France and the USA as well as Britain. For several years the United States continued to refuse to sell equipment having potential military uses, but did not try to prevent its allies from doing so. The French sold some helicopters in 1974, and Britain signed a very large contract for Rolls-Royce jet engines in 1975.

In a step with an even greater potential for subverting the purity of the Revolution, China began sending a few students to Britain to study at the end of 1972. The number of students sent to capitalist countries increased dramatically later in the decade.

The Right was more enthusiastic about very broad contacts, commercial and intellectual as well as diplomatic, than the Left. Mao and the leftists stressed that the Chinese economy should be fundamentally self-sufficient. They accused the rightists of wanting to enslave China to the foreigners physically by depending on imported goods, which would have to be paid for by the export of vital raw materials, and also mentally by depending on imported technology and scientific ideas, and by accepting foreign technologies without change where the leftists wanted to make extensive modifications in imported designs. But the difference was only one of degree; the leftists accepted the need for substantial foreign imports, and the rightists did not want as much as the leftists charged.

9

China since Mao

Mao Zedong and Zhou Enlai presided over a government that was, by the mid 1970s, an uneasy balance of Left and Right. In a sense they were the leaders of opposing factions, but they were both to some degree compromisers. Zhou Enlai, the pragmatic administrator, had done what he could to protect many of the individuals attacked for Right-wing views during the Cultural Revolution, but had not defied Mao. Mao, the extreme leftist, had a lifelong faith in the ability of human beings to change. He was convinced that individuals with incorrect views could be reformed. He had tolerated the restoration of some of his most important opponents to positions of considerable power in the early 1970s, under conditions that forced them to adapt their behaviour to his views. When both Zhou and Mao died in a single year, however, their respective factions were left under the leadership of people much less disposed to compromise.

The Right soon won an overwhelming victory. Some important leftist leaders were under arrest within a month of Mao's death, and the Right consolidated its control of the government and the Communist Party over the next two years. The rightists then began a remarkable series of reforms, undoing much of the legacy of Maoism.

The deaths of Zhou and Mao

Zhou Enlai died, after a lingering illness, in January 1976. He quickly became, in death, a greater symbol of resistance to radical policies than he ever had been in life. His enemies on the Left, led by the group later known as the 'Gang of Four' (Jiang Qing, Yao Wenyuan, Zhang Chunqiao, and Wang Hongwen), cut the official ceremonies of mourning for him to only a few days. However, in late March and

9.1   In April 1976, thousands of Chinese crowded into Tiananmen Square
to present wreaths in memory of Zhou Enlai and read the inscriptions
attached to wreaths others had presented. When the authorities tried to
interfere, shortly after this photograph was taken, the crowd rioted.

early April many cities saw public demonstrations in honour of
Zhou's memory, some of which involved open attacks on the
leftists, and all of which were at least acts of implicit defiance after
the way the leftists had cut short the formal ceremonies of mourning
in January. The best publicized of these incidents was at
Tiananmen, the place in the centre of Beijing where major parades
and important official ceremonies were usually held. The Qing
Ming (Ch'ing Ming) festival, during which the Chinese have
traditionally commemorated their dead, came early in April.
Thousands of people brought wreaths in memory of Zhou, many
with politically oriented poems attached, and presented them at the
Monument to the Heroes of the People in Tiananmen Square. When
the radicals removed the wreaths the demonstration became a riot.
The radicals, instead of trying to co-opt Zhou's memory, had
handed it over to their enemies by acknowledging openly that any
strong gesture of respect for Zhou was equivalent to a gesture of
hostility against themselves. They blamed Deng Xiaoping for the
Tiananmen disorders, and he was purged for a second time two
days after the incident.

The leftists seemed on the surface to have a strong position, but they were crucially dependent on the support of Mao Zedong. The 'Gang of Four' had neither Mao's prestige nor his political skill. Only one of them, Zhang Chunqiao, even had proven ability as an administrator. They might have been adequate as spokesmen for a national consensus, but what they were trying to do was to maintain a policy line that ran against both the beliefs and the personal interests of most of the Chinese national leadership. The radicals said that maintaining the purity of the revolution should take precedence over economic development. Beyond this, they were arguing that people with special knowledge, talents, and skills make a contribution to national construction that is only moderately greater than the contribution of the ordinary workers and peasants who do most of the actual labour, and that to the extent that the skilled people do make an extra contribution, they should be willing to do so without expecting special privileges or rewards in return. Some of these ideas were inherently defensible, but even if they had been honestly applied they would not have been likely to attract much support from the educated élite of China. Most educated Chinese felt that the main purpose of the revolution was to develop and modernize China. Many of them were very proud that they possessed skills useful in the tasks of economic development; they felt entitled to be rewarded very substantially for what they could do. Most members of the Chinese élite felt that they had been harmed by the Cultural Revolution. They could argue with sincerity that the policies they preferred were more just and more in the interests of the nation. They felt that Maoist policies were not only denying educated people the rewards they had earned by their work, but also denying them the conditions they needed to work effectively on national construction. Deng Xiaoping commented bitingly on the practice of 're-educating' senior scientific personnel, to prevent them from becoming too separated from the masses, by requiring them to spend much of their time doing unskilled manual labour: 'The Academy of Sciences is an academy of sciences and not an academy of production or of education. It is not an academy of cabbage cultivation; it is not an academy of beans.'

Beyond this, the egalitarian principles of the radicals were sometimes marred by favouritism and corruption; the Maoist élite that had arisen in the Cultural Revolution contained many individuals who flagrantly failed to practise what they preached. The technocrats felt that they were being asked to give up the power and privilege they had earned by their work on national construction not in order to make everyone equal, but so that power, privilege, and illicit personal luxuries could be enjoyed by those who had 'waved the Red Flag' with exceptional vigour. Old revolutionary veterans did not admire Mao's leading supporters in the Politburo, who had been promoted very rapidly, on the basis of Mao's personal favour rather than any solid record of accomplishments. Wang Hongwen in particular was labelled 'the helicopter' for the speed with which he had risen out of a Shanghai textile mill to take, at the age of thirty-six, the number three position in the CCP hierarchy. It is easy to see why sentiment against the radicals among the most influential elements in China was over-whelming.

The moderates even manipulated the radicals into an implicit admission that radical egalitarianism was inconsistent with rapid economic growth. The moderates used public slogans calling for greater economic construction, with the implied message that there should be rewards and political promotion for the technocrats who alone were capable of leading this economic construction. The radicals, opposing the idea of rewards and promotion for the technocrats, felt impelled to attack the slogans. By doing so they implicitly accepted the notion that only the technocrats could lead economic growth, and allowed themselves to be cast in the role of opponents of growth. They also reinforced the stereotype of the moderates as a group of technically skilled people, and lost the opportunity to attack the moderates by concentrating propaganda attacks on the considerable number of important moderates who did not in fact have any conspicuous skills.

The leftists protested feebly that the slogan of modernizing the economy was being misused by people whose real goal was a restoration of capitalism in China, that the rightists' ability to orbit earth satellites was just a sham, while the sabotaging of revolutionary politics was the real content of rightist policies. They claimed, in fact, that modernization would be more successful under leftist policies. However, when they issued statements condemning the idea that economics and professional proficiency could be as important as politics, they were implicitly admitting the obvious: that they dared not let themselves be judged by standards of economic results and professional proficiency. The result was to isolate the radicals; they were neither liked nor respected by most of the administrative apparatus through which China was ruled.

Mao died on 9 September 1976. The first stage of the ensuing power struggle was brief; the Gang of Four were under arrest within less than a month. There were two main factions among the winners of this struggle. One was made up of the less extreme Maoists, people who had risen to power during the Cultural Revolution and its aftermath, and who wished to preserve many of Mao's policies, but who (unlike the Gang of Four) were convinced of the need to cooperate with more conservative elements. Their most important leaders were Hua Guofeng (Hua Kuo-feng), an administrator from Hunan whom Mao had designated as his successor a few months before dying, and Wang Dongxing (Wang Tung-hsing), the former commander of Mao's bodyguard, whose control of military forces in the city of Beijing had played a crucial role in the arrest of the Gang of Four. Hua Guofeng came to occupy, simultaneously, the posts of Premier, Communist Party Chairman, and Chairman of the Party's Military Affairs Commission. Even Mao had not held such a combination of offices. This group published an editorial in the *People's Daily* on 7 February 1977, saying that whatever Mao had said must be obeyed and whatever he had decided must be upheld. Critics called this slogan the 'Two Whatevers', and sometimes referred to its advocates as the 'Whatever' faction.

The other main group was made up of Right-wing leaders who had been purged in the Cultural Revolution. Some of them were back in positions of power by the time Mao died, but others were still in disgrace. Deng Xiaoping, the most important member of this group, was not publicly rehabilitated until July 1977. The slogan of this group was 'Seek truth from facts'.

The balance of power appeared fairly even at first. Deng and other recently rehabilitated rightists, while they pushed to reverse much of what Mao Zedong had done during the ten years of the Cultural Revolution, had to mute their public statements to avoid antagonizing the 'Whatever' faction too badly. They blamed leftist excesses on Lin Biao and the Gang of Four, not on Mao himself. They pretended to regard the Cultural Revolution as a great and good thing, whose spirit had been violated by the vile actions of Lin Biao and the Gang of Four. However, as the months went by the Right wing consolidated its position, and the Left weakened. The extent to which the Cultural Revolution as a whole was being re-evaluated was suggested by the changing evaluation of the Red Guards. People began to refer to them, in public discussions of the Cultural Revolution, as the 'beating, smashing, and looting elements'.

Each rightist rehabilitated and restored to a position of influence was another voice to support the rehabilitation of further rightists, and further reductions in the influence of the Left. When the Central Committee of the Communist Party met in the famous Third Plenum[1] in December 1978, the Right-wing elements led by Deng Xiaoping were able to establish effective control.

Wang Dongxing, the most radical person remaining in the top Party leadership after the arrest of the Gang of Four, had lost almost all of his real power by the time of the Third Plenum; other leftists had lost even their nominal positions. Hua Guofeng's status as Mao's chosen heir was losing its value, and perhaps even becoming a liability as veiled remarks began to appear about the foolishness of believing in the 'Two Whatevers'. He lost his major offices soon after; Zhao Ziyang replaced him as Premier in September 1980, Hu Yaobang (Hu Yao-pang) replaced him as Party Chairman in June 1981, and Deng Xiaoping replaced him as Chairman of the Party's Military Affairs Commission in June 1981. China was increasingly dominated by those who wanted to move quickly and decisively away from Mao's policies. As they became more open in repudiating the actions of Mao's last years, they began to discuss in public his responsibility for those actions. By 1980, Mao's portraits and statues were coming down.

The Gang of Four, Mao's most fervent disciples, finally went on trial in the winter of 1980–81 along with some followers of Lin Biao. The trial was intended to complete the discrediting of their Left-wing policies, but also to show China's return to the rule of law. The government said, very loudly, that the defendants were not on trial for having lost a power struggle, but for having used illegal means – committed crimes – in trying to win it. Some of the crimes were rather political in nature, such as saying terrible things about Deng Xiaoping in order to persuade Mao to purge Deng in the spring of 1976, but others were things which would be considered crimes anywhere. Several of the defendants were accused of having framed innocent people of various crimes during the Cultural Revolution, and of having used torture to extract false confessions as part of these frame-ups.

Two of the Gang, Yao Wenyuan and 'helicopter' Wang Hongwen, confessed their crimes and expressed repentance; they were given long prison terms. The other two, Zhang Chunqiao and Mao's widow Jiang Qing, refused to admit they had done anything wrong. Jiang Qing defended herself vocally, denying that she had committed some of the acts attributed to her, and saying that everything she actually had done had been at Mao's orders. Zhang Chunqiao simply refused to dignify the proceedings by saying anything what-

9.2   Jiang Qing during the trial of the Gang of Four, 1981.

ever. Both were given suspended death sentences; they were supposed to have two years to show signs of repentance, at the end of
which time the decision would be made whether to execute them.
(Neither was particularly repentant, but their sentences were com-
muted to imprisonment anyway.)

The anathema pronounced on Lin Biao and the Gang of Four,
the most conspicuous leftist leaders, was reflected on the lower
levels of the Chinese power structure. Deng Xiaoping could not
carry out a clean sweep, but he did remove large numbers of leftists
from Party and government positions.

The new leadership launched a formal reversal of the verdicts
on almost all the people, whether still living or (like Peng Dehuai

and Liu Shaoqi) long since dead, who had been criticized or purged by the Maoist element during the previous twenty years. Deng Xiaoping is said to have reported, in January 1980, that 2,900,000 people had been rehabilitated. The most important group among those being rehabilitated was made up of Communists who had been purged in the Cultural Revolution as followers of the 'capitalist road'. The CCP as a whole was adopting large portions of their path. But beyond this, many victims of the 1957–58 'Anti-Rightist' campaign were rehabilitated, in the flesh or posthumously. Members of the pre-revolutionary capitalist class came once again to enjoy some of the respect which had been shown them, as economic managers, in the mid 1950s just after their factories came under government control.

Even the landlord and rich peasant classes benefited from the change of attitudes. The Communist Party expressed no regret for the harsh way these people had been treated during the land reform of the 1940s and 1950s, but the way the CCP made class status hereditary was making some class labels somewhat ridiculous by the late 1970s. Families classified as landlords were beginning to include children whose *parents* had not even been born at the time these families' lands had been confiscated and distributed to the poor. In 1979 the CCP decided that their days as exploiters were far enough in the past so that most of them no longer needed to be categorized according to their former class status.

The fact that some members of the 'bad classes' were supposed to have their class labels removed did not eliminate discrimination against them. Indeed, some administrators simply did not obey the decision on allowing them to change their class label. However, discrimination was significantly reduced.

The programme of the new leadership was summarized as the 'Four Modernizations' – modernization of agriculture, industry, science–technology, and national defence. These policies involved abandoning important parts both of the details and of the spirit of Maoism. Explicitly, they involved the adoption of Western-style technology, some of which had to come from foreign countries. Implicitly they involved placing much less reliance on the collective spirit of the masses.

The status and privileges of the intellectuals increased tremendously. In education there was a renewed stress on academic achievement and a downgrading of egalitarian ideals. Leftist leaders had stressed the goal of giving at least some sort of education to everyone; they had hoped to make not only primary education but also several years of secondary schooling universal as quickly as possible. The moderate leadership that came to power in 1976 did not completely abandon these goals, but it assigned them a lower priority. The main thrust after 1976 was on providing a really good education to a limited number of people. The Cultural Revolution had led to a tremendous expansion in secondary education, while college enrolments had dropped. This naturally affected the quality of secondary schooling; in Guangxi province, for instance, it created a situation in which only about 30 per cent of the senior-middle-school teachers were college graduates. After 1976, as leftist policies were repudiated, college enrolments expanded rapidly, while the growth of secondary enrolments slowed and in some areas was even reversed.

Academic standards were raised. Some schools at every level were designated as 'key' institutions; they were given the best teachers, the best students, and more funds. Some of the key secondary schools, in turn, chose to concentrate on teaching their best students, the ones likely to shed glory on the school by achieving college admission, and gave little attention to the average and below-average students. ('Key' schools and the use of streaming within schools seemed rather extreme departures from egalitarian ideals, even by post-Maoist standards, and these concepts therefore came under attack late in 1981.)

Students were once more admitted to colleges primarily on the basis of written entrance examinations. Students were allowed to proceed directly from secondary school to college, without an intervening period in productive labour. The requirement that they devote a large proportion of their time to manual labour during their years as students was also relaxed. The idea that China must import large amounts of foreign technology was once more accepted, and thousands of Chinese students were sent to study in capitalist countries. The rewards for academic excellence increased significantly; not only could one win a place in the next higher level of the educational system, but when one was through with school one could generally avoid being assigned to work in the countryside.

Competition for entrance to colleges and universities was very keen. Education was once more the main channel of upward mobility, and China could not, in the foreseeable future, hope to give a college education to more than a fraction of the people wanting one. In 1980, only 4.6 per cent of the graduates of senior middle schools passed the entrance examinations for institutions of higher learning.

The number of peasants in secondary and tertiary institutions may have been significantly lower under these policies than under the Maoist line. However, one should note that under these policies a small number of peasants received a first-rate academic education, while under the Maoists no peasants at all received such an education, because no such thing was available to anyone of any class.

By 1979 the programmes for sending educated youth from the cities to the countryside were being cut back sharply, and those young people who did well in secondary school were no longer in serious danger of being 'sent down'. The government was not even able to keep in the countryside those who had been sent down in previous years. These young people became quite aggressive about asserting their newly restored status; some from Shanghai, allowed to visit their homes for a holiday in the spring of 1979, rioted and stopped rail traffic for several hours to protest the fact that they had not received permission to return to the city permanently. Of the 10 million in the countryside in late 1978, about half had returned to the cities, legally or illegally, by the autumn of 1979; most of the remainder had done so by the end of 1980. Those in the cities illegally posed the greatest social problems. They had neither a great respect for authority, nor much access to gainful employment. This combination produced the same result in China as in many other societies: a wave of crimes committed by unemployed youths.

Improvements in the status of the educated had both positive and negative implications for the economy. The extent to which technically trained people could be fitted into crucial jobs, and the extent to which the best qualified candidates could be chosen for training, clearly improved. In 1980, Hu Yaobang (soon to replace Hua Guofeng as Chairman of the Chinese Communist Party) argued that recent improvements in the position of the intellectuals were not only desirable, they needed to go much further than they had.

> We must value intellectuals and attach due importance to culture and education. Intellectuals play an important role. In our country there is a general lack of learning among our people, and learning is inseparable from intellectuals. We have not yet finished our job of implementing the relevant policies towards intellectuals. Intellectuals have not been used appropriately enough. They still face many practical problems, such as housing, separation from spouses, and wages. Yet, surprisingly, there are comrades who have declared that our

treatment of intellectuals is overdone and that intellectuals are beginning to show conceit. The existence of this attitude shows that there are great obstacles to implementing policies on intellectuals. Now when the intellectuals have just begun to raise their heads, a few comrades are trying to beat them down. This demands that we work on these comrades.

For years our attitude towards learning and intellectuals has been in many respects neither materialist nor Marxist. Today we must change this state in which intellectuals are discriminated against.

On the other hand, the improved status of the educated gave them freedom to do as they wished, and this sometimes went against the short-term and even the long-term interests of the economy. The return of educated young people from the countryside to the cities was sometimes very clearly against the national interest. In cities where there was not work for them, local officials sometimes ended by creating jobs for them, jobs that did not make much use of their education. Their political influence had proven adequate to make the government go out of its way to provide work for them where they wanted to live, rather than send them to where they were needed.

The question of individual freedom

It is possible to exaggerate the extent to which personal freedom was expanded after the fall of the Gang of Four. Serious opposition to the Communist system, or actions likely to compromise national unity, were not permitted. Also, the Party maintained and even strengthened some policies that by the standards of most societies would be remarkable intrusions on the life of individuals. That secondary-school graduates were no longer shipped out to the countryside *en masse* did not mean that people were allowed to live where they wished; what it meant was that the bureaucrats who told people where they had to live were more friendly to secondary-school graduates than they formerly had been. Most peasants were still bound to the villages. In the cities the government used a great array of very strong pressures to make people postpone marriage, and avoid having many children once they did marry (see below).

Some dissidents came into the open, especially in Beijing, to demand increased democracy, but they were repressed quite severely when the government felt they had gone too far. For a few months there was a 'Democracy Wall' in Beijing, where dissidents were allowed to display wall posters criticizing the regime. It was established in November 1978, just as the balance of power within the Communist Party was swinging decisively in favour of Deng Xiaoping. Posters began to appear demanding that the legacy of Maoism be repudiated much more completely than was occurring at that time, that a wide range of misbehaviour by cadres and officials be corrected, and that the range of personal freedom be expanded drastically. Some of these posters actually criticized Mao by name, something unheard of until that time. Once it had become apparent that the Party had decided at least temporarily not to interfere, the wall became a medium for the expression of a startling range of ideas. Some posters commented openly on the fact that the Chinese people had less freedom and less control over their government than the people of many foreign countries. The posters could reach far more than just the people who came physically to read them; foreign journalists regularly visited the wall, read important posters, and sent out of the country summaries which were then incorporated into radio news broadcasts. Chinese in many cities could listen to foreign radio broadcasts and keep track of what was appearing on the wall in Beijing. Within a few weeks the dissidents moved from writing wall posters to publishing journals and establishing formal organizations, such as the China Human Rights Alliance.

The posters on the 'Democracy Wall' represented the next stage of the development that had begun in the Tiananmen demonstrations of April 1976, when political statements defying the current Party line had been attached to many of the wreaths commemorating Zhou Enlai. Indeed one of the major demands in posters on the Democracy Wall was that the officials responsible for the suppression of the Tiananmen demonstrations be punished.

The dissident movement, in Beijing and elsewhere, was profoundly disturbing to the typical Communist bureaucrat, who had grown accustomed to an environment in which Party policy could not be questioned or criticized. Even Deng Xiaoping, who agreed with some of the criticisms voiced on the Democracy Wall, and was not terrified of the notion that views with which he disagreed could be aired in public, may have been annoyed with the more extreme of the dissidents. The most conspicuous was Wei Jingsheng, a twenty-eight-year-old electrician who had been a Red Guard in Beijing during the Cultural Revolution. Wei attacked the whole Communist political system. He argued that the Four

Modernizations would be a sham unless a fifth modernization – democracy – were added. He denounced Deng for making only a pretence of introducing democracy while in fact practising dictatorship. The bureaucrats must have been greatly relieved when Wei gave them an excuse to act against him: they inflated his willingness to talk to foreigners about the border fighting between China and Vietnam into a charge of furnishing military secrets to foreigners. He was arrested in March 1979, and before the end of the year he had been tried and sentenced to fifteen years in prison. Others were also arrested.

The Party leadership, ending the period of uncertainty that had allowed dissidents even as extreme as Wei Jingsheng to speak out for a few months, announced that the four fundamental principles under which the PRC operated were: (1) the socialist road; (2) the people's democratic dictatorship (dictatorship of the proletariat); (3) the leadership of the Communist Party; (4) Marxism–Leninism and Mao Zedong Thought. As the Central Committee put it in 1981, 'Any word or deed which denies or undermines these four principles cannot be tolerated'. The Democracy Wall in Beijing was closed down in December 1979; most of those in other cities had already been abolished. During 1980 the Party decided to remove from the Constitution a provision guaranteeing the right to put up wall posters.

The Party had not, however, restricted speech to anything like the extent that had occurred in Mao's last years. It was sometimes possible to disagree with particular policies of the Party without attacking, or being accused of having attacked, the four fundamental principles. Perhaps even more important than this widening of the limits of permitted speech was the change in the spirit with which the limits were enforced. The citizen who wished to ignore politics and get on with his or her own affairs could do so in relative safety. Few political cadres were inclined to leap at the first sign of ideological deviation, and place the worst possible construction on it. Only through the most extraordinary bad luck did the person who had made a single careless statement, or who had said something ambiguous which might be interpreted as an attack on Party policies, get into serious trouble. It was even possible

9.3 (a)   'Democracy Wall', Beijing, 1979. Chinese reading posters critical of the Beijing Government on a brick barrier around a bus depot that became the focal point of dissent.
9.3 (b)   'Democracy Wall', Beijing, 1979. Workers attacking the famous wall to remove all posters except the one banning posters from the wall.

for dissidents to test the limits of the system, doing things which they knew might lie beyond the range of permissible action, gambling on the probability that if they did not venture far beyond the limits they would not be punished too severely. China's situation was roughly equivalent to that which had existed in the Soviet Union since Khrushchev dismantled Stalinism in the 1950s, though controls on expression were probably still a bit more stringent in China. This was far from constituting free speech, but it represented a tremendous loosening of the restrictions that had existed up to 1976.

Freedom of artistic creativity followed approximately the same path as freedom of political expression. There was a burst of liberalism in the late 1970s, when Deng Xiaoping and the moderates were just consolidating their power, but soon the Party renewed demands that art and literature serve the cause of socialism.

China and the world

Chinese foreign policy after the death of Mao continued to be dominated by hatred of the Soviet Union. This was extended to Vietnam, which after the end of the Vietnam War in 1975 drew increasingly close to the Soviet Union. By the end of 1975 a single Vietnamese government had effective control over all of Vietnam and Laos; in 1978, after bloody border skirmishes, it moved in addition to conquer Cambodia. China felt that for a Soviet ally to have this much power in Southeast Asia was intolerable. China supported Cambodian resistance to Vietnam both diplomatically and through an invasion of Vietnam in early 1979, designed to draw off Vietnamese troops from Cambodia.

Chinese diplomats all over the world urged other nations to distrust and oppose the Soviet Union. In a striking reversal of earlier pronouncements, China even took the attitude that strong NATO armed forces were a contribution to world peace.

China greatly expanded its contacts with the United States and Western Europe after 1976. In some areas, as with the establishment of full diplomatic relations with the United States in 1979, China was simply continuing to work on the goals Mao had set in the early 1970s. But by 1979 the Chinese and US governments were even willing to cooperate in military matters if they could do so quietly. The United States agreed to supply very advanced equipment for an electronic observation post in Xinjiang, to eavesdrop on the communications of missile-testing ranges in the Soviet Union. The equipment was manned by Chinese, but the data which it acquired was shared with the United States. In 1980, in the aftermath of the Soviet invasion of Afghanistan, military cooperation became more public. The US Secretary of Defense, Harold Brown, toured Chinese defence installations, and the USA announced its willingness to sell non-lethal military equipment to the PRC. In 1981 this was broadened to include the possible sale of military weapons, but the USA continued to restrict the sale of high technology, both in regard to weapons and to civilian items such as computers which might be turned to military uses.

In 1983, the USA decided to ease the restrictions even on advanced technology, but some limits still remained, as was indicated by the arrest in February 1984 of five people charged with conspiring to smuggle over $1,000 m. worth of very advanced military equipment to China in violation of US law.

The willingness of the Western powers to sell weapons to China had much smaller results than might have been expected. The principal problem was simply money; China could not even begin to pay for all of the equipment its antiquated armed forces needed. Officers who for years had been told that they could not have a lot of modern weapons because what mattered in warfare was the human factor – fighting spirit and the support of the masses – were told instead that they could not have modern weapons because the country could not afford them. The result was a great deal of negotiation over arms purchases, but few deals actually consummated. A £100 m. agreement for Britain to equip destroyers of the Chinese Navy with electronic equipment and Sea Dart missiles, for instance, fell through in 1983 because the Chinese decided they could not afford such a purchase.

Economic contacts with the West, already broadening in the early and mid 1970s, continued to develop. In Mao's last years the Chinese were buying considerable numbers of factories from foreign capitalists; by 1983 they were negotiating for the purchase of four nuclear reactors. The tourist trade continued to expand; over 200,000 foreigners visited China in 1981. China even entered into joint business ventures, in which a foreign capitalist helped to build a factory in China and remained part-owner, with a right to part of the output. Major petroleum companies such as British Petroleum (BP), Atlantic-Richfield (ARCO), Exxon, and Shell obtained contracts to explore for oil in China's territorial waters.

Educational exchanges had much more far-reaching implications. In a direct sense, China accepted the fact that the type of knowledge in which the West surpassed China was vitally important, and that China had to learn from the foreigners. This carried the implication that having learned from the Westerners could be a legitimate source of prestige and perhaps even power for a Chinese. The limited expansion of the number of foreigners permitted to study in China, and in some cases teach in Chinese colleges, seemed unlikely to have massive effects. However, a much larger number of Chinese were going abroad for study. By 1983 there were 9,000 or more Chinese studying just in the United States. Such students learned about the much higher standard of living abroad, and encountered a range of ideas and permitted behaviour incomparably greater than that found in China in recent decades. There was a clear possibility that some of them might become profoundly subversive influences when they returned home.

The CCP did its best to minimize contact between Western visitors and the Chinese people, but it was aware that some such contact would occur none the less. The *People's Daily* commented that in the process of borrowing and learning from the outside world, some things would be brought into China which should not have been, but that people should not become alarmed and should not use this as grounds to cut off importation of foreign things.

There were, of course, a variety of sources of friction between China and the West. Some were momentary, such as the US decision to grant political asylum to the Chinese tennis-player Hu Na in 1983. Of the long-term problems, the most important was Taiwan, where the government of the Republic of China (the Guomindang regime) still claimed to be the government of all China. The PRC suggested that the problem of reunification might be settled by a compromise, in which Taiwan would retain substantial autonomy and even its own armed forces, but the Guomindang firmly rejected such offers.

The USA, the last major power maintaining full diplomatic relations with the Republic of China, announced in December 1978 that it intended to break off those relations, and did so early in 1979. The USA also terminated (with one year's notice) its mutual defence treaty with the Republic of China. However, the USA and other nations continued to maintain informal diplomatic ties with Taiwan. The PRC expressed annoyance at such ties, and especially at the sale of arms to Taiwan.

The problem of Hong Kong, while not involving a hostile confrontation, had to be settled somehow. Most of the land area of

9.4   China's Premier, Zhao Ziyang, toasts British Premier Margaret Thatcher at a banquet in Beijing, 1982.

Hong Kong (89 per cent) was legally part of China; Britain had only leased it from China, and the lease ran only until 1997. In the early 1980s, the Chinese indicated that they wanted to recover all of Hong Kong (not just the leased portion). A visit to Beijing by British Prime Minister Margaret Thatcher in 1982 did not settle the conflict between the British view that British rule was in the best interests of Hong Kong, and the Chinese view that Hong Kong was Chinese territory and had to be returned to China. In September 1984 the British agreed that all of Hong Kong would revert to Chinese sovereignty in 1997. With the leased territories gone, the colony of Hong Kong would have been too small to be viable if the Chinese did not approve of it.

Hong Kong's prosperity was economically very important to China, and the PRC agreed to allow capitalism to persist there for fifty years after the resumption of Chinese rule, but many in Hong Kong remained fearful. The very limited toleration of private enterprise in China, in the early 1980s, would not have come close to satisfying the freewheeling capitalists of Hong Kong.

By 1982, offended by US restrictions on trade and by the continuing relationship between the United States and Taiwan, the Chinese began to distance themselves from the USA and to improve

9.5   President Ronald Reagan and China's Premier Zhao Ziyang outside the White House, 10 January 1984.

their relations with the Soviet Union. This ended, at least for the moment, prospects that the USA and China might actually become allies. Sino-Soviet trade revived to some extent, and in 1983 the two countries began exchanging a small number of students, for the first time in over twenty years. However, there was no real thaw between China and the Soviet Union; China remained sharply critical of Soviet behaviour in Afghanistan and Indo-China. In the second half of 1983, after a substantial loosening of US restrictions on trade with China, the relationship between China and the USA began to improve again. Early in 1984, Chinese Premier Zhao Ziyang visited the USA as well as Canada; US President Reagan soon visited China in return.

In search of prosperity

China's great problem remained its fundamental poverty. Most of the people still lived in poor villages, where they scraped out a living without enough machinery, fertilizer, or land. Most villages were still not far above subsistence level; when crops failed through drought or flood, as they did in parts of two provinces in 1980, the peasants went hungry.

The most obvious way to attack poverty was to increase production, in all sectors of the economy. The problem here was that the easiest way to increase production was to increase capital inputs, and China could only afford a limited amount of capital construction. When the Four Modernizations first won acceptance as guidelines for government policy, many industrial planners assumed they would get the large modern factories of which they had dreamed for so long. China went on a construction binge. Whole factories were purchased from abroad; others were built with local resources. Coordination was poor; sometimes two factories were built where there were only enough raw materials, or only enough electric power, for one factory actually to function. Besides this, the range of projects being started simply ran beyond what the Chinese economy could pay for. By 1978 the frenzy for new projects reached a level that reminded some people of the Great Leap Forward. In 1981 the government was forced to adopt stern restrictions on capital construction.

There were also shifts in the structure of the economy. The Party turned away from the doctrine that each commune should be as self-sufficient as possible, taking grain production as the 'key link', and thus minimizing the capitalist behaviour patterns implicit in specialist production units which produced a few items, which they sold to other units in return for the things they needed. Under Deng Xiaoping, economic units were permitted to take more initiative in producing what they could produce well, for the market, even when this reduced their self-sufficiency. Enterprises were supposed to run at a profit. If they could not do so – if the value of their output did not exceed their costs – the government would at least consider closing them down, and a correct revolutionary attitude would not necessarily save them.

In an effort to promote agricultural production, the government released many of the restrictions on the 'spontaneous capitalist tendencies' of the peasantry. The income of a family came to depend much more on the production of that family, rather than being the family's share of the production of a larger group. Experiments with the 'responsibility system', in which a family or a small group of families was given responsibility for a piece of land or an enterprise owned by their production team, brigade, or commune, occurred quite widely in 1979. Soon afterwards some of the provincial officials who had played a major role in these experiments were promoted to top positions in Beijing; Zhao Ziyang from Sichuan became Premier, and Wan Li from Anhui became Vice-Premier. The responsibility system was spread rapidly on a nationwide basis.

Families signed contracts with the collective organizations that owned land, by which the family promised to achieve a certain level of production, and would be rewarded very handsomely for exceeding the contract level. Some were even allowed simply to take any production above the contract level and sell it, for their own benefit, in local markets. In some versions of the responsibility system, there was still effective central planning. The brigade or production team decided what crops would be grown on a certain piece of land, how much fertilizer would be applied, and so forth, and the individual families were simply responsible for carrying out the plan competently. In other versions, nearly universal by 1984, individual families made almost all the decisions.

Late in 1980, the government decided to expand the scope of private marketing. The next step was to increase the amount of land assigned to the peasants as private plots to about 15 per cent of all agricultural land. The peasants were not responsible to the government for the use they made of their private plots; they could simply grow what they wished, for sale to the government or in private markets.

The peasants were still forbidden to go into commerce – to buy things that other people had produced, for resale at a profit. However, they had opportunities to adapt their productive activities to the goal of maximum personal profit which would have been unthinkable a few years earlier. In 1981, the *People's Daily* told peasants who were thinking of getting rich quickly by going into illegal commercial activities (which did exist on a significant scale) that instead they should try something like taking over management, on contract, of communally owned fish-ponds or banana groves. They were told that by doing this they could enrich themselves quite rapidly *without* violating current government policies. Three years later, even the restrictions on private commerce were loosening.

The Chinese press admitted openly that this represented an abandonment of radical egalitarianism; if incomes were keyed to results, some people would do better than others.

> Let some localities in the country and a section of the peasants prosper first . . .
> Facts have proved that it amounts to sheer illusion to suppose that socialism can be built by deliberately preventing

9.6   Fruit for sale in a market at Jinan, the capital of Shandong Province.

people from getting rich . . .

It is equally absurd to maintain a low income level for people in relatively prosperous areas or units to prevent a possible polarization of society.

In some communes the system of assigning land on contract to individual families, which managed it as if they were operating family farms, amounted in practice to a dismantling of the collective economy, and a return to private farming. Furthermore, it was suggested as early as 1980 that this *should* be carried to the point of *de facto* abolition of collective agriculture, in very large areas. There was opposition to this proposal, and most Party leaders emphasized that individual management of farmland operated within a framework of collective ownership, that the peasants had only the use of the land (not rights such as sale or rental, which they would have had if they had been its owners), and that cadres should not associate individual family management with actual ownership by forming the habit of assigning to people, for individual management, precisely the farms that their families had owned before collectivization. The amount of land allocated to a family was to depend on the present number of people in the family, not on how much land it had contributed when cooperatives were formed in the 1950s. By 1984, however, the government announced that almost all land was to be allocated to the peasants on fifteen-year contracts. Some peasants were in fact renting out their contract land. Collective agriculture was virtually dead.

In 1982 the government decided to strip the communes of their main political and administrative functions, reducing them essentially to economic units.

The shift towards free enterprise methods in agriculture required that the principal showcase of Maoist methods be discredited. This was the Dazhai production brigade, located in the hills of Shanxi province in northern China. The peasants of Dazhai had, through monumental exertion, transformed unusable hillsides and gulches into fertile fields. They operated on highly egalitarian principles, without the usual amount of land devoted to private plots. The whole country had been urged to learn from Dazhai. It seemed a textbook case of Maoist ideals in action; it demonstrated that peasants working in a collectivist spirit, casting off personal greed and the desire for individual rewards, relying on their own powers rather than on money and modern technology, could accomplish anything to which they set their minds. Through correct application of Maoist ideas, Dazhai was credited with having built a prosperous agriculture in one of the least promising areas of China.

The rightists may or may not have suspected all along that this was too good to be true. In any case, after investigation they announced that it had not been true. Dazhai's supposed spirit of self-reliance had in fact been supported by substantial government subsidies, and even with the subsidies the actual level of production attained had not always been as high as the Maoists had claimed.

A certain amount of capitalist enterprise also came to be accepted in industry. A Chinese who had funds could invest them in a workshop, hire people to work, and earn a profit out of the work done by the employees. In other words he could, quite openly, engage in what was by Marxist economics a form of exploitation. Special zones were established in which capitalists from outside China could set up factories, and make a profit from the labour of Chinese workers. The CCP seemed unsure just how far it would permit either of these practices to go, but the fact that they were occurring at all represented an astonishing abandonment of former policies.

Finally, market principles were introduced into socialist industrial enterprises. In November 1981, the government began (very cautiously and hesitantly) to introduce policies under which urban workers had a certain degree of freedom to search for jobs on their own, rather than simply being assigned jobs. At the same time, factories and other enterprises were given greater authority to fire workers who flagrantly failed to do their jobs. By 1983, the contract system (under which socialist enterprises contracted out certain operations to private individuals) was beginning to spread into retail distribution, service industries, and some light manufacturing industries.

Controlling population growth was as vital as increasing production. Even the Maoists had understood the need for population control, despite the way their ideology made them reluctant to acknowledge in clear language that China had too many people. In the early 1970s they had developed one of the most vigorous birth-control programmes in the world. Deng Xiaoping and his colleagues, feeling less obligated to 'respect the people', were even more determined to slow and eventually reverse the growth of population. By 1979, the growth rate was reported down to 1.17 per cent.

The problem was that once population growth had built up momentum, it was very hard to stop. In the early 1980s, when the Chinese population passed the 1,000 million level, it contained a high proportion of people just approaching marriagable age, but only a small proportion of very old people. Even if the government could have succeeded in its effort to persuade every married couple to settle for one child, the number of couples reaching the age of marriage each year, and having their one child, would have been greater than the number of old people who died, and the population would have continued to grow until the age distribution had adjusted itself. The best the Chinese even hoped to accomplish was to bring the growth of the population to a halt by about the year 2000, at a level of about 1,200 million. It could then start shrinking to a more reasonable figure.

The government tried to encourage the use of contraception not only by moral suasion, but also by offering preference to small families in the distribution of ration coupons, in admission to higher education, and in job placement. The system for allocating land to peasant households either as private plots or under the responsibility system, which at first assigned land to each family in proportion to the number of people in the family and thus encouraged childbearing, was modified to reward smaller families.

The government continued to encourage postponement of marriage as a birth-control device, but it did not rely so heavily on this tactic as had the Maoists. In 1980 the minimum legal age for marriage was set at twenty years for women, twenty-two years for men. This was higher than the previous legal age limit, but not as high as the *de facto* limits of twenty-three for women and twenty-five for men that the government of the mid 1970s, in line with its determination to eradicate selfishness and the search for individual gratification, had tried to enforce. Both the government and the population assumed that virtually all young people would marry; the family system remained strong enough to make a life without marriage almost unthinkable. (Some young people who really did not want marriage found that they could not defy social pressures to wed, but could arrange to marry someone whose work assignment was in a distant province, and thus ensure that the marriage would be purely a formality.)

Compliance with government policies was far from universal. Many people had a sense of proper family life that led them to want numerous children. This applied especially to households that had produced only daughters and were determined to keep trying until they got a son. In 1981, there were about 1,700,000 children born into families that already had five or more children. The government was better able to limit births in the cities than in the countryside, where the traditional family structure was much stronger and where children were often a major economic asset for a family.

Government efforts to persuade people to limit their reproduction were supplemented by sheer coercion. Every woman was required to plan her childbearing in consultation with local cadres, and although the basis of the system was supposed to be voluntary, women who became pregnant without permission were sometimes in fact forced to have abortions. A family-planning conference in Guangdong province, in mid 1983, decided that family-planning personnel should concentrate their efforts on compulsory sterilizations for parents having two or more children. By this time the ideal of the one-child family was an effective reality in many cities and even some areas of the countryside. There were cases in which parents killed female infants so as to be able to try for a son without violating the prohibitions against having too many children.

The CCP faces the future

In June of 1981, the Central Committee of the CCP produced an official re-evaluation of the history of the Party, summing up the lessons of its thirty-two years in power. This document contained a total repudiation of the Cultural Revolution. It mentioned some constructive accomplishments which had been made during the Cultural Revolution, but at the end of the list it commented: 'Needless to say, none of these successes can be attributed in any way to the "cultural revolution", without which we would have scored far greater achievements for our cause.' One sees no mention of any useful results of the Cultural Revolution which really were connected with its fundamental goals, such as the spread of 'barefoot doctors', or the fact that individual peasants in at least some areas, however helpless they remained when faced with arbitrary decisions made in Beijing, really did have a better chance of resisting an unjust decision by an individual village cadre after the Cultural Revolution than before it. One sees, indeed, no acknowledgement that the Cultural Revolution had any goals worthy of serious consideration. Mao, seeing Communist functionaries behaving in a way he felt was unpleasantly reminiscent of the pre-revolutionary bourgeoisie, had spoken out in vague and apocalyptic language suggesting that the Party was becoming a bourgeois organization. The Central Committee position of 1981 was that since it was not true that the pre-revolutionary bourgeoisie had infiltrated and taken over the Party, Mao must simply have been suffering from some sort of delusion. The Central Committee wished to sweep under the rug the real complexity of Mao's views. It was able to do so, at least for the moment, partly because most of the people who wrote and talked about such issues were intellectuals who had suffered in the Cultural Revolution and had no desire to bring up the idea that it might have had some rational motivation, and partly because Mao had never presented his views to the public in a clear and rational form.

Repudiation of the Cultural Revolution, however, did not mean repudiation of Mao; he was still treated as a great revolutionary, whose merits far outweighed his errors. China's new leaders may genuinely have respected Mao's tremendous accomplishments during the early stages of the revolution; in any case they did not wish to see his memory become a rallying point for opposition to them, the way Zhou Enlai's ghost had become the leader of opposition to the leftists in 1976. They said that Mao was the man who, more than anyone else, had originally set the revolution on the correct path: 'Our Party and people would have had to grope in the dark much longer had it not been for comrade Mao Zedong . . .' He was the one who had adapted Marxism–Leninism to fit the concrete conditions of China, and the synthesis he had worked out, Mao Zedong Thought, was and should remain the guiding light of the CCP. The Central Committee dealt with the question of the Cultural Revolution, in this context, in a startlingly simple manner: it decided that Mao Zedong Thought consisted only of Mao's correct (earlier) ideas; that what Mao as an individual believed in the last decade of his life had nothing to do with 'Mao Zedong Thought', and indeed contradicted it. This seemed breathtakingly cynical, but it allowed Mao's name to be used as a symbol and a prop for a system Mao had spent ten years trying to destroy.

China's new leaders faced tremendous challenges. They said that their supreme goal, to which everything had to be subordinated, was developing the Chinese economy – bringing the country out of the state of extreme poverty which still afflicted it. Almost all Chinese approved this goal, but there were many groups which might, someday, challenge the way the goal was being pursued. The wild swings in policy that the Party had undergone in the past twenty-five years had undermined its authority; only a total amnesiac could believe that whatever the Communist Party said must, *ipso facto*, be correct.

Would intellectuals and writers remain satisfied with the limited expansion of free speech? They were in contact with foreign countries where the range of personal freedom was very much greater, and some of them wanted the same degree of freedom in China. Many veteran bureaucrats, on the other hand, were shocked by even the modest degree to which controls had been loosened after 1976. They published attacks on 'bourgeois liberalism' in art and literature, and if they felt sufficiently threatened they might demand a clampdown far more severe than the one that had led to the closing of the Democracy Wall and the imprisonment of Wei Jingsheng in 1979.

Allowing people to follow their own economic self-interest worked out well in the short run, giving the economy needed flexibility. However, the Party was permitting people to try to get rich quickly; it would increasingly face the concrete question of dealing with wealthy individuals within a system in which egalitarian goals, even if muted, formed part of the ideological underpinnings. Consider the problem posed by a certain tractor driver in Guangdong. Fellow villagers had helped make arrangements, and possibly paid part of the cost, for him to get training in handling a tractor. They had expected that once trained he would use his new skills to plough their fields. However, in the spring of 1981 he bought his own tractor, hired an assistant, and went into the transport business, hauling cargo on a trailer pulled by the tractor. He was able to earn what was by local standards a princely income. His neighbours' fields went unploughed; they could not afford to pay him, for the very time-consuming job of ploughing, the hourly rate he could earn in the transport business. The most fascinating thing about this was that he got away with it, at least in the short run. Such an extreme of selfishness was in violation of CCP policy even in 1981, but local cadres could not or would not put a quick stop to it.

Concentrations of wealth in private hands strengthened some other aspects of traditional culture that the CCP did not like. In Guangdong province, by the early 1980s some of this money was going to restore the old clan organizations, and even clan feuds were reviving.

Deng Xiaoping and his cohorts stressed order, stability, unity, the rule of law, and prosperity. They were trying to restore confidence in impersonal institutions, to reverse the trend of the 1960s which had made Chinese politics so much a matter of conflicts between individuals and factions. They criticized the 'cult of personality' which often gave a single individual absolute power over his subordinates, either at the national level or in provincial and local organizations. They distinguished offices from the individuals who held them; they repudiated the unwritten rule under which Party leaders had lifetime tenure in their jobs, unless purged for some ghastly doctrinal error. They also tried to streamline administration. By the second quarter of 1982, restructuring of the central government's ministries had reduced the number of ministers and vice-ministers from 505 to 167.

Conversion to the rule of law was more difficult. Party policy for many years had taken precedence over formal law. This not only coloured attitudes and expectations, it left China with only the most rudimentary laws, and hardly any lawyers. Deng had new legal codes written, but there remained the problems of training lawyers to interpret and implement them, and persuading Party functionaries into the habit of obeying them. The networks of *guanxi* (personal relationships and obligations) among bureaucrats often remained more influential than formal rules.

The great advantage of the new policy line, which quickly won it considerable success, was that it relied much more on the carrot and less on the stick in winning compliance with its policies. Coercion was still substantial, but it played a much smaller role in government policy than it had before 1976. The Maoist line of economic development had called for self-sacrifice; it had called on the people to work hard and unselfishly to build a better China, in which all would someday benefit. Deng Xiaoping felt that the quickest way to build a better China was to improve living conditions immediately, to give people the level of morale they needed for further development. The economic readjustment of 1981 called, quite deliberately, for cutting back on capital construction to allow more production of consumer goods. Aside from the fact that Deng's policies seemed likely to lead to a higher level of long-term growth, they proved more tolerable to the people in the short run. However, one should bear in mind that while standards of living were rising, they were still very low, and most Chinese were likely to be very poor, by any reasonable standard, for many years to come.

The Communist Party's authority had been compromised by the turmoil of the years since 1966, and it was by no means able to impose total unity and discipline on a society where many people were seriously dissatisfied with their lives. The Party itself, 40 million strong, had considerable internal divisions; in the autumn of 1983, the leadership announced still another drive to deal with corruption and Left-wing factionalism within the Party.

Many young people were frankly cynical about politics. Some students treated their compulsory courses in Marxist theory with undisguised apathy, even with contempt; this would have been unthinkable a few years earlier. China was plagued by social ills that the Communist had once believed could not occur to any serious extent under socialism – smuggling, embezzlement, robbery, rape, and so forth. The Sichuan provincial government found it necessary in June 1982 to issue an order forbidding anyone to carry weapons, explosives, or pornographic books into a school.

The future and the past

The Right wing had prevailed over the Left, but the Right was itself subject to serious internal divisions. For one thing, there was the conflict pitting dictatorially minded bureaucrats against advocates

9.7 In the second half of 1983, the PRC staged numerous well-publicized executions in an effort to deter a serious crime wave, which included drug-trafficking. Here, convicted drug-dealers in black gowns, their legs manacled and hands tied behind their backs, arrive at the execution ground at Beijing. Such an execution would be preceded by the public burning of large amounts of drugs, and followed by the dumping of the corpses into crude coffins for the criminals' cemetery.

of increased personal freedom. In the economic sphere, the expansion of what might be called the 'free-enterprise' sector of the Chinese economy was so great as to guarantee eventual conflict over just how large it should be permitted to grow. Disputes over freedom of political expression were not such a major issue, since in this regard the bureaucracy was more united and more firmly in control of the situation, but the suppression of the Democracy Wall did not settle this issue completely.

Within the bureaucracy itself, rising young technocrats struggled for power against entrenched office-holders. Many key positions were held by ageing men without much technical training, who had come to office when educational standards were very low. Forty per cent of the cadres in China had a junior middle school education or below. These men had always assumed that they would hold office as long as they lived, and they were prepared to resist strenuously any suggestions to the contrary. Deng Xiaoping was determined to promote people really capable of modernizing and streamlining China's economy, but he had no magic wand capable of conveniently eliminating China's 'geriatric leadership'.

The most extreme Left-wing leaders – the Gang of Four and their allies – seemed totally discredited. Most politically articulate Chinese saw the egalitarian ideals they had preached as mere posturing, as a set of rationalizations for policies that harmed development without really promoting equality. Such leaders were unlikely to make a comeback. However, the egalitarian tradition was firmly rooted both in Marxist theory and in the history of the Chinese Revolution. As long as the CCP continued to treat Marx and Mao as great revolutionary thinkers, people dissatisfied with the system as they found it would have the option of trying to revive the more radical aspects of Marxist and Maoist ideas. Intellectuals could use these ideas in a struggle against the bureaucracy; the bureaucrats could use them either against the intellectuals or against the private sector. It was noteworthy that Li Xiannian (Li Hsien-nien), who became Chief of State in 1983, was a man who had got along with the Maoists, before 1976, much better than had Deng Xiaoping.

A look at the salient surface issues in Chinese politics might have suggested that China had almost totally escaped its past. None of the great traditions – Confucian, Legalist, Daoist, or Buddhist – still had a central role in intellectual life. They had been replaced by the imported and radically different ideology of Marxism. The intellectuals had been westernized. China was still ruled by a centralized bureaucracy, but it was different in organization and function from the one that had ruled in previous centuries. Those Chinese who chose to rehash old political disputes seldom went further back than 1955.

Much continuity with the past remained, however. Educational attainment was still the first step in upward mobility. The startling dichotomy between a people of great commercial talent and a government that did not respect commerce remained. The bulk of the population was still made up of peasants, who remained much closer to the Chinese past than the urban minority. Their lack of adequate land, technology, and education left them very poor. Furthermore, the post-Mao reforms had brought the methods by which the peasants dealt with these problems much closer to the family-centred pattern of past centuries. Male domination of the family, while not as blatant as in past centuries, was still very strong, Even traditional religious beliefs and superstitions were reviving to some extent.

China's long-term prospects remained very unclear. There was no visible prospect of a return to the Cultural Revolution. However, the CCP was experimenting with a degree of liberalization that went far beyond a mere repudiation of the Cultural Revolution, and there was no guarantee that it would like the results. It might move either back towards traditional Communist orthodoxy, or towards some modified form of Maoism. On the other hand, there was the possibility that the reforms would go even further than they had. Only after the post-Mao leaders had not only developed a new ideological framwork, but proven it stable over a long period, proven it capable of serving as the basis for an effective authority system, would it be possible to say that they had succeeded in putting the nation on a new course.

Notes

1. This was the third plenary meeting the Central Committee had held since the Party Congress of August 1977.

Suggestions for Further Reading

Serials

The most important all-purpose journal dealing with China is the *China Quarterly*, which contains not only articles, but also reviews of recent books, and a 'Quarterly Chronicle and Documentation' section, which summarizes events in China's domestic and international affairs and sometimes gives full translated texts of major documents. *Modern China*, which also appears on a quarterly basis, contains only full-length articles.

Beijing Review (formerly *Peking Review*) is a weekly magazine published by the Chinese government. It deals with events in China, and with major world developments as seen in Beijing. The best weekly coverage of Chinese affairs published outside China is in the *Far Eastern Economic Review*, published in Hong Kong.

Translations are also available on a day-to-day basis of articles from the Chinese press, and of Chinese radio broadcasts. In Britain, see the BBC's *Summary of World Broadcasts*. In the USA and some other countries, the US government's Foreign Broadcast Information Service *Daily Report* is more readily available.

Books

The Cambridge History of China (Cambridge University Press, 1978–), when it is finally completed, will probably be the definitive history of China in the English language. The planned total is sixteen volumes. For a less lengthy account see *A Short History of China*, by Hilda Hookham (Longmans, 1969).

China's Imperial Past, by Charles Hucker (Stanford U.P., 1975), gives a good summary of Chinese history up to the beginning of the modern era. *Sources of Chinese Tradition*, edited by DeBary, Chan, and Watson (Columbia U.P., 1960), is a selection of excerpts from the writings of the early philosophers, Buddhist scriptures, and other documents. *The Death of Woman Wang*, by Jonathan Spence (Viking, 1978), gives a detailed look at life in one unimportant county of China in the seventeenth century. It is extremely useful in establishing the background against which the later modernization of China can be seen.

For the early stages of the Western impact, and China's reaction to that impact, see *The Opium War*, by Peter W. Fay (North Carolina Press, 1975), and *The Last Stand of Chinese Conservatism*, by Mary C. Wright (Stanford U.P., 1957).

China in Revolution, edited by Mary C. Wright (Yale U.P., 1968), is a collection of articles on the Revolution of 1911. For analysis of early twentieth-century patterns of social mobility, see 'Downward Social Mobility in Pre-revolutionary China', by Edwin E. Moise, in *Modern China*, vol. 3, no. 1.

China in Disintegration, by James Sheridan (Free Press, 1975), traces the overall history of China from 1911 to 1949. Lloyd Eastman has written two good volumes on the Guomindang regime: *The Abortive Revolution* (Harvard U.P., 1974) covers the period from 1927 to 1937, and *Seeds of Destruction* (Stanford U.P., 1984) covers the period from 1937 to 1949. *One Day in China*, edited and translated by Sherman Cochran, Andrew Hsieh, and Janis Cochran (Yale U.P., 1983), is a fascinating collection of short pieces written in 1936, discussing Chinese society and China's situation at that time.

The U.S. Crusade in China, by Michael Schaller (Columbia U.P., 1979), and *Stillwell and the American Experience in China*, by Barbara Tuchman (Macmillan, 1971), give a good picture of relations between Chiang Kai-shek and the United States during the Second World War. *Two Kinds of Time*, by Graham Peck (Houghton, Mifflin, 1970), and *Thunder out of China*, by Theodore White and Annalee Jacoby (Sloane, 1946), are important contemporary accounts of the Second World War in China.

The Long March to Power, by James Harrison (Macmillan, 1973), traces the history of the Chinese Communist Party from its founding in 1921 up to its victory in 1949. The official Beijing edition of the *Selected Works of Mao Tse-tung* (Foreign Languages Press, 1965–77), gives the most important of Mao's writings (with the original texts slightly altered in some places). *Red Star Over China*, by Edgar Snow (Gollancz, 1937; Grove Press, 1968), is an excellent account of Chinese Communism in the 1930s, by an American journalist who succeeded in visiting the Communist base area in Shaanxi province in 1936. It contains the autobiography of Mao Zedong, as Mao told it to Snow. For the way the Communist Party won the support of the peasants through land reform in the 1940s, see the classic *Fanshen*, by William Hinton (Monthly Review Press, 1966), and also *Land Reform in China and North Vietnam*, by Edwin Moise (North Carolina Press, 1983).

Peasant China in Transition, by Vivienne Shue (U. of California Press, 1980), gives a good picture of the initial transformations China underwent after the revolution of 1949. Roderick Mac-Farquar's study, *Origins of the Cultural Revolution* (O.U.P., 1979–   ), will probably be the definitive history of the period from 1956 to 1965, when it is finally complete; so far two volumes, covering the period from 1956 to 1960, have appeared.

On the Cultural Revolution itself there is an excellent eye-witness account, *Son of the Revolution*, by Liang Heng and Judith Shapiro (Knopf, 1983). *Mao's Way*, by Edward Rice (U. of California Press, 1972), gives a good chronological framework for the Cultural Revolution, from a strongly anti-Maoist perspective. Mao Zedong's speeches and writings from the period 1956–71 are not really very good, but for those who are interested, some have been collected by Stuart Schram in a volume that has been published as *Mao Tse-tung Unrehearsed: Talks and Letters, 1956–71* (Penguin, 1971), in Britain and as *Chairman Mao Talks to the People* (Pantheon) in the USA.

The accounts by Westerners who visited China in the early 1970s are seldom of much use today, whether they were admiring like Ross Terrill's *80,000,000: The Real China* (Little, Brown, 1971), or hostile like Simon Leys' *Chinese Shadows* (Viking, 1977).

There is no fully satisfactory biography of Mao Zedong. Stuart Schram's was at one time the best, but it is now badly outdated. Ross Terrill's concentrates too much on details of Mao's personal life, and does not deal adequately with his political views and policies.

On the transformation China has undergone since the death of Mao, there are two good accounts by Westerners who were in China in the late 1970s: *Coming Alive* by Roger Garside (Deutsch, 1981), and *Alive in the Bitter Sea* by Fox Butterfield (Times Books, 1982).

On the international relations of the PRC, see *Chinese Foreign Policy* by Joseph Camilleri (Robertson, 1980), *China Crosses the Yalu* by Allen Whiting (Macmillan, 1960) on the Korean War, *The Chinese Calculus of Deterrence* by Allen Whiting (U. of Michigan Press, 1975) on the Sino-Indian boundary dispute and China's involvement in Vietnam, and studies of the Sino-Soviet dispute by Edward Crank-shaw, David Floyd, and William Griffith.

John Fairbank's *The United States and China* (Harvard U.P., various dates) is not just a study of China's relations with the USA; it is in effect a short history of modern China, with a particular focus on relations with the USA. (Recent revised editions are much more complete than the original.)

Index